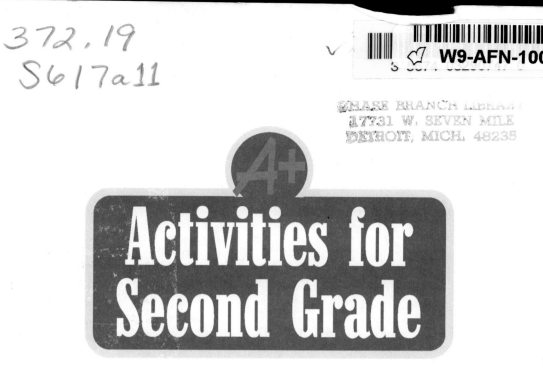

Activities for Second Grade

Hundreds of fun and creative activities that will help kids
advance in math, language, science, and more!

Naomi E. Singer & Matthew J. Miller

Adams Media Corporation
Holbrook, Massachusetts

Published by
Adams Media Corporation
260 Center Street, Holbrook, MA 02343. U.S.A.
www.adamsmedia.com

ISBN: 1-58062-276-3

Printed in the United States of America.

J I H G F E D C B A

Library of Congress Cataloging-in-Publication Data
available upon request from the publisher.

This publication is designed to provide accurate and authoritative information with regard to the
subject matter covered. It is sold with the understanding that the publisher is not engaged in
rendering legal, accounting, or other professional advice. If legal advice or other expert assistance is required, the services of a competent professional person should be sought.
   —From a *Declaration of Principles* jointly adopted by a Committee of the
American Bar Association and a Committee of Publishers and Associations

Interior illustrations by Kurt Dobler and Kathie Kelleher.
Cover photo by Bob Jacobson/International Stock.

This book is available at quantity discounts for bulk purchases.
For information, call 1-800-872-5627.

TABLE OF CONTENTS

INTRODUCTION / XI

SKILLS LIST / XIII

LANGUAGE ARTS ACTIVITIES / 1

MATH ACTIVITIES / 73

SCIENCE ACTIVITIES / 125

SOCIAL STUDIES ACTIVITIES / 173

BIBLIOGRAPHY / 195

RESOURCES / 205

ABOUT THE AUTHORS / 216

INTRODUCTION

When offered the opportunity to write a book of second-grade activities, concurrent with our writing a book of first-grade activities, we readily agreed. How better to support our belief that children learn best when we build from what they know than by extending the ideas put forth in our first book into a second. The close of first grade marks the end of just one stage along the learning continuum. Completing that all important first year does not mean, however, that all ideas, concepts, and skills put forth at the start of second grade are brand new. Review, reinforcement, and even reteaching are essential and common practice. As your child moves into and through second grade, exploring new ideas and developing new skills, remember to build on the known. Support your second grader's learning by showing interest in and enthusiasm for all that occurs in your child's workplace. Our goal in *A+ Activities for Second Grade* is to assist you in this effort.

We teach in an inclusive school system that celebrates diversity. The parents, teachers, and administrators of our school communities have developed core values that emphasize a love of learning, respect for self and others, academic excellence, and commitment to school and community. Each of these values has been a driving force in the writing of this book and in the work we do each day with our students. Just as we embrace these values in our classrooms, so do parents embrace them at home.

We truly believe that parents working in partnership with teachers make a huge and positive difference in the education of young children. Extend classroom learning to the world around you. As you use these activities, build on your child's strengths to enhance your second grader's self-confidence, positive self-image, and knowledge. Have fun, celebrate, and enjoy learning! Take an active and participatory part in your child's learning not only to enhance your second grader's burgeoning skills but also to demonstrate the value you place on learning.

We extend thanks to all of our friends and to our families for their encouragement and patience. We especially thank our parents, Herbert and Shirley Singer and Denny and Helaine Miller, for their support of us and our work. We also thank Marilyn, Andy, Joe, and Caitlin for the creative ideas they so generously shared and encouraged us to include and Dr. Margery Miller (no relation), director of the Graduate Reading Programs at Lesley College in Cambridge, Massachusetts, for recommending our authorship to Adams Media Corporation. Finally, we thank our editors, Cheryl Kimball, Linda Spencer, and Anne Weaver.

SKILLS LIST

Generic skills covered in the range of activities presented include: vocabulary development, brainstorming, imaginative thinking, visual discrimination, visual memory, auditory discrimination, expressive language, receptive language, interviewing, listening comprehension, following directions, fine motor skills including drawing, painting, cutting, coloring, and sculpting. The language arts skills, by their nature, are embedded in math, science, and social studies activities.

LANGUAGE ARTS

READING
Phonological Awareness
Alphabetical Order
Sight Word Recognition
Phonetic Analysis
Oral Reading
Silent Reading
Reading Comprehension
Literature Appreciation
Poetry Appreciation

WORD STUDY
Parts of Speech
Compound Words
Homonyms
Synonyms
Antonyms
Contractions
Plurals
Abbreviations

Syllabication
Prefixes
Suffixes
Possessives
Homographs

FIGURATIVE LANGUAGE
Alliteration
Personification
Onomatopoeia
Simile
Hyperbole
Metaphor

WRITTEN EXPRESSION
Mechanics
Spelling
Sentence Structure
Sentence Construction

Paragraphing
Writing Process
Story Form
Letter Writing
Narrative Writing
Persuasive Writing
Expository Writing
Poetry Writing

HANDWRITING
Letter Formation
Letter Recall
Near Point Copying

STUDY SKILLS
Dictionary
Researching
Note Taking
Organization

MATH

NUMERATION & COUNTING
Math Appreciation
Math Awareness
Number Awareness
Number Recognition
Connecting Math &
  Literature
Counting
Number Writing
Number Sequence
Calculator
Place Value
Equivalent Names
Number Patterns
Fractions

OPERATIONS & RELATIONS
Addition
Subtraction
Multiplication
Division
Problem Solving
Number Relations

MEASURES & REFERENCE FRAMES
Time
Calendars
Ordinal Numbers
Linear Measure
Weight
Capacity

Distance
Perimeter
Area
Temperature
Timelines
Equivalents

EXPLORING DATA
Predicting
Estimating
Tables, Graphs, & Charts
Frequency Distribution

GEOMETRY
Shapes
Symmetry
Polygons
Three-Dimensional
  Objects
Using a Straightedge

MONEY
Coin Recognition
Coin Values
Dollars
Making Change
Coin Sorting
Notation
Estimating Costs

PATTERNS & ATTRIBUTES
Visual Patterns
Odds & Evens
Sorting

SCIENCE
Brainstorming
Asking Questions
Observation
Surveying
Gathering Information
Identifying
Collecting
Sorting
Classifying
Categorizing
Cataloguing
Sequencing
Recording Data
Making Comparisons
Hypothesizing
Prediction
Experimentation
Measurement
Application
Constructing
Symmetry
Drawing Conclusions
Researching
Referential Writing
Theorizing
Connecting Science &
  Literature

SOCIAL STUDIES
Self-Awareness
Family Awareness
Community Awareness
Social Action
Cultural Awareness
Respecting Human
Differences
Map Skills

LANGUAGE ARTS

A large sign printed in vibrant colors rests on an easel facing the door of the classroom that your child enters each morning of second grade. *Good Morning Super Second Graders! Please sign in. Drop your homework in the homework box. Copy and correct the sentence on the board in your Before School Log. Choose a book from your book bin and read by yourself or with a buddy. See you at 8:45 in the meeting area. Morgan will lead today's morning meeting.*

Thus the day begins in a language-rich second grade classroom. Children are immersed in print as they develop skills to complete tasks independently or cooperatively, make constructive choices, assume responsibility for their learning, and take risks. They enter the classroom with just the right mix of expectation, confidence, and trepidation, exhibiting a sense of purpose that requires nurturing, consistency, and encouragement at school and at home.

Second grade is a time of enormous growth and transition in language arts. The skills that were introduced in first grade become the building blocks for the skills introduced in second grade. As second graders move toward becoming more fluent, independent, and confident readers and writers, they seek and welcome more challenges. Picture storybooks continue to delight their fancy while chapter books add a new dimension to their reading experience. As the world of independent nonfiction reading becomes more accessible, curiosity is sparked. Like sponges, children soak up information about people, places, animals, and natural phenomena. With eyes wide open in amazement, second graders are eager to read of the wonders of the world.

As they delve into more literary and longer texts, second graders extend their writing into a range of genres. They incorporate newly developing sentence and paragraph writing skills in letter, journal, review, research, song, and poetry writing. They persuade, they convince, they argue, they explain, they report, they describe. Young writers begin to imitate the language of the authors they read. They experiment with figurative language and have fun playing with words of multiple meaning. As developing authors, they stretch their thoughts, paint pictures with words, and play with the language of prose and poetry.

To foster true enjoyment of reading and writing and to develop fluent, excited, and successful readers, writers, and communicators, we present an integrated and balanced array of activities that encourages the use of rich literature and language. As you use the activities with your second grader, be aware of where your child is in the development of literacy skills. Gather for a Vowel Jamboree, or create Delicious Digraph ice cream sundaes. Scan the daily newspaper for the Mover and Shaker verbs, or Ham It Up by acting out an adjective. Squiggle a Synonym to liven up the language, or draw a Personification Picture to give life to a leaf or chair. Join the Fan Club of a favorite book character, or spin the spinner to build recognition of facts and details. Serve a Sentence Buffet, spread a Peanut Butter Paragraph, share a poem to tickle the senses, or Scramble a Spelling Egg!

No matter what the activity, read together, write together, and share a joyful celebration of language.

TWO-TO-FOUR RHYME

SKILLS: Phonological Awareness/Brainstorming/Categorizing/Rhyme/Written Expression/Drawing

Phonological awareness is the awareness that a word is made up of individual sounds or phonemes that are represented by letters. Strong phonological awareness enhances reading development. It is important to hear where a sound occurs within a word. Write a rhyme to strengthen the ability to recognize sounds that are the same at the end of words.

Brainstorm and list words in a category such as animals or foods. Together, write a two-word rhyme for each word in the category. In the animal category, rhymes might include "Bee Knee," "Funny Bunny." Write each two-word rhyme on a separate sheet of paper. Now, extend the two-word rhyme into a two- or four-line rhyme.

> See the buzzing busy bee,
> It won't sting me on my knee!
> *or*
> See the buzzing busy bee,
> As it flies from tree to tree,
> Keep the bee away from me,
> It won't sting me on my knee!

> REQUIRED:
> • Paper and pencil
> • Crayons
>
> OPTIONAL:
> • Stapler
> • Hole punch
> • Ribbon/yarn/string

Illustrate each rhyme. Staple the pages together, or punch a hole in the upper left-hand corner of each page and tie the pages together with yarn, ribbon, or string. Read the rhymes and add the book to your child's personal library.

CLAP, JUMP, STOMP, AND ROMP

SKILLS: Phonological Awareness/Chant/Rhyme/Written Expression

Children love to chant and rhyme as they clap their hands, jump rope, bounce a ball, or stomp their feet. Invite your child to Clap, Jump, Stomp, and Romp. Select a favorite chant such as, "*A my name is Annie and my brother's name is Allan. We live in Alaska and we sell apricots.*" While chanting, jump rope, clap, or bounce a ball. Try a favorite rhyme such as:

> Down by the bay, where the watermelons grow,
> Back to my home, I dare not go.
> For if I do, my mother will say:
> Did you ever see *a bear*
> *combing its hair*,
> Down by the bay?

> REQUIRED:
> • Paper and pencil
>
> OPTIONAL:
> • Library/bookstore visit
> • Jump rope
> • Ball

Write and replace your own rhyming verse for the words in italics.

Finally, work with your second grader to write a chant or rhyme. To get your ideas going, share books such as *Bug in a Rug* and *Miss Mary Mack and Other Children's Street Rhymes*, both by Joanna Cole and Stephanie Calmenson.

LINGUINI LETTERS

A little pasta goes a long way in reviewing and reinforcing the letter recognition and letter formation skills of a beginning second grader.

If the *b*'s and *d*'s, *p*'s and *q*'s, *m*'s and *w*'s, and *n*'s and *u*'s are occasionally trading places, boil the water, throw in the linguini, cook, drain, cool, and pass the plates to doodle with a noodle. On the surface of a plate or wax paper, shape two strands of linguini into a lowercase *b,* one for the line down, one for the rounded portion of the *b.* Encourage your second grader to trace the *b,* gently following the strands from top to bottom and left to right with the index and middle finger of his or her writing hand. Use a third strand of linguini to demonstrate that one can reconfirm that *b* is really *b,* not *d,* by adding a third strand of linguini to the lowercase *b* to make uppercase *B.*

Use linguini to form any letter or number that remains confusing in regard to directionality. Multisensory strategies of this nature enhance visual discrimination skills by enlisting the help of the sense of touch.

REQUIRED:
- Cooked linguini
- Plates

OPTIONAL:
- Wax paper

CATEGORIZE AND ALPHABETIZE

In order to find a word in the dictionary, look up a phone number in the telephone directory, check a reference in an encyclopedia, locate a book by title or author at the library, and read an index in a book, newspaper, or magazine, children need to have facility with alphabetical order.

To enhance your second grader's alphabetizing skills, alphabetize anything that comes to mind. Brainstorm a list of fruits, vegetables, or ice cream flavors. Write each word in each category on a small sticky tag. Then, put the tags in ABC order. Store each category in an envelope. Try kinds of cars, trees, flowers, birds, or insects and do the same.

To practice alphabetizing to the second, third, or even fourth letter, brainstorm a list of things that begin with a specified letter, *p,* for example: popcorn, pretzel, peanut, peppermint, potato, pin, pill, pumpkin, pear, plum, peach, poem, palm, puppy, paper. As you say each word, write it on a sticky tag. When you have 10 to 20 words, alphabetize.

With this kind of reinforcement and practice, your child will have categorizing and alphabetizing skills that are *te*rrific, *to*pnotch, and *tr*emendous!

REQUIRED:
- Sticky tags
- Envelopes
- Pencil

MINI PICTIONARY

SKILLS: Brainstorming/Categorizing/Alphabetical Order/Dictionary Skills/
Researching/Note Taking/Drawing/Written Expression

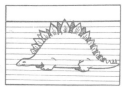

Capitalize on your second grader's special interests to make a Mini Pictionary.

Perhaps insects, dinosaurs, ocean animals, mammals, methods of transportation, or sports intrigue your child. Choose a topic. Brainstorm and list nouns that fit the topic. Select four to six words from the list and write each on an index card. Alphabetize the cards.

On your next visit to the library, take the index cards with you and do a little research to find facts about each word. Use the dictionary, encyclopedia, or any book you find about the topic. Jot notes on each index card.

Use the information gathered to make your Mini Pictionary. Fold two sheets of paper together and staple on the left edge. Label the cover with a title that fits the topic, "Mara's Mammals," for example. On each page, write one word, draw and color a picture of the word, and write two or three sentences to tell about the picture. Make this completed picture dictionary the first in a series to add to your child's personal library of resources.

REQUIRED:
- Index cards
- Paper and pencil
- Crayons
- Stapler
- Library visit

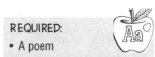

POETIC, PEACEFUL, AND PRACTICAL

SKILLS: Near Point Copying/Handwriting/Poetry Appreciation/Drawing/Painting

Young children care about the appearance of their work. In a Poetic, Peaceful, and Practical way, enjoy poetry, music, and manuscript.

Choose a favorite poem to share from a book such as *Talking Like the Rain* by X. J. Kennedy and Jane Dyer or *The Great Frog Race* by Christine O'Connell George. Listen to the language and talk about the picture or feeling created with words. Then tune in to a classical music station on the radio or pop in a favorite cassette or CD. Keep the volume low. Read the poem again to the flow of the music. Then, sit together in a comfortable writing spot with the poem before you. Copy the poem or a portion of the poem on lined paper, paying attention to spacing on the line and the page. Remind your child to print letters from top to bottom, left to right. When the writing is done, ask your child to read the poem, read the poem together, or alternate reading line by line. Finally, add artistry by drawing or painting a picture to accompany the copied poem.

REQUIRED:
- A poem
- Paper and pencil
- Music
- Crayons/markers/paint/
  paintbrush

OPTIONAL:
- Library/bookstore visit

DAILY DICTATE AND DRAW

SKILLS: Auditory Memory/Handwriting/Spelling/Punctuation/Capitalization/
Proofreading/Making Comparisons/Drawing

Find a few minutes a day for a Daily Dictate and Draw. Using words from your child's reading or weekly spelling list, dictate a sentence for your second grader to write and draw. For example, when your child's spelling list contains words with *ou* and *ow*, dictate a sentence such as, "A big red flower grew by the house." Say the sentence; ask your child to repeat the sentence. Then ask your child to write the sentence, using neat top-to-bottom, left-to-right handwriting.

Encourage your second grader to reread the finished sentence, self-checking or proofreading for spelling, initial capital letter, and end-mark punctuation. Praise all efforts and provide assistance as needed.

Suggest that your child draw a picture to match the sentence. For added pleasure, you draw the picture, too, and compare the results. Finally, make a cumulative Daily Dictate and Draw Diary. Decorate a cover and punch a hole in the upper left-hand corner of each dictate and draw sheet. Tie with a bow. Add each dictation done to keep a running record of your child's development throughout the year.

REQUIRED:
• Paper and pencil
• Crayons/markers

OPTIONAL:
• Hole punch
• Yarn/ribbon/string
• Decorations

BUILD TO 225

SKILL: Sight Word Recognition

Children use both sight word recognition skills and phonetic analysis skills to read. During second grade, the sight words in your child's treasury should include approximately 225 high-frequency words. Here's a list to get you started as you reinforce your child's sight word recognition skills. Write each word on an index card and use for flash card drill. Hide cards about your home and ask your child to seek and read. Double up the words and use for Concentration or Go Fish.

HIGH-FREQUENCY WORD BANK: to the in and he you it at is we she see on not can said that are do up for one they two be me too go down mother my little was big so box by into his had like did him her old as baby but this with will dog what out father then came no come when some get have there about from here who just or if girl think work make blue them an around ball long cat once saw green going eat away how say yes went run three put jump help six black brown kitten now before children name new over ran after day were write only would am very has feet many again right pretty

REQUIRED:
• Index cards
• Pencil/pen

MASTER 225 . . . ADD 25 MORE

Continue to review and reinforce sight word recognition skills by adding to those words your child already knows. Here are the words you need to reach 225. Write each on an index card. Use for flash card drill, Hide-and-Seek Read, Go Fish, or Concentration. Store all in a box that your child can decorate as a personal treasure chest of words. When 225 are mastered, add 25 more!

HIGH-FREQUENCY WORD BANK: any take back under its play made must been ride walk soon fly dinner where their save why on let daddy well street tree call cold home find man may car drink stop milk us tell these night which school give sit keep bed bird want door does pets read head off four round book open funny cake use fall first birthday small laugh friend five hold circle don't could bring our got water much other know found house hot together please better something every pull always looked best hand because fast love sleep gray ate thank try kind show cut shall far

25 MORE: goes fall buy answer feel never done hope draw grow fine gave hurry wish seem those hear start sure own animal both guess morning until

REQUIRED:
• Index cards
• Pencil/pen

OPTIONAL:
• Box
• Decorations

ROADSIDE READ

Roadside Read is the perfect antidote to the age-old question, "Are we there yet?" The next time the family takes to the highway for a drive to visit friends or to take a vacation by the sea, use print to make the time pass productively!

Look for advertisements as you pass restaurants, shopping malls, schools, public buildings, houses, apartment complexes, and billboards. Read "Shell" at a gas station and rhyme around the car with "bell," "dell," "fell," "gel," "sell," "smell," "swell," "tell," "well," "yell." Read bumper stickers or advertisements on the sides of trucks and buses and chat about the meaning or content. Find single words like "school," "hospital," and "deer" to use in sentences. Read phrases to generate storytelling. See a sign such as "Rest Area Six Miles Ahead" and put the words in alphabetical order. Read a street name that includes a vowel team as in "Main Street" or one that begins with a consonant blend, digraph, or cluster as in "Cherry Street." Brainstorm other words that include *ai* or *ee* or begin with *ch* or *str*. Before you know it, you'll reach your destination having engaged in a fun-filled and skill enhancing Roadside Read.

REQUIRED:
• A car ride

SHORT AND SWEET

SKILLS: Abbreviations/Sight Word Recognition/Spelling

Mr.	Wed.	Dr.
Aug.	St.	Mon.
Mon.	Oct.	Rd.

Enhance your child's familiarity with common abbreviations by playing Short and Sweet. Cut a supply of 3″ × 5″ index cards in half. On each half, write a word that has a common abbreviation. Next, make a 3 × 3–grid gameboard for each participant. In each square of each gameboard randomly write the abbreviation for one of the words on the cards. Shuffle the cards and place between players. Give each player a supply of sweet game markers: Skittles, Gummy Bears, or M&Ms.

Alternate turns. Draw a card from the center pile. Read the word. All players scan their gameboards for the matching abbreviation. The player who has the abbreviation covers it with a candy. Continue play until one player has covered all the abbreviations on his or her board.

Enjoy the sweets and play again to practice recognition of abbreviations.

WORD BANK: mister/Mr., mistress/Mrs., doctor/Dr., street/St., avenue/Ave., road/Rd., January/Jan., February/Feb., March/Mar., April/Apr., August/Aug., September/Sept., October/Oct., November/Nov., December/Dec., Monday/Mon., Tuesday/Tues., Wednesday/Wed., Thursday/Thurs., Friday/Fri., Saturday/Sat., Sunday/Sun.

REQUIRED:
- Index cards
- Construction paper
- Markers
- Candy game markers
- Ruler

I'LL BE THE EMPEROR

SKILLS: Oral Reading Fluency/Oral Reading Expression/Sight Word Recognition/Phonetic Analysis/Punctuation/Paragraphing/Characterization

"I'll be the Emperor; you be the swindler!" "I'll be the mouse; you be the fox!" Young readers welcome the opportunity to have a turn to read aloud, especially when they can play the part of a story character. The next time you share a favorite book such as *The Emperor's New Clothes* by Hans Christian Anderson, retold by Ruth Gross, or *Dr. DeSoto* by William Steig, give your child the lead role!

Invite the whole family to read a selected book together. Talk about the characters and events, noting that words inside quotation marks are words said by a character. Point out that each time the speaker changes, a new paragraph begins.

Select a portion of the story with dialogue and assign parts. Include a narrator to read all text that isn't dialogue. Encourage your child to read a character's words as that character would say them. Use the punctuation as an aid to phrasing and expression.

Ready on the set? Take one! Bring the story to life as you enhance oral reading fluency, oral reading expression, and understanding of character.

REQUIRED:
- Book

OPTIONAL:
- Library/bookstore visit

TWENTY-MINUTE READ

SKILLS: Literature Appreciation/Oral Reading Fluency/Oral Reading Comprehension/ Silent Reading Comprehension/Predicting Outcomes/Drawing Conclusions

Set aside time from your busy schedule, sometime each afternoon or evening, to give your child the gift of a Twenty-Minute Read. When children recognize that the adults in their lives value reading, they are more likely to become avid readers, too!

During your shared reading time, try different models. Start by reading a book that your child has chosen. Take turns reading aloud, alternating for paragraphs or pages. Engage in discussion about the main idea and the details that support it. Make predictions and draw conclusions. Talk about characters and their feelings and actions. Read the dialogue of selected characters so that conversations come to life. Talk to characters if you wish. Children love to hold imaginary conversations with characters they meet in books! If *Nate the Great* is puzzled, offer suggestions. If *Amelia Bedelia* is confused, give advice. Have fun with the story!

Try a silent read during which all participants choose reading material. Sit together in the living room, den, or yard. The place isn't as important as the shared experience. At the end of twenty minutes, take a few moments for each family member to tell about the material read.

REQUIRED:
• Books

OPTIONAL:
• Cookies and milk

CONSONANT COMEBACK

SKILLS: Phonetic Analysis/Initial, Medial, Final Consonants/Spelling

Second graders know the consonants and the sounds they usually make. They recognize, read, and write them at the beginning, in the middle, and at the end of words. Play Consonant Comeback and have fun as you reinforce consonant awareness for reading and spelling.

Tell your child that you have lost the consonants and are now having trouble writing words. Sit beside your child. On a piece of paper, write, for example, "__ a __ e __." Say, "I'm trying to put a big, two-humped animal on my paper, but I seem to have lost the consonants. Please help them make a comeback. What letter do you think is at the beginning, in the middle, and at the end?" Your child should say, "It's a camel. You need *c* at the beginning, *m* in the middle, and *l* at the end!"

Ask your child to fill in the missing letters. Provide additional clues if needed.

Visit the library to read *The Story of Z* by Jeanne Modesitt. This delightful tale will concretely illustrate the importance of each consonant in the alphabet.

REQUIRED:
• Paper and pencil

OPTIONAL:
• Library visit

WORD BANK: robot, tiger, hotel, seven, cabin, lemon, wagon, donut, baker, label, novel, medal, favor, timer, carrot, mitten, ribbon, wallet, muffin, parrot

APPLE BASKET

SKILLS: Phonetic Analysis/Short *a*/Drawing/Cutting/
Brainstorming/Spelling/Handwriting/Expressive Language

Phonetic analysis skills need regular review and reinforcement until they are mastered. Put all your apples in one basket as your second grader reviews short *a* for both reading and spelling. Join in the fun as you draw and cut 20 to 30 apples from construction paper. Work together to brainstorm words that include short *a* as in "apple" and "basket." As you say a word, clearly print the word on an apple. Remind your second grader to print neatly, forming letters from left to right and top to bottom. Place the apples in a basket. Then, take turns apple picking. Choose one apple from the basket, read the word, and use it in a sentence. Continue play until the basket is empty. Add apples to the basket each time you play. Enhance the experience by munching and crunching on a juicy Granny Smith or Red Delicious apple while you work.

REQUIRED:
- Red, yellow, green, and brown construction paper
- Safety scissors
- Basket
- Pencil/marker

OPTIONAL:
- Apples

WORD BANK: cab, bat, lap, hand, sack, stamp, crack, trash, blast, class, backpack, paddle, rattle, dragon, splash, happen, wagon, cabin, rabbit, grasshopper

BOUQUET OF A

SKILLS: Phonetic Analysis/Long *a*/Drawing/Cutting/Brainstorming/Spelling/Handwriting

There is more than one way to spell long *a*. Second graders know that *a* is long when it says its own name. They know that silent *e* or magic *e* at the end of a word often makes the first vowel long as in "cake" and "plate." They also know that when two vowels are side by side, the first is usually long while the second silently tags along as in "sail" or "day." Children need to have regular review and reinforcement of long *a* for reading and spelling.

Draw and cut several 3″ flower patterns from colored construction paper. Brainstorm words with long *a*. As you and your child generate words, ask your child to print each word neatly in the center of a flower, forming letters from left to right and top to bottom. Attach each flower to a straw or Popsicle stick. Read the long *a* flowers as you arrange them in a vase to make a beautiful Bouquet of *A*.

Apply long *a* as you share a book such as *Nate the Great and the Stolen Base* by Marjorie Weinman Sharmat.

REQUIRED:
- Construction paper
- Nontoxic glue/tape/stapler
- Safety scissors
- Straws/Popsicle sticks
- Pencil/marker
- Vase

OPTIONAL:
- Library/bookstore visit

THE LONG AND SHORT OF A

SKILLS: Phonetic Analysis/Short & Long *a*/Cutting/Drawing

The long and short of it is that vowels can be confusing to young readers. Initially, we teach children to recognize, read, and spell short *a* as in "apple" and "bag." Then we complicate matters by teaching them to recognize, read, and spell long *a* as in "made," "rain," "clay," and "fable."

To review and reinforce your child's ability to recognize and read the Long and Short of A, design a collage of words, some with short *a*, others with long *a*.

Look through magazines, newspapers, and catalogues. Read advertisements and articles, watching for words with *a*. Cut out the words, emphasizing that your child select words of varied size, font, and color. Arrange the words in an inviting design on a large sheet of construction paper. Glue them to the paper, add illustrations if desired, and read the words. Label the collage with "*Aa*" and display for all to see.

For added practice, share a book such as *Jack Takes the Cake* by Marni McGee or *Commander Toad and the Planet of the Grapes* by Jane Yolen.

Variation: Make a long and short collage for *e*, *i*, *o*, or *u*.

REQUIRED:
- Magazines/ newspapers/catalogues
- Safety scissors
- Nontoxic glue
- Marker

OPTIONAL:
- Library/bookstore visit

ELEPHANT HELP

SKILLS: Phonetic Analysis/Short *e*/Drawing/Brainstorming/Spelling/Handwriting

An *e*lephant can help as you review and reinforce short *e* with your second grader.

Make the Elephant Help gameboard from a file folder. Open the folder vertically. In the lower left-hand corner draw a 1″ square. Label this square "Elephant Pen." Draw a 1″ square in the upper right-hand corner. Label this square "Circus Tent." Connect the two squares by drawing 20 to 30 squares from the Pen to the Tent. In six selected squares, write messages such as "Elephant fell. Miss 1 turn." "Smell peanuts. Run ahead 3." "Get fed. Go back 2." "Help the clown. Extra turn." "Messy den. Go back 1." "Do your best. Go ahead 2." Brainstorm short *e* words and clearly print one word in each of the remaining squares. Use buttons or coins as game pieces.

Place game pieces on Elephant Pen. Alternate turns. Toss a die, move that number of spaces, read the word, and use it in a sentence. The first player to reach Circus Tent is the winner. Fold the file for easy storage.

REQUIRED:
- File folder
- Marker
- Pen/pencil
- Game pieces
- Die

WORD BANK: jet, nest, bell, men, sled, bend, sent, felt, dress, fresh, present, pepper, better, metal, setting, bedroom, pencil, seven, shelf, telephone

A+ ACTIVITIES FOR SECOND GRADE

SHEEP, GEESE, PEAS, AND BEANS

SKILLS: Phonetic Analysis/Long *e*/Brainstorming/Spelling/Handwriting/Counting/Categorizing

 Second graders know that *e* is long when it says its own name. They know that silent *e* or magic *e* at the end of a word often makes the first vowel long as in "Pete" and "Zeke." They also know that when two vowels are side by side, the first is usually long while the second silently tags along as in "deer" and "peach." Children need to have regular review and reinforcement of long *e* for reading and spelling.

Provide each player with paper and pencil. Set the timer to three minutes and say, "Go!" Independently, players brainstorm and print neatly a list of long *e* words. When time is up, read the lists, crossing out any word that appears on more than one list. Award a point for each long *e* word on a list that no one else included. Tally the results to determine the winner.

REQUIRED:
• Paper and pencils
• Timer

OPTIONAL:
• Library/bookstore visit

For added challenge, play by category, asking everyone to write words with long *e* that are animals, "Sheep, Geese," or foods, "Peas, Beans."

Apply long *e* as you share books such as *No Peas for Nellie* by Chris L. Demarest or *Say "Cheese"* by Patricia Reilly Giff.

SEND A LETTER PLEASE

SKILLS: Phonetic Analysis/Long & Short *e*/Written Expression/Handwriting/Spelling

1000 Main Street
Young America, MN

By applying phonetic analysis rules to authentic reading and writing, children move closer to mastery of the different sounds of the vowels. They know that *e* is short in words such as "elephant" and "bed" and long in words such as "Pete," "green," "treat," "key," and "repeat."

Send a Letter Please to your second grader in clearly printed manuscript, asking about his or her day in school. Highlight or underline every word that has a short or long *e*. You might write, "Tell me about your day. What did you read? Did you add twenty-three plus ten? Did you enjoy eating your snack?" Encourage your child to read the letter aloud, noting the words with *e*. Ask your child to write back. Tell your young writer to include words with *e* and to underline each one used. Also request that your second grader use neatly formed left-to-right, top-to-bottom handwriting.

REQUIRED:
• Paper and pencil

OPTIONAL:
• Library/bookstore visit

For added practice with *e*, read a book such as *Ivy Green, Cootie Queen* by Joan Holub or *The Beast in Ms. Rooney's Room* by Patricia Reilly Giff.

Variation: Send a letter that highlights short and long *a, i, o,* or *u.*

BINGO LINGO

BINGO		
pig	will	lit
flip	dim	tip
bit	Sing	king

Review and reinforce the sound of short *i* by playing Bingo Lingo. Make a bingo card for each player. Write "Bingo" across the top of the cards and divide each into nine equal sections, three rows across and three rows down. Work together to brainstorm and print short *i* words such as "clip" and "sing" on small slips cut from construction paper. Clearly print the same short *i* words in random order on the cards, one word per section. Put the paper slips in a bowl. Distribute a card to each player, including the caller. Place a supply of game pieces in the center of the playing area and begin.

The designated caller for the first game pulls a short *i* word out of the bowl and calls it out. If a player has that word on his or her bingo card, that player covers the word with a game piece. Continue until one participant gets three in a row and calls, "Bingo!" The winner uncovers and reads each short *i* word.

Variation: Challenge players to cover words to make an *X, L,* or border for bingo. You may want to make additional bingo boards to practice the other short vowels, *a, e, o,* and *u.*

WORD BANK: fix, lips, will, bit, grin, sink, king, picnic, visit, mitten, drink, bring, trip, blink, glitter, slipper, fiddle, little

REQUIRED:
- Construction paper
- Marker
- Paper and pencil
- Game pieces
- Safety scissors
- Bowl

MICE EAR RHYME

Second graders know that *i* is long when it says its own name in "bike" and "pie." Second graders also know that *y* is sometimes a vowel that says long *i* in "fly."

Use paper mice to review and reinforce long *i* for reading and spelling.

Fold a piece of construction paper. Cut a 4" heart and a 2" heart along the fold. Hold the large heart, the body, with the fold at the top. Slip the small folded heart, the ear, over the large folded heart and staple just below the fold. Be sure that the points face in the same direction. Draw an eye on both sides of the body, a half inch from the point. Attach a paper or yarn tail.

Neatly print a long *i* word on an ear. Challenge your child to think of a rhyming word. Lift the ear and print the word. Flip the mouse. Follow the same procedure on the second ear. Make several mice to read and rhyme.

Share books such as *Mice Twice* by Joseph Low or *Blue Skies, French Fries* by Judy Delton to see long *i* in context.

REQUIRED:
- Construction paper
- Marker
- Safety scissors
- Stapler

OPTIONAL:
- Library/bookstore visit
- Yarn

RIDDLE WRITE AND READ

SKILLS: Phonetic Analysis/Long & Short *i*/Brainstorming/Written Expression/Handwriting/Spelling

Engage your second grader in authentic reading and writing practice to enhance recognition and application of developing phonetic analysis skills. Riddle Write and Read will move your youngster toward mastery of the short sound of *i* as in "igloo" and "pin," and the long sound of *i* as in "ice," "bike," "tie," and "final."

Riddles delight second graders, who enjoy telling them and solving them. Take a few minutes for a short *i*, long *i* riddle write. Independently, think of words that include *i*. Then write a riddle for each one. Remind your child to print the riddles in neatly formed left-to-right, top-to-bottom handwriting. Come together for a short *i*, long *i* riddle read. Alternate turns asking and answering riddles.

For added practice with *i*, read books such as *The Littles and Their Friends* by William T. Little and John Peterson and *Pinky and Rex and the Mean Old Witch* by James Howe.

Variation: Write and read riddles with short and long *a, e, o,* and *u*.

RIDDLE BANK:
He is married to the queen. (king)
You skate on this in winter. (ice)
Make this when you blow out birthday candles. (wish)

REQUIRED:
• Paper and pencil

OPTIONAL:
• Library/bookstore visit

OCTOPUS HOP AND STOP

SKILLS: Phonetic Analysis/Short *o*/Drawing/Brainstorming/Spelling/Handwriting/Rhyme

Hop from word to word but stop to read and rhyme. Use Octopus Hop and Stop to review and reinforce reading and spelling words with short *o*.

Draw a large octopus on construction paper. Make the tentacles wide enough to accommodate printed words. Brainstorm words with short *o*. Clearly print each word on a tentacle, leaving space to hop from word to word as you complete a list of four words per tentacle. For example, on the first tentacle, your second grader prints, "Job," "Plop," "Lock," "Box"; on the second, "Rod," "Hot," "Frog," "Mom." Continue in this manner until all tentacles have four words.

Now you are ready to toss the die, hop, and stop. Place a marker just above the word at the top of the first tentacle. Alternate turns as you roll the die and hop from word to word the number of times indicated. Hop down the first tentacle, across to the second tentacle, up the second, across to the third, and so on to the top of the eighth tentacle. When you stop on a word, read the word and say a word that rhymes. On five, hop to "Rod." Read "Rod," and say "Nod."

REQUIRED:
• Construction paper
• Pencil/marker
• Game pieces
• Die

BEAT THE TOAST

SKILLS: Phonetic Analysis/Long *o*/Brainstorming/Spelling/Handwriting

Make the review and reinforcement of long *o* as in "cone," "boat," "crow," and "toe" an exciting and fun breakfast game. Challenge your second grader to Beat the Toast.

Provide your child with paper and pencil. Put slices of bread in the toaster and say, "Go!" While the bread is toasting, your second grader brainstorms and prints words with long *o*. When the toast is ready, spread the butter and jam and read the words. Each time you play, try to write more long *o* words.

Variation: Write words with long *a, e, i,* and *u.*

Apply the long *o* rules when you share books such as *A New Coat for Anna* by Harriet Ziefert, *Koko's Kitten* by Dr. Francine Patterson, *Lon Po Po* by Ed Young, and *Spectacular Stone Soup* by Patricia Reilly Giff.

REQUIRED:
• Bread
• Toaster
• Paper and pencil

OPTIONAL:
• Library/bookstore visit
• Butter/jam

CHEER FOR O

SKILLS: Phonetic Analysis/Long & Short *o*/Brainstorming/Handwriting/Spelling

Use Cheerios to enhance your child's ability to recognize and apply the short sound of *o* as in "ox" and "flop" and the long sound of *o* as in "home," "coat," "toe," "crow," and "open."

Label one sheet of paper "Short *O*" and another sheet of paper "Long *O.*"

Have Cheerios and glue handy as you alternate saying a word with *o*. Decide whether the *o* is long or short. Then ask your child to print the word in neatly and correctly formed handwriting on the appropriate *O* sheet, gluing a Cheerio in place of each *o*.

When the lists are complete, read the words and Cheer for *O*. "Give me a rock! Give me a toe! Stand up, sit down, cheer for O!"

For added practice with *o,* read books such as *Ox-Cart Man* by Donald Hall and *Cam Jansen and the Mystery of the Monster Movie* by David A. Adler.

REQUIRED:
• Paper and pencil
• Marker
• Cheerios
• Nontoxic glue

OPTIONAL:
• Library/bookstore visit

BUBBLE STUFF

SKILLS: Phonetic Analysis/Short *u*/Brainstorming/Spelling/Handwriting/Counting

Count the bubbles, one by one, to practice short *u* and have some fun! Get out some bubble stuff to review and reinforce short *u* for reading and spelling.

Brainstorm and list words with short *u* as in "bubble" and "stuff." Remind your second grader to print neatly, forming letters from left to right and top to bottom.

Take your list, a bottle of bubble stuff, and go outside. Dip the wand into the bubble stuff and blow. Count as many bubbles as you can. Then read that number of short *u* words from the list. Alternate turns blowing bubbles and reading.

Variation: Repeat the activity for short *a, e, i,* and *o.*

WORD BANK: gum, tub, but, hug, sun, bud, pup, puff, skull, fuss, duck, hunt, fuzz, jump, must, hulk, drum, grub, trunk, stuck, club, glum, plus, slug, lunch, scrub, strung, butter, button

REQUIRED:
- Paper and pencil
- Bubble stuff
- Bubble wand

SHAKE, RATTLE, AND RULE

SKILLS: Phonetic Analysis/Long *u*/Brainstorming/Spelling/Handwriting/Drawing/Painting/Cutting/Rhyme

Add rhythm and chant to the review and reinforcement of long *u* for reading and spelling. Don't discard the tube inside the roll of paper towels. Instead, encourage your second grader to decorate the tube with the letter *u*: big *U*, little *u*, green *u*, dotted *u*, striped *u*, plain *u*, fancy *u*, squiggled *u*. Draw and color, cut and glue, or paint the Shake, Rattle, and Rule tube.

When the decorations are complete, cover the bottom of the tube with foil, secured with a rubber band. Put a handful of popcorn kernels, beans, or rice inside the tube. Cover the top with foil and secure.

Brainstorm and neatly print a list of long *u* words in rhymed pairs or groups such as "mule/rule," "cute/flute," "cube/tube," "tune/June/dune," "due/true/blue/clue/glue."

While shaking and rattling the tube, your child reads the pairs and groups of words, keeping time to the rhythm of reading.

Read long *u* words in context in books such as *The Legend of the Bluebonnet* by Tomie dePaola and *The Mystery of the Blue Ring* by Patricia Reilly Giff.

REQUIRED:
- Paper towel tube
- Art supplies
- Paper and pencil
- Kernels/beans/rice

OPTIONAL:
- Library/bookstore visit

HIDE AND SEEK U

SKILLS: Reading Comprehension/Phonetic Analysis/Long & Short *u*/Handwriting

Take notice of *u* in any book you read with Hide and Seek *U*. Alternate turns as you read aloud with your child. Enjoy the story as you discuss characters, setting, theme, and illustrations.

Fold two sheets of paper in half, one for your child and one for you. On each paper, label one column "Short *U*" and one column "Long *U*." Then pick two facing pages and look for words with short *u* as in "puppy" and "lunch" and long *u* as in "tune," "due," "suit," and "music." As you explore the left page, your child explores the right. Independently, record short and long *u* words found. Share the words found by reading them to each other. Tally the results. Then, repeat the activity on two other pages.

Have fun and be challenged in your efforts to find *u* in books such as *Buddy The First Seeing Eye Dog* by Eva Moore and *The Pee Wee Jubilee* by Judy Delton.

REQUIRED:
• Paper and pencils
• Book

OPTIONAL:
• Library/bookstore visit

VOWEL JAMBOREE

SKILLS: Phonetic Analysis/Long & Short Vowels/Spelling/Handwriting

To review and reinforce the vowels, long or short, invite your child and other family members to a Vowel Jamboree.

In advance, prepare two recording sheets for each participant, one headed "Short Vowels," the other, "Long Vowels." Divide each sheet into five equal columns, labeled "*a*," "*e*," "*i*," "*o*," and "*u*."

Gather participants at a starting point. Explain that a *jamboree* is a celebration or gathering. Since your child knows all the short and long vowels, it is time to gather them together. Set a timer to 15 minutes. Challenge players to walk around the house or yard, looking for items with short or long vowels. Find at least one item for each sound. Say, "Go!" and begin the jamboree.

As each item is discovered, the player records the name in the appropriate column on the short-vowel or long-vowel recording sheet. When time is up, all players return to the starting point. Call out, "Short *a*!" Players read "pan," "mattress," "glass." Call out, "Long *a*!" Players read "table," "radio," "frame." Continue in this manner until all words have been shared.

For a fun-filled romp with the vowels and consonants, read *The War Between the Vowels and the Consonants* by Priscilla Turner.

REQUIRED:
• Paper and pencils

OPTIONAL:
• Library/bookstore visit

THE SOMETIMES VOWEL

SKILLS: Phonetic Analysis/*y* as a Vowel /Brainstorming/Spelling/
Drawing/Adjectives/Nouns/Written Expression

Young readers can be challenged by The Sometimes Vowel, alias *y*. Initially, children meet *y* as a consonant, as in "yellow" and "yoyo." Next they learn that *y* can stand for the vowel sound of long *e* as in "puppy" or long *i* as in "shy." You can have fun with language while reinforcing recognition of the two sounds of *y* when it is used as a vowel.

Start by thinking of book titles or book characters such as *Henny Penny* by Paul Galdone, *Humpty Dumpty* by Moira Kemp, or *Why Can't I Fly* by Rita Golden Gelmen. Notice while reading the title and the book that *y* sometimes sounds like long *e* and sometimes sounds like long *i*.

Now brainstorm and list pairs of words that include *y* as a vowel. Try to think of an adjective and a noun for each pair, for example, "cry baby," "cloudy sky," "sparkly butterfly," "my bunny," "silly fly," "yummy candy," "busy city." Encourage your child to select one phrase to illustrate. Then write a story to accompany the illustration. Again, in any of the words that include *y*, note the sound as long *e* or long *i*.

REQUIRED:
• Paper and pencil
• Crayons/markers

OPTIONAL:
  Library/bookstore visit

MULTISYLLABLE SCRAMBLE

SKILLS: Syllabication/Brainstorming

A syllable is a word or part of a word that has one vowel sound. Words have as many syllables as vowels heard. The word "basket" has two syllables, "bas" and "ket," because each vowel sound is heard. We determine the number of syllables in a word by how many vowels we hear, not by how many vowels we see.

Enhance your child's ability to read two-syllable words by playing Multisyllable Scramble. Put a blue dot in the upper left-hand corner of 20 index cards. On each card, brainstorm and write a two-syllable word, leaving a space between the syllables. Cut the cards in half between the syllables. Scramble the cards faceup on the table. Remind your child that the cards with the blue dot are first syllable cards.

Set a timer to five minutes and say, "Go!" Provide word clues as needed as your child reassembles the words. When time is up, read completed words.

For added fun, include more words and players and keep score. Finally, for extra challenge, add a red dot in the middle and a green dot in the upper right-hand corner. Write three-syllable words such as "fan-tas-tic," cut between syllables, and scramble!

REQUIRED:
• Pencil
• Index cards
• Safety scissors
• Crayons/markers
• Timer

SKITTLE SYLLABLES

SKILL: Syllabication

When words are too long to sound out, divide them into parts or syllables. Some words divide between double consonants, "kit-ten." Others divide between two different consonants, "thun-der." Some divide after a vowel, "ho-tel."

Play Skittle Syllables to enhance your second grader's ability to read two-syllable words. Write each word in the word bank on a slip of paper. Make a 4 × 4 game card for each player. Randomly write the syllables of eight words on one playing card, filling the sixteen squares. Write "mon" in one square and "key" in another. Fill the card in this manner. Do the same on the second card, using the eight remaining words.

Provision each player with a game card and a supply of Skittles. Place the slips of paper in a container between players. Alternate turns to select a word, read the word aloud, say the word in syllables, and repeat the word. Players look for the two syllables of the word and cover each syllable with a Skittle. Play continues until a player makes a border of Skittles or fills the card. Eat the Skittles and play again.

REQUIRED:
- Paper and pencil
- Ruler
- Skittles
- Container
- Safety scissors

WORD BANK: monkey, puddle, locate, pencil, follow, decide, barrel, trumpet, happy, stolen, ladder, pattern, hammer, little, reply, tumble

TONGUE TWISTER BLENDS

SKILLS: Phonetic Analysis/Initial Consonant Blends/Alliteration/Written Expression/Expressive Language/Drawing

A consonant blend is formed when two consonants combine their sounds. The consonant blends include *r* blends as in "bring," "crush," "drop," "fresh," "grow," "present," "train"; *l* blends as in "blue," "clay," "flip," "glow," "plant," "slip"; and *s* blends as in "score," "skin," "smile," "snore," "spin," "stick," "sweet."

Practice the initial consonant blends by writing and reading Tongue Twister Blends. In writing the tongue twisters, you provide your second grader with the opportunity to manipulate language, practice blends, and use *alliteration*, a figure of speech formed when words begin with the same sound.

Make a book of tongue twisters. Encourage your child to draw illustrations to accompany each one. Examples include:

Great green grass grows in the grand garden.
Blue blimps blow by the bay.
Spinning spiders spy spotty spittlebugs.

Over time, on separate sheets of paper, write a tongue twister for each consonant blend. Staple together or punch a hole in the upper left-hand corner of each page. Tie the pages together with yarn, ribbon, or string. Read the tongue twisters and add the book to your child's personal library.

REQUIRED:
- Paper and pencil

OPTIONAL:
- Crayons/markers
- Stapler
- Hole punch
- Yarn/ribbon/string

A+ ACTIVITIES FOR SECOND GRADE

BLEND A SENTENCE

SKILLS: Phonetic Analysis/Initial Consonant Blends/Brainstorming/Nouns/Verbs/
Adjectives/Application/Sentence Structure/Written Expression

The consonant blends are formed when *r, l,* or *s* joins a second consonant as in *br, gl, st.*
By applying the consonant blends to reading and writing, second graders move toward
mastery of these phonetic elements.

Blend a Sentence that incorporates words with consonant blends. Prepare for this
activity by brainstorming nouns, verbs, and adjectives that begin with consonant blends.
Write each word on a slip of paper. Fold the slips and place the words in three bowls,
one for nouns, one for verbs, and one for adjectives.

Invite your second grader to choose one word from each bowl. Open the folded papers
and read the words. Work independently to write a sentence that incorporates the three words in any
form. Read your sentences aloud. Then choose again to make new sentences.

NOUNS: brother, creature, drum, frog, grasshopper, principal, treehouse, blanket, clown, flower,
gloves, plane, scarecrow, skunk, slippers, smoke, snowman, spoon, star, swimmer

ADJECTIVES: brave, crowded, drab, frightened, great, proud, tremendous, blue, cloudy, flat,
glamorous, pleasant, scary, skinny, slimy, smart, sneaky, special, stuffed, sweet

VERBS: bring, cry, drip, freeze, grow, prance, trick, blow, clap, fly, glow, play, scatter, skate,
slide, smell, sneeze, speak, stop, swing

REQUIRED:
• Paper and pencils
• Bowls

LIBRARY BLEND BLAST

SKILLS: Phonetic Analysis/Initial Consonant Blends

Have a blast the next time you visit your personal, school, or local library. Remind
your child that a consonant blend is formed when *r, l,* or *s* joins a second consonant, as in *dr, pl,* and *sn.* Look for books with initial consonant blends in the titles.
Find one title with an *r* blend, one with an *l* blend, and one with an *s* blend. Read
book jackets, view illustrations, and make a selection. Enjoy and discuss the story,
making note of initial consonant blends.

Delight in the antics of *Sheila Rae, The Brave* by Kevin Henkes. Celebrate sharing
in *The Paper Crane* by Molly Bang. Travel the world with *My Great-Aunt Arizona* by Gloria Houston. Join
a second-grade outing in *Triplet Trouble and the Class Trip* by Debbie Dadey and Marcia Thornton Jones.
Outfox a fox in *Flossie & the Fox* by Patricia C. McKissack. Climb to the moon in *Papa, please get the
moon for me* by Eric Carle. Mail *Flat Stanley* by Jeff Brown. Make up inven-
tions in *Snaggle Doodles* by Patricia Reilly Giff. Help as *Nate the Great
Saves the King of Sweden* by Marjorie Weinman Sharmat.

REQUIRED:
• Library visit

THE END BLEND BOWL

SKILLS: Phonetic Analysis/Final Consonant Blends/Brainstorming

Invite family members to gather around the table for The End Blend Bowl. Remind your second grader that a final consonant blend is made when two consonants blend their sounds at the end of a word. Each sound is still heard, as in "lamp," "mask," "raft."

To begin, write final blends *ft, lk, mp, nd, nk, nt, sk, st* on individual slips of paper. Fold each and place in a bowl in the center of the playing area. Ask your second grader to go first by selecting one slip of paper from the bowl and reading the final blend aloud.

Now get ready to think fast! Set a timer to two minutes and say, "Go!" All participants brainstorm and write words that include the final blend chosen. When time is up, read the lists, crossing out any words that appear on more than one list. Award a point for each final blend word written on a list that no one else has included. Continue clockwise around the table, each time selecting a different final consonant blend. When play ends, tally the results to determine the winner.

REQUIRED:
- Paper and pencils
- Timer

DELICIOUS DIGRAPHS

SKILLS: Phonetic Analysis/Consonant Digraphs/Brainstorming

Create a tasty treat to reinforce that a consonant digraph is formed when two consonants work together to make one new sound, as in *ch, sh, th,* and *wh.* Imagine the mouthwatering digraph sundaes you can make either at home or at your favorite ice cream parlor.

While preparing, selecting, and eating your sundaes, brainstorm all the words related to the sundae that include a consonant digraph. Perhaps you'll have *ch*ocolate *ch*ips, *ch*ocolate sprinkles, or *ch*ocolate sauce on your ri*ch* *ch*ocolate ice cream. Maybe you'll add a scoop of pea*ch* *sh*erbet topped with butterscot*ch* sauce. Try mar*sh*mallow topping or mountains of *wh*ipped cream. If you have a sweet too*th,* add *ch*ewy Baby Ru*th* candy bars, cracked bits of Hea*th* Bar, *wh*ite *ch*ocolate bits, or hunks of Her*sh*ey kisses. *Ch*opped nuts are always yummy, along with cru*sh*ed pineapple topping. No matter what the ingredients, enjoy this amazingly mun*ch*y confection. Then wa*sh* away your *th*irst with a smoo*th* cold drink. Finally, work with your second grader to brainstorm and list, on a four-column sheet of paper, other words that include the digraphs in initial, medial, or final position.

REQUIRED:
- Paper and pencils
- Ice cream sundae ingredients

OPTIONAL:
- Ice cream parlor visit

TRIPLE C

SKILLS: Phonetic Analysis/Consonant Clusters/Brainstorming/Handwriting/Spelling/Expressive Language

A consonant cluster is made when three consonants or a consonant digraph and a consonant work together to blend their sounds. Each sound is still heard, as in "screech," "sprout," "splint," "strong," "shrill," and "thrift." Play Triple *C, Consonant Cluster Concentration,* to review and reinforce consonant clusters for reading and spelling.

Brainstorm a list of 24 words, each with a consonant cluster. Neatly print each word two times on a 3″ × 5″ index card, once on the left side of the card and again on the right. Cut the cards in half and shuffle. Place the cards facedown in rows on the table, eight cards per row. Alternate play, turning over two cards. If the words don't match, turn them facedown in the original position. If the words do match, pick them up, read them, use each in a sentence, and go again. The one with the most pairs at the end wins!

WORD BANK:		
	scr:	scrap, scribble, scream, describe
	shr:	shred, shrimp, shrink, shrug
	spl:	splash, splatter, split, splot
	spr:	spray, spread, spring, sprinkle
	str:	strawberry, stream, instruct, instrument
	thr:	thread, three, threw, thrust

REQUIRED:
- Index cards
- Marker
- Safety scissors

REACH FOR THE STAR

SKILLS: Phonetic Analysis/*r*-Controlled Vowels/Brainstorming/Expressive Language

Second graders know the sound of short *a,* as in "cat," and the sound of long *a,* as in "cake," "pail," and "tray." They have been exposed to the sound *a* makes when *r* comes along to take charge, as in "bark." Play Reach for the Star to reinforce recognition of *ar* in reading and writing.

Make a file folder gameboard. Open the folder vertically. In the lower left-hand corner, draw a red square, labeled "Yard." In the upper right-hand corner, draw a yellow star, labeled "Star." Draw a winding path of 20 to 30 circles to connect Yard and Star. In six selected circles, write messages such as "Jump far, move ahead 2." "Sticky tar, lose one turn." "Hot sparks, race ahead 3." "Park the car, go back 1." "Rocket starts, go again." "Large comet, go back 2." Brainstorm *ar* words. Print one word in each of the remaining circles. Use buttons or coins as game pieces.

REQUIRED:
- File folder
- Pencil/marker
- Die
- Game pieces

Place game pieces on Yard. Alternate turns. Toss a die, move that number of spaces, read the word, and use it in a sentence. The first player to reach Star is the winner. Fold the file for easy storage.

AT THE SHORE

Second graders know the sound of short *o* as in "mop" and the sound of long *o* as in "home," "goat," and "toe." They have been exposed to the sound *o* makes when *r* comes along to take charge as in "sport." Play At the Shore to reinforce recognition of *or* in reading and writing.

Make a file folder gameboard. Open the folder horizontally. In the upper left-hand corner draw a pink circle labeled "Coral." In the lower right-hand corner draw a tan rectangle labeled "Shore." Draw a winding path of 20 to 30 shell shapes to connect Coral and Shore. In six selected shells, write messages such as "Ride a seahorse, move ahead 3." "Storm alert, lose one turn." "Sunny morning, go again." "Foghorn blows, go back 3." "Go snorkeling, swim ahead 2." "Torn shorts, go back 2." Brainstorm *or* words. Print one word in each of the remaining shells. Use buttons, coins, or shells as game pieces.

Place game pieces on Coral. Alternate turns. Toss a die, move that number of spaces, read the word, and use it in a sentence. The first player to reach Shore is the winner. Fold the file for easy storage.

REQUIRED:
- File folder
- Pencil/marker
- Die
- Game pieces

TREASURE CHEST

Since *er, ir,* and *ur* sound the same in words such as "her," "third," and "purse," second graders use phonetic analysis and sight word recognition skills to read and write *r*-controlled words. Reinforce recognition of these words by playing Treasure Chest.

Make a lotto card for you and your child. Divide each card into nine equal sections. Brainstorm and list *er, ir,* and *ur* words. Print three of each in random order on the cards, one word per section. Don't use a word on more than one card. Cut gold coins from yellow paper. Write a word on each coin to match each word on the cards. Put the coins into a box decorated as a treasure chest.

Alternate turns picking a coin. Read the coin and look for a match on your card. If you have a match, cover the word with the coin. If not, return the coin to the box. Continue until one of you has filled a card.

REQUIRED:
- Yellow construction paper
- Markers
- Safety scissors
- Box
- Art supplies

WORD BANK: clerk, fern, ruler, sister, butter, germ, dessert, serve, herd, stir, girl, dirt, skirt, bird, thirst, chirp, twirl, squirt, fur, burst, hurt, turn, nurse, surf, turtle, curl, purr

R-CONTROLLED READ

SKILLS: Phonetic Analysis/*r*-Controlled Vowels

Put the focus on the *r*-controlled vowels as you share a book with your second grader. By applying phonetic analysis rules for reading *r*-controlled vowels, children internalize the rules and make application automatic.

Select any book with an *r*-controlled word in the title. Sit down, relax, and read together. Enjoy and discuss the story while noting words with *r*-controlled vowels. Upon completion of the story, if you wish, go back and list words found. A list of possible titles follows.

*Three Sm*a*rt Pals* by Joanne Rocklin, <u>*Argyle*</u> by Barbara Brooks Wallace, *Cam Jansen and the Mystery of the C*a*rnival Prize* by David A. Adler, *Poppleton F*o*rev*e*r* by Cynthia Rylant, *The Sw*o*rd in the Stone* by Grace Maccarone, *The Littles Go Expl*o*ring* by John Peterson, *Walt*e*r the Bak*e*r* by Eric Carle, *The St*o*ry of F*e*rdinand* by Munro Leaf, *There's A Hamst*e*r In My Lunchbox* by Susan Clymer, <u>*Bi*</u>*rthday Presents* by Cynthia Rylant, *The Thi*<u>*rd*</u>*-St*o*ry Cat* by Leslie Baker, *The Fi*<u>*rst*</u> *Day of School* by Tony Johnston, *The Amazing Panda Advent*u*re* adapted by Grace Kim, *Don't Eat Too Much T*u*rkey!* by Miriam Cohen, *A Day with Wilb*u*r Robinson* by William Joyce.

REQUIRED:
- A book

OPTIONAL:
- Library/bookstore visit
- Paper and pencil

R-CONTROLLED WRITE

SKILLS: Phonetic Analysis/*r*-Controlled Vowels/Brainstorming/Story Form/
Written Expression/Spelling/Handwriting/Drawing

Put the focus on the *r*-controlled vowels as you encourage your second grader to write a story. By using *r*-controlled vowels in their writing, children internalize the rules and make application automatic.

Begin by selecting a topic. Then work with your child to brainstorm *r*-controlled words that are specific to the topic. For example, choose baseball or softball. The list you'll generate is long, including words such as "ballpark," "superstar," "ice cream bars," "vendor's cart," "Cardinals," "baseball cards," "sports," "popcorn," "score," "scoreboard," "souvenir store," "Orioles," "spectators," "error," "pitcher," "catcher," "batter," "players," "manager," "bleachers," "homer," "banner," "Mariners," "Dodgers," "Brewers," "first base," "third base," "turnstile," "frankfurter."

No matter what the topic, select words from your list and weave them into a story that has a beginning, a middle, and an end. Remind your child to include a main character, a setting that tells where and when the story takes place, and a wish or problem that drives the story forward. While your child writes, you write, too. Take time to share your stories. Illustrate and bind to add to your family library.

REQUIRED:
- Paper and pencil
- Markers/crayons
- Stapler

OPTIONAL:
- Yarn/ribbon/string for binding
- Hole punch

MOUSE OR OWL

SKILLS: Phonetic Analysis/Diphthongs/Drawing/Cutting/Brainstorming/
Spelling/Expressive Language/Counting

A diphthong is made when two vowels work together to make one sound as in "mouse" and "owl." Note that *w* acts as a vowel when paired with *o*.

Draw and cut a 6" mouse and 6" owl. Place the figures in the center of a table. Provide each player with a pencil, a scorecard divided into two columns—one labeled "Mouse," the other, "Owl"—and two plastic chips. Point out that *ou* and *ow* make the same sound.

Alternate turns. Use one chip to snap the other chip to "Mouse" or "Owl." If the chip lands on "Mouse," the player says an *ou* word. If the chip lands on "Owl," the player says an *ow* word. In either case, use the word in a sentence and write it in the appropriate column on the scorecard. If a player lands on "Mouse" but says "cow," ask that player to try another word for *ou*. Play several rounds. Count all *ou* words and *ow* words to see whether "Mouse" or "Owl" wins.

For reinforcement read *Mouse Tales* or *Owl at Home* by Arnold Lobel and *Town Mouse Country Mouse* by Jan Brett.

REQUIRED:
- Construction paper
- Paper and pencils
- Safety scissors
- Marker
- Plastic chips

OPTIONAL:
- Library/bookstore visit

ROYAL FOIL

SKILLS: Phonetic Analysis/Diphthongs/Brainstorming/Spelling/Counting

A diphthong is made when two vowels work together to make one sound. Your child may know that *oi* and *oy* make the same sound in familiar words such as "join" and "boy," words probably read from sight. Your child also needs to apply the diphthongs *oi* and *oy* to read and spell unfamiliar words such as "moisture" and "annoy."

Provision yourselves with small slips of paper, pencils, and two sheets of foil. Mold each sheet of foil into a Royal Foil shallow cup; one for you, one for your child. Set the timer to three minutes and say, "Go!"

Independently, you and your child quickly brainstorm and write *oi* and *oy* words, one word per slip of paper. Put the words, as they're generated, into your individual Royal Foil cup.

When time is up, alternate turns. Remove a slip, read the word, and place it on the table before you. When all words have been read, remove any that you have in common. Receive a point for all remaining words from your cup. Tally the results to determine the winner.

For reinforcement read books such as *Corduroy* by Don Freeman and *Night Noises* by Mem Fox.

REQUIRED:
- Foil
- Paper and pencils
- Timer

OPTIONAL:
- Library/bookstore visit

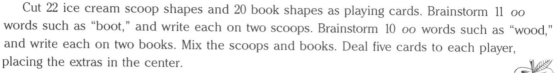

SCOOPS AND BOOKS

SKILLS: Phonetic Analysis/Diphthongs/Brainstorming/Auditory Discrimination/Spelling/Cutting/Counting

Play Scoops and Books, a variation of Go Fish, to build your child's facility with *oo*, a diphthong that has two sounds, as in "tool" and "hook."

Cut 22 ice cream scoop shapes and 20 book shapes as playing cards. Brainstorm 11 *oo* words such as "boot," and write each on two scoops. Brainstorm 10 *oo* words such as "wood," and write each on two books. Mix the scoops and books. Deal five cards to each player, placing the extras in the center.

In turn, ask an opponent for a word. If the opponent has the word, he or she hands it over. Place the pair faceup on the table and go again. If the opponent doesn't have the word, the opponent says, "Scoops and Books!" The asker takes a card from the center pile. Play continues until all cards from the center are gone or one player has no cards left. The player with the most pairs wins.

For fun, enjoy scoops of ice cream and books such as *The Big Balloon Race* by Eleanor Coerr or *Bookworm Buddies* by Judy Delton.

REQUIRED:
- Construction paper
- Pencil
- Safety scissors

OPTIONAL:
- Library/bookstore visit
- Ice cream

HAUNTED HAWK

SKILLS: Phonetic Analysis/Diphthongs/Brainstorming/Spelling/Sentence Structure/Written Expression

A diphthong is made when two vowels work together to make one sound, as in "sauce" and "fawn." Note that *w* acts as a vowel when paired with *a*.

Have rousing fun creating silly sentences that incorporate words with *au* and *aw*. Brainstorm *au* words and write each on a slip of paper. Do the same with *aw* words. Fold the slips. Put the *au* words in one container, labeled "au," and the *aw* words in another, labeled "aw."

Choose one word from each container. Open the folded papers and read the words. Work independently to write a silly sentence that includes both words. For example, choose "haunted" and "hawk" and write, "A dizzy hawk flew into the haunted house and scared the socks off a ghost." Read your sentences aloud to recognize the amazing power of the imagination.

Apply *au* and *aw* to reading when sharing books such as *The Mapmaker's Daughter* by Mary-Claire Helldorfer, *Mufaro's Beautiful Daughters* by John Steptoe, *Little Hawk's New Name* by Don Bolognese, and *Scrawny the Classroom Duck* by Susan Clymer.

REQUIRED:
- Paper and pencil
- Container

OPTIONAL:
- Library/bookstore visit

WORD BANK: applaud, astronaut, author, automobile, exhaust, faucet, laundry, launch, naughty, saucer, awful, claw, dawn, draw, fawn, jaw, jigsaw, paws, seesaw, strawberry

LANGUAGE ARTS ACTIVITIES

SHEW PLEW

In the diphthong *ew*, *w* acts as a vowel, working with *e* to make the sound heard in "flew" and "grew." Change the old card game Slap Jack to Shew Plew to enjoy lively reinforcement of the diphthong *ew*.

Cut index cards in half to make a deck of cards. Together, design a buglike creature called a "plew." Draw and color the plew on three cards. Print "Shew Plew" above each bug. Brainstorm words that include *ew*. Write each word on a card.

Sit opposite your child. Shuffle the cards, randomly including the three "Shew Plew" cards. Deal all the cards, placing the piles facedown before the players. Alternate turns to draw a card, place it in the center, and read the word. When a "Shew Plew" card appears, be the first to slap the pile, call "Shew Plew," and take all the cards in the pile. Continue play until one player has won all the cards.

Apply *ew* to reading by sharing books such as *The Wind Blew* by Pat Hutchins or *Franklin's New Friend* by Paulette Bourgeois and Brenda Clark.

REQUIRED:
- Index cards
- Pencil/marker
- Safety scissors

OPTIONAL:
- Library/bookstore visit

WORD BANK: dew, few, mew, pew, brew, crew, drew, renew, screw, skewer, stew, strew

RICE CAKES

Reinforce your child's awareness of the two sounds of *c* by pointing out the difference. Young readers regularly meet familiar words with initial, medial, and final *c*. Combining their phonetic analysis skills and their sight word recognition skills, children read "cat," "cold," "cute," "crib," "clock," "attic," "mice," "city," and "lacy" without stopping to note that *c* sounds like /k/, the hard sound, in some words and like /s/, the soft sound, in others. Usually, *c* is hard when followed by *a, o, u, l, r,* or nothing. *C* is usually soft when followed by *e, i,* or *y*.

Write the phrase "Rice Cakes," leaving a big space between the two words. Ask your child to notice something unusual about *c*. Set to work on a newspaper or magazine Rice Cakes search. Find and circle words with *c*. Look at the letter following *c*, read the words, listen to the sound of *c*, and write the words on the paper under "Rice" or "Cakes."

While munching on a rice cake, apply the rules of *c* when you share a book such as *Cross Country Cat* by Mary Calhoun or *Just Plain Fancy* by Patricia Polacco.

REQUIRED:
- Paper and pencil
- Newspaper/magazine

OPTIONAL:
- Library/bookstore visit
- Rice cakes

GOAT OR GIRAFFE?

SKILLS: Phonetic Analysis/Hard & Soft *g*/Sight Word Recognition/Auditory
Discrimination/Drawing/Brainstorming/Spelling

Reinforce your child's awareness of the two sounds of *g* by pointing out the difference. Young readers regularly meet familiar words with initial, medial, and final *g*. Combining their phonetic analysis skills and their sight word recognition skills, children read "gas," "good," "gum," "grass," "glow," "rug," "large," "giant," and "gym" without stopping to note that *g* sounds like /guh/, the hard sound, in some words and like /j/, the soft sound, in others. Usually, *g* is hard when followed by *a*, *o*, *u*, *l*, *r*, or nothing. *G* is usually soft when followed by *e*, *i*, or *y*.

Draw a goat on one piece of paper and a giraffe on another. Brainstorm words that include either hard or soft *g*. If the *g* is hard, write the word below the goat. If the *g* is soft, write the word below the giraffe. Read all the words and use each in a sentence.

Apply the rules of *g* when you share a book such as *The Three Billy Goats Gruff* by Paul Galdone or *A Giraffe and a Half* by Shel Silverstein.

REQUIRED:
- Paper and pencil
- Crayons/markers

OPTIONAL:
- Library/bookstore visit

SPIN FOR C OR G

SKILLS: Phonetic Analysis/Hard and Soft *c* & *g*/Sight Word Recognition/
Auditory Discrimination/Drawing/Brainstorming/Spelling

Reinforce your child's awareness of the sounds of hard and soft *c* and *g* for reading and spelling by playing Spin for *C* or *G*.

For the spinner, divide a 6″ square of cardboard into four sections. Draw a cat in one square labeled "Cat," mice in another labeled "Mice," a dog labeled "Dog," and a giraffe labeled "Giraffe." Cut a cardboard arrow and connect it to the center with a paper fastener.

For the gameboard, open a file folder vertically. In the lower left-hand corner, draw a car labeled "Car." In the upper right-hand corner, draw a garage labeled "Garage." Draw a path of 30 squares from Car to Garage.

Brainstorm words with soft *c* as in "city," hard *c* as in "candy," soft *g* as in "ginger," and hard *g* as in "gum." Write the words in mixed order, one word per square, from Car to Garage.

Place game pieces on Car. Alternate turns as you spin the spinner, move to a word with the matching *c* or *g* sound, read the word, spell the word, and use it in a sentence. The first to the garage wins!

REQUIRED:
- Cardboard
- Pencil/marker
- Paper fastener
- File folder
- Game pieces
- Safety scissors

NARROW IT DOWN TO A NOUN

SKILLS: Nouns/Vocabulary Development/Expressive Language

In grade one, we call them naming words. In grade two, we call them *nouns*. Nouns are words that name a person, place, or thing. *Proper nouns* name a specific person, place, or thing: John Glenn, America, Challenger. *Common nouns* are not specific: astronaut, country, space shuttle.

Narrow It Down to a Noun to reinforce your child's knowledge of nouns. Follow the basic rules of Twenty Questions. Alternate turns to think of a person, place, or thing. When you are "it," tell the other players that the word you have in mind names a place, for example. The players then ask questions that require a *yes* or *no* answer. The object of the game is to narrow it down to the noun you have in mind.

Say, "I'm thinking of a place. It is a common noun."

QUESTION:	Do we go there every day?	ANSWER:	No.
	Can we get there by car?		Yes.
	Do we go there in the daytime?		Yes.
	Can we eat there?		Yes.
	Is it a restaurant?		No.
	Do we play there?		Yes.
	Is it the park?		Yes.

REQUIRED:
• Your time

OPTIONAL:
• Library/bookstore visit

To learn more about nouns, read *Merry-Go-Round: A Book About Nouns* by Ruth Heller.

NOUNS ABOUND

SKILLS: Nouns/Brainstorming/Vocabulary Development/Categorizing

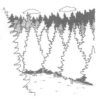

Gather the family around to discover that Nouns Abound. Sit around the kitchen table or spread a blanket on the grass in the yard or park. Then with paper and pencil in hand, take turns as caller to name a category such as:

• things you see in a forest, jungle, desert
• places that begin with *B, T, A*
• kinds of candy
• occupations
• articles of clothing
• means of transportation
• animals that live in the ocean

REQUIRED:
• Paper and pencil
• Timer

OPTIONAL:
• Countable treat

All players write the category at the top of the page. When the category caller says, "Go!" all players individually brainstorm and write words that fit the category. Keep the action quick, limiting each round to three minutes. When time is up, compare lists. Get one M&M, jellybean, gumdrop, or pretzel for every noun listed that no one else had. Play several rounds but don't eat the treats until the very end. The player with the most wins!

THE MOVERS AND SHAKERS

SKILLS: Verbs/Vocabulary Development

In grade one we call them action words. In grade two we call the action words *verbs*. Second graders recognize that verbs show physical action we can see, such as "run," "dance," "jump," "fall." They also understand that verbs show mental action we can't see, such as "wonder," "dream," "know."

Impress your second grader by introducing The Movers and Shakers, the all-important verbs that make our oral and written language strong. Every sentence must have a verb, and your child can enjoy finding them as you scan the morning paper to search for verbs.

Take a few minutes and a couple of red markers and collaboratively or independently circle verbs. Share your findings by reading the verbs and discussing meaning. Notice the different endings and forms of verbs, but don't get into any kind of detailed explanation of tense, number, or person. Simply check out the verbs.

You may want to learn more about verbs by reading *Kites Sail High: A Book About Verbs* by Ruth Heller.

REQUIRED:
• Newspaper
• Markers

OPTIONAL:
• Library/bookstore visit

ONE UP THE ACTION

SKILLS: Verbs/Vocabulary Development/Synonyms/Sentence Structure/Making Comparisons

Invite your second grader to One Up the Action by replacing "flat" verbs with "big, chunky, powerful" ones.

Write a sentence such as, "The elephant walked into the pond." Draw a squiggle under the word "walked" to show that you'd like your child to replace the verb "walked" with a strong and powerful synonym.

Pass the paper and pencil to your child to make the change. Responses might include, "The elephant tromped, clomped, lumbered, splashed into the pond."

Try another sentence: "Six children ran across the field." Draw a squiggle under "ran" and pass the paper to your child. Responses might include, "Six children galloped, raced, charged, sprinted across the field."

Invite all family members to participate as you use verbs to make things happen. Be sure to compare the results.

REQUIRED:
• Paper and pencils

WHICH TEDDY, WHICH TRUCK?

SKILLS: Adjectives/Brainstorming/Vocabulary Development

"Look at the bird!"

"Which bird?"

"The *black* bird with the *small red* patch on *its* wing."

Adjectives are words that describe or tell about people, places, things, actions, or qualities. During second grade, children become familiar with adjectives that describe appearance and behavior.

Review and reinforce, in a concrete way, your child's facility with adjectives that tell how something looks. Gather a collection of five similar objects. Use teddy bears or toy trucks, action figures or dolls, t-shirts or hats. Place the objects on a table or countertop. For example, put a baseball hat, sun hat, beret, bonnet, and winter hat on the table. Say to your child, "Please hand me the hat."

Your child might look at you with a puzzled expression and ask, "Which hat?"

To determine which hat, take time to brainstorm and record five adjectives for each hat. The sun hat adjectives might include "tan," "floppy," "flowered," "lightweight," "straw." When all adjectives have been generated, place the hats about the room. Then say, "Please bring me the woolly, soft, blue, fuzzy, warm hat."

Your child will have no trouble retrieving each requested hat using adjectives to guide the way!

REQUIRED:
- Paper and pencil
- Collection of five similar objects

HAM IT UP

SKILLS: Adjectives/Vocabulary Development/Expressive Language/Imaginative Thinking

Concretely demonstrate that adjectives show how someone or something acts when you Ham It Up. Tell your child in advance that you are going to act out a behavior with actions and words. Your child needs to watch and listen as you walk in, stretch, yawn, rub your eyes, and say, "I didn't get to bed last night until midnight . . ." Be sure not to say "tired," "sleepy," "exhausted," or "drowsy." Continue with your performance until your child provides an appropriate adjective. Invite the whole family to participate, taking turns to demonstrate adjectives that describe behavior.

WORD BANK: excited, scared, grouchy, impatient, angry, cold, hot, annoyed, happy, sad, hungry

REQUIRED:
- Your time

A+ ACTIVITIES FOR SECOND GRADE

CARET A WORD

SKILLS: Adjectives/Vocabulary Development/Written Expression/Imaginative Thinking/Making Comparisons

Anytime your child writes, anytime you write, share your work and Caret a Word. As you read your child's latest book review, weekend adventure, favorite place description, or letter to a book character, look for places to pop in a *caret* (^). A caret is a revising tool that suggests the spot as a good one for an adjective, a word that describes how a person, place, or thing looks or acts. Challenge your second grader to write an appropriate adjective just above the caret. Remember that adjectives can also tell how many and show ownership.

To get started, copy the sentences below onto two sheets of paper. Pop a caret or two into each one. Then encourage your child to add an adjective for each caret while you do the same. Compare sentences and note the differences that result from including adjectives.

1. At the beach, girls floated in the water.
2. A puppy barked at the ball.
3. The airplane flew into the clouds.
4. We had fun on our trip to the mountains.

To learn more about adjectives, enjoy *Many Luscious Lollipops: A Book About Adjectives* by Ruth Heller.

> **REQUIRED:**
> - Paper and pencil
> - Written work
>
> **OPTIONAL:**
> - Library/bookstore visit

THE SUBSTITUTE WORDS

SKILLS: Pronoun Usage/Vocabulary Development/Sentence Structure

Just as a substitute takes the place of a teacher, so does a *pronoun* take the place of a noun. The job of pronouns is to stand for nouns in sentences.

To enhance your child's use of pronouns, write "I," "You," "He," "She," "It," "We," "They," "him," "her," "us," and "them" on small sticky tags, one pronoun per tag. Place the sticky tags faceup on the table. Using a marker and construction paper, write a sentence such as "Mom ran six miles." Make the print large enough to accommodate the sticky tag as a substitute for the noun.

Ask your second grader to read the sentence aloud. Next find the sticky tag pronoun that can substitute for "Mom." Place "She" over "Mom" and reread the sentence.

Use the following sentences to get started; then alternate turns making up sentences and substituting the sticky tag pronouns for nouns.

Learn more about pronouns by reading *Mine, All Mine: A Book About Pronouns* by Ruth Heller.

> **REQUIRED:**
> - Sticky tags
> - Construction paper
> - Marker
>
> **OPTIONAL:**
> - Library/bookstore visit

SENTENCE BANK:

Dad made popcorn.
My sister and I went swimming.
Tell the children to come home.

Deidre and Bob walked to town.
Give the book to Jeff.
Don telephoned Patty.

STAND UP, SIT DOWN

SKILLS: Pronoun Usage/Oral Reading Fluency

Since pronouns stand for nouns, invite your second grader to stand for pronouns!

To enhance your child's use of pronouns, Stand Up, Sit Down each time you hear a pronoun. Choose any book, poem, or story from your child's personal library. Line up the kitchen chairs, one chair for each participant. Alternate turns as the reader. As the reader slowly and clearly presents a page or poem, all participants listen for a pronoun. When they hear one, they stand up. Participants remain standing until they hear the next. Then they sit down. Hear another, stand up. Then the next, sit down.

Be sure to focus on the "doers" (I, you, he, she, it, we, they), the "receivers" (me, you, him, her, us, them), and the "owners" (my, mine, your[s], his, her[s], its, our[s], their[s]).

REQUIRED:
- A book or poem
- Chairs

SWITCH AND READ

SKILLS: Pronoun Usage/Oral Reading Fluency

Imagine how repetitive language would be without the pronouns, the words that stand for nouns! Try Switch and Read to reinforce and enhance your second grader's facility with pronouns.

Choose any story or poem from your child's personal library. Read a paragraph or verse aloud. Pay special attention to the pronouns used.

Now try to read the same paragraph or verse without the pronouns. Switch every pronoun you read with the noun it replaces. By the time you've read a few paragraphs or verses, your second grader will recognize that pronouns are useful, necessary, and important. To get started, try the following rhyme:

There was a young lady named Sue.
When *she* had nothing to do,
She ran to the kitchen
Because *she* was itchin'
For candy and cookies and goo!

She started on shelf number one.
Peanuts and popcorn what fun,
On shelf number two
She found marshmallow stew
She ate everything under the sun!

REQUIRED:
- A book or poem

STICKY TAG IT

SKILLS: Compound Words/Brainstorming/Vocabulary Development/Spelling

"Pop" without the "corn" doesn't taste salty and buttery! "Base" without the "ball" isn't quite the same! A *compound word,* "popcorn" or "baseball," is made when two words join to make one.

Use sticky tags to reinforce your child's facility with compound words. Write the first half of a compound word on a sticky tag. Stick the tag, with a blank one beside it, anywhere in your home—on a cabinet, vase, mirror, cereal box, cookie jar, or door. Repeat the process for 10 words.

Provide an example to remind your child that a compound word is made from two words put together. Ask your second grader to search for 10 sticky tags that need partners. Find the word "sea"; write "weed," "shell," or "sick" on the blank tag beside it. Continue in this manner until all the compound words have been found. Gather all words to read.

As a variation, write the second half of the word and ask your child to provide the first half. Sticky tag both beginnings and endings for extra challenge.

REQUIRED:
- Sticky tags
- Pencil

WORD BANK: cupcake, backpack, oatmeal, sunshine, doghouse, gumdrop, paintbrush, pigpen, blueberry, downtown, sidewalk, scarecrow, railroad, football, basketball, rainbow

COMPOUND COLLECTION

SKILLS: Compound Words/Spelling/Handwriting/Sentence Structure/Drawing

Authenticate compound words by recognizing and applying them in reading and writing. The next time you share a book or story together, begin your child's Compound Collection. Remember that a compound word, "snowman," is made of two words joined to make a new word.

Label the cover of a notebook "Compound Collection." After enjoying a story, return to the text. For each compound word you find, make a page entry. Write the word "tiptoe," for example, followed by "tip + toe = tiptoe." Then encourage your second grader to write a sentence that includes the word. Finally, draw an illustration to accompany the sentence. To enhance the appearance of the Compound Collection, encourage left-to-right, top-to-bottom handwriting that is neatly formed. Add to the collection whenever you meet a compound word in reading or whenever a new one comes to mind. Reread the compound words and sentences for reinforcement.

REQUIRED:
- Notebook/journal
- Pencil
- Crayons/markers
- Book

OPTIONAL:
- Library/bookstore visit

Consider starting your collection by reading a book with a compound word in the title, such as *Horrible Harry and the Kickball Wedding* by Suzy Kline. In chapter one alone you'll find "anything," "stinkbug," "eyebrows," "whatever," "everyone," "something," "sweatshirt," "hourglass," "outside," "kickball," and "funnybone."

HEART TO HART

SKILLS: Homonyms/Brainstorming/Vocabulary Development/Spelling/Drawing

Homonyms are words that sound alike, are spelled differently, and have different meanings. Learning to *write* the *right* homonym can be *too* confusing because there are *two* or more spellings or meanings *to* learn.

Reinforce and enhance your second grader's facility with homonyms for reading, writing, and spelling by playing Heart to Hart. (A hart is a red deer!) Open a file folder horizontally. In the lower left-hand corner, draw a heart labeled "Heart." In the upper right-hand corner, draw a heart labeled "Hart." Connect the two with a winding path of 40 hearts.

Brainstorm a list of 20 pairs of homonyms. Randomly write each word in one of the hearts along the path. Place game pieces on Heart. Alternate turns as you roll the die and move that number of hearts. Read the word you land on, spell the word, and use the word in a sentence. The first to reach Hart wins.

REQUIRED:
- File folder
- Pencil/marker
- Game pieces

WORD BANK: base/bass be/bee beat/beet board/bored buy/by cellar/seller fair/fare chews/choose close/clothes break/brake cent/sent deer/dear heel/heal peak/peek guessed/guest knot/not steal/steel some/sum weak/week wood/would

HOMONYM HUNT

SKILLS: Homonyms/Vocabulary Development/Spelling/Sentence Construction/Drawing

The next time you share a book, hunt for homonyms: words that sound the same, are spelled differently, and have different meanings.

Label a notebook, "Homonym Helper Glossary." Label each page with one letter from *A* to *Z*.

After reading and discussing a story, return to the text to search for homonyms.

Work together to scan the pages. As soon as you find a homonym, call out, "Found one!" Look at the homonym, reread it in context, and discuss the meaning. Then turn to the alphabetical page in your glossary to make the first entry. For example, find "grown." Turn to the *G* page. Ask your child to write "grown" and an original sentence that incorporates "grown." Just beneath "grown," write "groan" and an original sentence that incorporates "groan." A sample entry thus appears:

G

grown   Flowers are grown in the garden.

groan   I groan when I stub my toe.

Add entries every time you hold a Homonym Hunt or whenever a homonym comes to mind. Keep the glossary handy as a homework helper for writing and spelling.

For extra reinforcement, enjoy *The King Who Rained* by Fred Gwynn. See what happens when a writer plays with homonyms.

REQUIRED:
- A book
- Notebook
- Pencil

OPTIONAL:
- Library/bookstore visit

SYNONYM SQUIGGLE

SKILLS: Synonyms/Expressive Language/Vocabulary Development/
Brainstorming/Written Expression/Making Comparisons

Synonyms are words that have the same or nearly the same meaning. A synonym for "smart" is "intelligent."

Share a book to search for synonyms and have fun with words. While reading a story such as *Cowardly Clyde* by Bill Peet, make a list of all the words used that mean the same as "said."

Next try a Synonym Squiggle. On two sheets of paper, write a sentence such as, "This cookie is tasty." Draw a squiggle beneath "tasty." Ask your second grader to write other words that mean the same as "tasty" beneath the word. You do the same and then compare lists. Now let your child provide a sentence and squiggle a word for both of you to try. *Close (shut, slam) the door when you leave (go, depart).*

Finally, use the Synonym Squiggle when your child writes a story or nonfiction report. Read the piece together and pencil in a squiggle under words that could use a bit of spice. If you see "nice," "good," or "said," add a squiggle so that your second grader can enliven the language with a synonym.

REQUIRED:
• A book
• Paper and pencils

OPTIONAL:
• Library/bookstore visit

SYNONYM SECRETARY

SKILLS: Synonyms/Expressive Language/Vocabulary Development/Brainstorming/Spelling/Handwriting

Synonyms are words that have the same or nearly the same meaning. Synonyms add color to our oral and written expression. Since everyone tends to overuse certain words in oral and written language, all family members benefit from a synonym logbook that is maintained and updated by your child.

Encourage your second grader to become the family Synonym Secretary. Provide a notebook or journal titled "Family Synonym Logbook." Head the first few pages with commonly overused words, such as "said" on page one, "nice" on page two, "good" on page three. Beneath each word, ask your child to write synonyms.

Brainstorm words for "said" to get started. Possibilities include: "giggled," "whispered," "shouted," "called," "asked," "replied," "squeaked," "laughed," "demanded," "commanded," "requested," "yelled," "screamed," "wondered."

As Synonym Secretary, your child can add to the logbook at any time and invite other family members to do so as well. Be sure to validate your child's efforts by referring to the logbook when looking for words to add color to your own writing.

REQUIRED:
• Notebook/journal
• Pencil

TOPSY-TURVY TALES

SKILLS: Antonyms/Brainstorming/Vocabulary Development/Written Expression/Story Form/Drawing

Antonyms are words that have opposite or nearly opposite meanings. Imagine what a topsy-turvy world it would be if antonyms took over! We'd eat breakfast at night and dinner in the morning! We'd walk when in a hurry and run when taking our time!

To enhance your child's facility with antonyms, create a Topsy-Turvy Tale. Find books with titles that can easily be changed with an antonym. Stories such as *Alexander and the Terrible, Horrible, No Good, Very Bad Day* by Judith Viorst, *Do Not Open* by Brinton Turkle, or *More Spaghetti, I Say* by Rita Golden Gelman work well. Make a list of topsy-turvy titles such as *Alexander and the Wonderful, Terrific, Fantastic, Very Good Day; Do Not Close;* and *Less Spaghetti, I Say!*

Encourage your child to write and illustrate a story for one of the topsy-turvy titles. Remind your child to include a beginning that introduces the main character, the setting and the wish or problem, a middle that tells what the main character does to make the wish come true or solve the problem, and an ending in which the wish is granted or the problem solved.

REQUIRED:
• Books
• Paper and pencil
• Crayons/markers

OPTIONAL:
• Library/bookstore visit

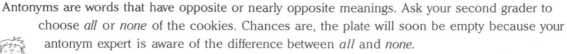

ANTONYM ALBUM

SKILLS: Antonyms/Brainstorming/Vocabulary Development/Sentence Construction/Spelling/Capitalization/Punctuation/Drawing

Antonyms are words that have opposite or nearly opposite meanings. Ask your second grader to choose *all* or *none* of the cookies. Chances are, the plate will soon be empty because your antonym expert is aware of the difference between *all* and *none*.

Reinforce and enhance your child's facility with antonyms for speaking, reading, and writing by making an Antonym Album.

Use a journal or notebook. Ask your child to label the front cover "Antonym Album." Draw a vertical line to divide each page in half. Next brainstorm a list of antonyms.

Working together, on the left half of each page, write one sentence that includes one word of an antonym pair. On the right half of each page, write the same sentence incorporating the other word of the antonym pair. For example, on the left print, "The child is *tall.*" On the right print, "The child is *short.*" Draw an illustration to accompany each sentence.

Encourage your child and all family members to add to the Antonym Album. Validate your child's efforts by regularly reading and reviewing the antonym sentences and drawings.

REQUIRED:
• Journal/notebook
• Pencil
• Ruler
• Crayons/markers

A+ ACTIVITIES FOR SECOND GRADE

CONTRACTION ACTION

SKILLS: Contractions/Vocabulary Development/Spelling/Handwriting/Sentence Structure

I am = I'm. We are = we're. A *contraction* is a short way to write two words. Leave out one or more letters, slip in an apostrophe, and you have a contraction. Recognize and apply contractions the next time you share a book.

Before reading, fold a piece of paper in half to make a booklet. Place the fold on the left to have a front cover, two interior facing pages, and a back cover. After enjoying a story, return to the text. Find a contraction. Write the contraction on the front cover of the booklet. On the left interior page, write a sentence that includes the contraction. On the right interior page, write the same sentence but substitute the two-word equivalent of the contraction. On the back page, write the contraction and its two-word equivalent. Encourage your child to use neatly formed, left-to-right, top-to-bottom handwriting. Make a booklet whenever you meet a new contraction. Reread the contraction booklets for reinforcement.

Consider reading a book with a contraction in the title such as *Can't You Sleep, Little Bear?* by Martin Waddell. You'll find contractions such as "can't," "couldn't," "I'm," "don't," "there's," "I've," and "that's."

REQUIRED:
• Paper and pencil
• A book

OPTIONAL:
• Library/bookstore visit

THE DO AGAIN PART

SKILLS: Prefixes/Vocabulary Development/Brainstorming/Sentence Structure/Rhyme

A *prefix* is a part you add to the beginning of a base word to make a new word. Enhance your second grader's vocabulary with "re-," a prefix that usually means "do again."

I heat myself a cup of tea
I'll reheat some for you and me.

Fill a teacup with slips of paper labeled "re." Brainstorm verbs; write each on a slip of paper and place in a second cup.

Sit beside your child. Alternate turns as you choose a verb from the cup. Read the verb, use it in a sentence, and place the slip on the table before you. Now pick a "re" slip to place at the beginning of the verb to make a new word. Read the new word and use it in a sentence. When all the new words have been read, reread the list, reheat the water, and enjoy a cup of tea!

For added fun, challenge your child to make a two-line rhyme that incorporates both verbs.

WORD BANK: tie, run, paint, tell, build, make, do, pack, write, wind, load, play, wash, think

REQUIRED:
• Paper and pencil
• Two cups

OPTIONAL:
• Tea

 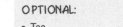

THE NOT PART

When the prefix "un-" is added to a base word, the new word is the opposite of the original word.

Pack your suitcase to go away,

Unpack your suitcase and stay today!

To build awareness of the prefix "un," keep a record, from morning until night, of the actions that you do and undo over the course of a day. Fold 10 sheets of paper in half. Place one inside the other and staple on the left margin. Label the cover "The Do and Undo Book."

Now encourage all family members to make an entry each time an action occurs that is likely to have an opposite action before the day is over. Write a sentence for the action, "I button my shirt," on the left facing page and a sentence for its opposite, "I unbutton my shirt," on the right facing page.

When the day is done, read the book together, focusing on "un." Ask your second grader to draw pictures to match the actions on each page.

REQUIRED:
- Paper and pencil
- Stapler

OPTIONAL:
- Crayons/markers

WORD BANK: dress, lock, tie, buckle, wrap, pack, load

S RULES

A *suffix* is a part added to the end of a base word. Whenever you share a book, magazine, or newspaper, review suffixes that form the plural.

For one reading, focus on "-s," the suffix that turns most singular nouns into plural nouns, as in "car/cars." Cut a large *S* from construction paper and ask your second grader to write all the plural nouns you find.

Next time you read, look for the suffix "-es," which is added to nouns that end in *s, x, ch,* and *sh,* as in "dresses," "foxes," "witches," and "wishes." Write each word found on an index card, store in a box, and use as flash cards for drill.

Finally, search for words that form the plural by changing *y* to *i* and adding "-es" as in "puppy/puppies." Begin a cumulative list that you keep handy. When you reach 25 words, share a handful of candy/candies.

REQUIRED:
- Construction paper
- Box
- Paper and pencil
- Book/newspaper/magazine
- Index cards

OPTIONAL:
- Candies

THE PAST PART

SKILLS: Suffixes/Verbs/Brainstorming/Phonetic Analysis/Vocabulary Development/Sentence Structure/Drawing

When the suffix "-ed" is added to a verb, the new word changes from present tense to past. Children *play* tag today. Children *played* checkers yesterday. Bakers *bake* cookies today. They *baked* muffins yesterday. Airplanes *land* today. Jets *landed* yesterday.

Make a "Yesterday Book" to enhance usage of past-tense verbs and heighten awareness that "-ed" has three sounds: /d/ as in "played," /t/ as in "baked," and /ed/ as in "landed." Cut a 12″ × 18″ sheet of construction paper into two 6″ × 18″ strips. Tape the two strips together to measure 6″ × 36″. Fold at 4″ intervals into an accordion. Work with your child to cut and decorate two 4″ × 6″ pieces of cardboard. Place a 24″ strip of ribbon across the front of the accordion book. Cover with cardboard and glue in place. Attach the second piece of cardboard to the back of the book.

Brainstorm verbs with "-ed." On each interior page, write a sentence that incorporates one verb in the form "Yesterday I painted a picture of a dog." Illustrate each sentence. Tie the ribbon around the book and add to your child's library.

REQUIRED:
- Construction paper
- Tape
- Cardboard
- Safety scissors
- Ruler
- Nontoxic glue
- Art supplies

WHO OWNS WHAT?

SKILLS: Possessives/Sentence Structure

Forming the possessive to show ownership can be confusing for adults and children alike! In second grade, children learn to follow two basic rules:

If the owner is singular, "boy," show ownership by adding "'s": "boy's dog(s)."

If the owner is plural, "girls," "children," place the plural noun before the apostrophe: "girls' cat(s)" or "children's room(s)."

Don't worry about exceptions to the rules at this time. Play Who Owns What? to enhance recognition of possessives.

On one set of 15 index cards, work together to write sentences, one per card, such as "Sara has a piano." "Mark owns two computers." "Cynthia has new shoes." "Lee has his own golf clubs." "Three girls own a pony." "Four boys have rabbits."

On a second set of index cards, write the matching possessive phrases, one per card: "Sara's piano," "Mark's computers," "Cynthia's shoes," "Lee's golf clubs," "girls' pony," "boys' rabbits."

Shuffle the cards and use to play a Who Owns What? game of Go Fish or Concentration. In either case, work to match the sentence with the corresponding possessive phrase. The player with the most pairs wins.

REQUIRED:
- Index cards
- Pencils

FAB VOCAB

SKILLS: Vocabulary Development/Context Clues/Dictionary Skills

Have you ever met an unfamiliar word while reading, tried unsuccessfully to determine meaning from context, and then moved on to the next page? The likelihood is that you have! Children do the same when they read. If meaning is unknown or not obvious from context, they continue. Get your child into the habit of noting unknown words, checking meaning, and then using the new word to build a Fab Vocab.

When your youngster sits down to read, provide a pad and pencil. Encourage your child to use context to help define words. Suggest that your child jot down any unfamiliar words met. After reading, find each word in the dictionary. Use guide words to assist you as you find the word and read the definitions. Which meaning fits the context of the story just read? Keep a running record of all words and definitions. Alternate turns to apply the new word by making up original sentences that incorporate the word.

Try a chapter book such as *Triplet Trouble and the Bicycle Race* by Debbie Dadey and Marcia Thornton Jones. In the first chapter alone you'll find "slumped," "moaned," "rude," "agreed," "pledges," and "bragged" to add to your Fab Vocab.

REQUIRED:
- A book
- Pad and pencil

OPTIONAL:
- Library/bookstore visit

FISHING WORD FUN

SKILLS: Vocabulary Development/Context Clues/Alphabetical Order/Expressive Language

Whenever you share a book or chapter, make note of new vocabulary. Discuss and enjoy a story such as *Henry the Sailor Cat* by Mary Calhoun. Use context clues to define words such as "pester," "lashed," "harbor," "hoisted," "squalled," "cockpit," "stowaway," "surefooted," "cormorants," "mast," "tiller," "slipknot," "sleek," "pranced," "spouting," "tacked," "drift," "strokes," "gasped," "heaved," "mainsail." After reading, apply dictionary skills to confirm definitions.

When your child has listed 21 words, write each on two index cards. Shuffle the cards. Deal five to each player. Put the extra cards in a pile, facedown on the table. Look for pairs in your hand and place faceup on the table. Alternate turns asking for a word to match a word in your hand. When you get a match, put the pair, faceup, on the table. Define the word, use it in a sentence, and go again. If you don't get a match, choose from the pile. If you fish your wish, go again. Play until one player has no cards left. While the winner of the game is the one with the most word pairs, everyone is a winner with all the new vocabulary!

REQUIRED:
- A book
- Paper and pencil
- Index cards

OPTIONAL:
- Library/bookstore visit

LEFTS AND RIGHTS

SKILLS: Homographs/Brainstorming/Vocabulary Development/Sentence Construction

Turn *left* at the corner and you'll find the park where I *left* my jacket. It isn't *right* that I have to get 10 *right* on the *right* side of the page. Enhance your second grader's familiarity with and application of *homographs,* multiple-meaning words.

Open a file folder horizontally. In the lower left-hand corner, draw a square labeled "Left." In the upper right-hand corner, draw a square labeled "Right." Connect the squares with a path of 20 circles.

Brainstorm 20 homographs and write each in a circle on the gameboard. Place game markers on Left. Alternate turns to roll the die and move that number of spaces. Read the word in the circle. Use it in a sentence for one meaning, get one point. Use it in another sentence for a second meaning, get a second point. Provide a third sentence, get a third point. When each player has moved from Left to Right, tally the score to determine the winner.

REQUIRED:
- File folder
- Paper and pencil
- Die
- Game markers

OPTIONAL:
- Library/bookstore visit

Share a book such as *Amelia Bedelia and the Surprise Shower* by Peggy Parish or *Deputy Dan Gets His Man* by Joseph Rosenbloom. Watch main characters cause riotous fun by misinterpreting multiple-meaning words.

WORD WEAVE

SKILLS: Personification/Brainstorming/Vocabulary Development/Nouns/Verbs/Adverbs/Sentence Structure

When the sun dances and stars sleep, when clouds fluff their dresses and the moon stretches long golden fingers to the ocean below, we have examples of *personification,* giving human characteristics to things.

Expose your child to personification while enhancing vocabulary and sentence-writing skills. Brainstorm things in nature. Write each on a slip of paper, fold, and put into a cup labeled "Things/Nouns." Next brainstorm action words. Write each on a slip of paper, fold, and place in a second cup labeled "Actions/Verbs." Finally, write the words "where," "when," "why," and "how" on slips of paper, one word per slip. Fold and place in a third cup labeled "Action Stretchers."

Provide paper and pencils. Randomly select one noun and one verb to place on the table. Each participant then writes, for example, "The wind smiles." Now select one word from the third cup. If the word is "when," each participant adds words to tell when the wind smiles. "The wind smiles as leaves fall." Share all sentences created, return "when" to the third cup, and repeat the process. Enjoy language as you weave words into personification sentences.

REQUIRED:
- Three cups/containers
- Paper and pencils

OPTIONAL:
- Library/bookstore visit

See personification at work in *Goodbye Geese* by Nancy Carlstrom.

PICTURE THIS

SKILLS: Personification/Vocabulary Development/Imaginative Thinking/
Making Comparisons/Drawing/Written Expression

The next time you share a book such as *Sun and Moon* by Marcus Pfister, look for examples of personification, a figure of speech that gives human characteristics to things.

After enjoying and discussing the story, provision yourselves with art supplies to create personification pictures. When "the sun tickles children's noses," discuss what the author means. Then on construction paper, all participants draw what the sun would look like if it really could tickle noses. Compare your drawings and admire your work.

Next write and illustrate original examples of personification. Draw pictures of the leaves that skip across the yard or the armchairs that invite you to sit.

REQUIRED:
- A book
- Paper and pencils
- Crayons/markers
- Construction paper

OPTIONAL:
- Library/bookstore visit

FABULOUS FAMILY FUN

SKILLS: Alliteration/Initial Sounds/Brainstorming/Sentence Construction/Written Expression/Poetry

Weekend With Wendell by Kevin Henkes, *Picking Peas for a Penny* by Angela Shelf Medearis, *Porcupine's Pajama Party* by Terry Webb Harshman, and *Dakota Dugout* by Ann Turner demonstrate that authors and poets often use alliteration, the repetition of the same sound at the beginnings of words, to create feelings and images with words.

Used to create tongue twisters, alliteration is a figure of speech that delights second graders, who continue to enjoy word play. Get the whole family involved in Fabulous Family Fun. Put the 26 letters of the alphabet on slips of paper, one letter per slip, in a bowl. Work individually or in pairs as you close your eyes, reach into the bowl, and select one letter.

Brainstorm and list words that start with the sound of the letter chosen. Then weave selected words into a sentence or poem. When everyone is done, take time to share and repeat each alliterative sentence or poem. Select *m* for example, write, "Magical monkeys make moonlight music at midnight."

REQUIRED:
- Paper and pencils
- Safety scissors
- Bowl

OPTIONAL:
- Library/bookstore visit

For extra fun, choose a book such as *The Amazing Bone* by William Steig. Find and enjoy examples of alliteration throughout the story.

A+ ACTIVITIES FOR SECOND GRADE

ONOMATOPOEIA ACTION

SKILLS: Onomatopoeia/Vocabulary Development/Brainstorming/Oral Reading Expression

Second graders are ready to be exposed to *onomatopoeia*, the figure of speech in which a word makes the sound it describes: the *hiss* of snakes, the *crash* of waves.

Have family fun with onomatopoeia. First look for examples of onomatopoeia by sharing a book such as *The Cow That Went Oink* by Bernard Most or *Crocodile Beat* by Gail Jorgensen. Encourage your youngster not only to read the word that sounds like the sound, object, or action it names, but also to act out the sound with expression and, when applicable, movement. When "Elephants' feet are thumping the ground, *Boom Boom Boom-boom-boom!*" act out the *"Booms"* in tone and movement. When "Birds swoop down to the river to play, *Swish Swish Swish Swish,*" swoop and swish in word and deed.

Finally, brainstorm and list words that are onomatopoeic. Then alternate turns as you say a word, "sizzle," and see what person, animal, object, or action the word calls to mind for all participants.

REQUIRED:
- A book
- Paper and pencil

OPTIONAL:
- Library/bookstore visit

WORD BANK: bang, beep, buzz, click, clink, creak, crunch, ding, drip, fizz, gurgle, honk, hoot, moo, moan, murmur, plink, plop, purr, quack, rattle, roar, snap, squeak, slurp, thump, tromp, whoosh, whisper, whirr

SIMILE STROLL

SKILLS: Simile/Vocabulary Development/Expressive Language/Making Comparisons

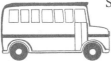

Second graders enjoy playing with words and being challenged by "million dollar" words that even adults may not be able to define. A *simile*, pronounced with two short *i*'s and one long *e*, is a comparison between two unlike nouns using the words "like" or "as" to make the comparison. By directly exposing young children to this figure of speech, we build a strong foundation for their being better able to recognize, appreciate, and apply figurative language to reading and writing prose and poetry.

Use a simple example and explanation to expose your second grader to the simile: "The baby's skin is like cotton." Then take your child on a Simile Stroll around your neighborhood. Point out anything that strikes your fancy and create a simile. As your child understands the concept, alternate turns making similes about the people, places, and things around you.

That school bus is like a giant stick of butter.

That flower is like a rainbow.

My shadow is like smoke.

When you get home, share a favorite story such as *Quick as a Cricket* by Audrey Wood. Find and enjoy similes at work.

REQUIRED:
- A neighborhood stroll

OPTIONAL:
- Library/bookstore visit

SIMPLE SIMILE POETRY

SKILLS: Simile/Vocabulary Development/Expressive Language/
Making Comparisons/Written Expression/Drawing

Can six- to eight-year-old children create poems that incorporate a simile, a comparison using "like" or "as"? Of course they can when given the necessary ingredients!

Similes tickle our senses. They capture sight, sound, taste, smell, and touch by combining just the right words. Give your child the recipe for a simile poem and enjoy the results.

Use crayons or markers to make splashes of color on slips of paper, one color per slip. Fold the slips and place in a basket. Next write the phrases "looks like," "sounds like," "tastes like," "smells like," and "feels like" on strips of paper, one phrase per strip. Fold and place in a second basket.

Find a cozy spot to write. Ask your child to choose a color slip from one basket and a phrase strip from the other. You and any other participating family members do the same. Then write and illustrate Simple Simile Poetry, combining the color and the phrase.

When all poets have completed a piece, take a moment to share and celebrate the language.

Orange feels like autumn,
Cold fat pumpkins,
Crinkled rusty leaves,
Crisp harvest moon.

REQUIRED:
• Paper and pencils
• Crayons/markers
• Two baskets/containers
• Safety scissors

WHEN PIGS FLY

SKILLS: Hyperbole/Vocabulary Development/Expressive Language/Imaginative Thinking

The incredibility of tall tales catches the fancy of second graders. In the book *Meteor*, by Patricia Polacco, each report of the meteor that crashed into a local farmyard outdoes the one before it. Writers and speakers apply *hyperbole*— pronounced "hi-PER-buh-lee"—a figure of speech that uses an exaggerated word or phrase, to create humor or emphasis.

When you're sitting in a restaurant waiting for food to arrive, make a statement such as, "Cats will bark before this food gets served!" or "I'm so hungry I could eat all the cakes in the bakery!" Invite family members to make similar exaggerated statements all the way around the table.

Whenever you want to pass the time productively—on a long car, plane, train, or bus ride—use hyperbole. By the time you get wherever you are going, pigs will fly!

REQUIRED:
• Your time
OPTIONAL:
• Library/bookstore visit

BOOK REGISTRY

Books are a spur to the young, a delight to the old; an ornament in prosperity, a consoling refuge in adversity; they are pleasure for us at home, and no burden abroad; they stay up with us at night, they accompany us when we travel, they are with us in our country visits.

CICERO

Often, when we finish a book and move on to the next, we forget the story of the first.

Encourage your second grader to join you in maintaining a family Book Registry. Work together to label each page of a notebook or journal for each entry. Include lines for the title, author, publisher, and date of publication. Assist your child as necessary in searching for this information on the title page and copyright page of each book read. Also include a line labeled "Date Started" and one labeled "Date Completed." Label the next area "Opinion and Impressions" and reserve several lines. Finally, near the bottom of the page, include space for "Recommended To."

No matter where you are, "at home, . . . abroad" or in your "country visits," take your book registry with you and record.

REQUIRED:
• Notebook/journal
• Pencil

BOOK DATE

"THIS BOOK BELONGS TO ROBERT R."

Be first in your neighborhood to change a play date to a Book Date. The next time your second grader invites a friend or two over for an afternoon of fun, add a "bit of lit" to the activities planned.

Request that each playmate come to your home with a favorite book to share. Join in as you seat the children in the family room, kitchen, or yard to talk books. While relaxing with soft drinks and snacks, alternate turns so that each participant has the opportunity to tell the group about the characters, setting, wish or problem, and main idea of the story. Remind participants to keep the outcome of each shared book a secret.

After everyone has had a turn to share, distribute stick-on labels and markers so that each child can decorate a personal bookplate to insert in the book shared. On the bookplate write "From the library of" with the child's name. Trade books so that each child has a new book to read. At the next Book Date gathering, return each other's books and share a few more. By including books and reading in leisure-time activities, you foster love of literature and learning.

REQUIRED:
• Books
• Stick-on labels
• Markers

OPTIONAL:
• Soft drinks and snacks

WORLDWIDE READ

SKILLS: Literature Appreciation/Map Skills/Multicultural Awareness/Facts & Details

Choose a book, take out a world map, and begin a worldwide tour! The books available to young readers are rich in story and reference to places, cultures, facts, and celebrations from all around the world. Combine literature appreciation, map skills, multicultural awareness, and factual knowledge as you share books during your child's second-grade year.

Begin your Worldwide Read with *Where to Look for a Dinosaur* by Bernard Most. As you meet Arctosaurus in the Arctic, Silvisaurus in Kansas, USA, Staurikosaurus in Brazil, Barosaurus in Zimbabwe, Spinosaurus in Egypt, Shantungosaurus in China, Indosaurus in India, Itemirus in Russia, Rhabdodon in Austria, or Austrosaurus in Australia, find each place on a world map. On a slip of paper, write the name of the book in which the country, state, or city appeared. Pin it to the location on the map.

Soar over New York City in *Abuela* by Arthur Dorros. Travel to Japan and across America in *Grandfather's Journey* by Allen Say. Enjoy a Mexican birthday celebration in *A Birthday Basket for Tia* by Pat Mora. Pin each book title shared to the world map as you tour the world without leaving your home.

REQUIRED:
• Books
• World map
• Pins/tacks
• Paper and pencil

OPTIONAL:
• Library/bookstore visit

AND THE WINNER IS • • •

SKILL: Literature Appreciation

Established in 1938 by the American Library Association, the Caldecott Medal is awarded annually to the illustrator of the American picture book for children selected as the most distinguished of the preceding year. The winner of the award must be a citizen or resident of the United States.

When you select a picture storybook to share with your child during a quiet reading time at home, choose from the list of Caldecott winners. As you enjoy the text, delight in the illustrations as well. Talk with your second grader about the style of the artist. Notice the medium used. Examine the details and the total effect of the design created to accompany the text.

A sampling of titles and illustrators follows.

1942 *Make Way for Ducklings* Robert McClosky
1953 *The Biggest Bear* Lynd K. Ward
1954 *Madeline's Rescue* Ludwig Bemelmans
1962 *Once a Mouse* Marcia Brown
1963 *The Snowy Day* Ezra Jack Keats
1971 *A Story, A Story* Gail E. Haley
1972 *One Fine Day* Nonny Hogrogian
1982 *Jumanji* Chris Van Allsburg

1985 *St. George and the Dragon* Trina Schart Hyman (Text by Margaret Hodges)
1996 *Officer Buckle and Gloria* Peggy Rathmann
1999 *Snowflake Bentley* Mary Azarian (Text by Jacqueline Briggs Martin)

REQUIRED:
• Library/bookstore visit

NOVEL IDEAS

SKILLS: Literature Appreciation/Reading Comprehension

As second graders add chapter books to their personal choice reading, parents ask, "What's a good novel to read at home?" Novel Ideas answers this question.

Try any book from the *Triplet Trouble* series at the second-grade reading level and, for more challenge, *The Bailey School Kids* series at third-grade level, both by Debbie Dadey and Marcia Thornton Jones. Children enjoy both!

Solve the mysteries of the *Cam Jansen* series by David A. Adler, the *Nate the Great* series by Marjorie Weinman Sharmat, or, for more challenge, the *Encyclopedia Brown* series by Donald J. Sobol.

Second graders also have fun with *The Kids of the Polk Street School* series and *The Polka Dot Private Eye* series by Patricia Reilly Giff.

Young readers travel to places all around the world in books of the *Magic Tree House* series by Mary Pope Osborne. They also delight in the adventures of the mouselike people of *The Littles* series by John Peterson. Have fun with the *Horrible Harry* series by Suzy Kline or try a Judy Delton adventure from the *Pee Wee Scouts* series.

REQUIRED:
• Library/bookstore visit

Sports fans enjoy any of the books written by Matt Christopher for primary-age children, such as *The Dog That Stole Home* or *All-Star Fever*.

FAN CLUB FUN

SKILLS: Characterization/Literature Appreciation/Written Expression/Recitation

Bring literature to life by inviting your child to join the fan club of a favorite book character. Imagine what fun you'll have when your child becomes a member, in good standing, of the fan club of *Mrs. Katz and Tush* or *Babushka Baba Yaga*, both by Patricia Polacco, or the fan club of *Wilfred Gordon McDonald Partridge*, by Mem Fox.

Share a book, any book, and discuss the challenges of the main character. What is the problem or wish of the character and what happens to solve the problem or make the wish come true? Enjoy the story, the illustrations, and the message conveyed.

REQUIRED:
• A book
• Paper and pencil
• Crayons/markers
• Safety scissors

OPTIONAL:
• Library/bookstore visit
• Cookies/lemonade

Then invite your child to design a fan club badge and membership card for the book character's fan club. Finally, work together to write a fan club pledge to recite in order to make membership official. Make badges and membership cards for all family members and friends who wish to join. Then, raise your right hands, recite the pledge, and celebrate the story and character with cookies, lemonade, and a family shared reading of the book.

HIP HIP HOORAY!

SKILLS: Characterization/Literature Appreciation/Imaginative Thinking/Drawing

One need not leap tall buildings in a single bound in order to be a hero. While the imaginations of young children are captivated by the super heroes who cross their paths on movie, television, and computer screens, children are also amazed by the courage and determination of the characters they meet in books.

In the 1993 Caldecott Medal book, *Mirette on the High Wire*, by Emily Arnold McCully, a young girl conquers fear with determination. In the 1979 winner, *The Girl Who Loved Wild Horses,* by Paul Goble, a Plains Indian girl finds the courage to pursue her dream. In the 1975 winner, *Arrow to the Sun: A Pueblo Indian Tale,* by Gerald McDermott, a young boy faces seemingly insurmountable challenges in order to find his father.

Each of these characters is representative of the many heroes your child meets in children's literature. Whenever you share a story in which a character demonstrates heroism, give a Hip Hip Hooray! Design a medal of honor, a badge of merit, a certificate of courage, or a clay statue of recognition. No matter what the honor bestowed, discuss the brave and astounding actions of the hero.

REQUIRED:
- Paper and pencil
- Crayons/markers
- Art supplies
- Safety scissors

OPTIONAL:
- Library/bookstore visit

HOME ADVENTURE HOME

SKILLS: Theme/Characterization/Making Comparisons/Written Expression

Home Adventure Home is a common theme in children's literature. The main character starts out at home, goes off on an adventure, and comes home changed. During the adventure, the main character has new experiences that result in changes and differences, perhaps in appearance, but more in nature, personality, and feelings.

Talk to your child about the Home Adventure Home theme before reading books such as *Cyrus the Unsinkable Sea Serpent* by Bill Peet or any book from the *Magic Tree House* series by Mary Pope Osborne. Discuss the main character at the start of the story. Write the character's name in a circle. Make a character web by surrounding the circle with adjectives that describe the character at the start of the story and through the early chapters or pages of the book. As you read through the book, continue to focus on the main character, noting any changes in nature. When you finish the story, make a new character web that describes the character upon return.

REQUIRED:
- A book
- Paper and pencil

OPTIONAL:
- Library/bookstore visit

Compare the two webs, noting similarities and differences. Graphically demonstrate that experience results in growth and change.

Finally, ask your child to recall and write about a personal "adventure" that resulted in personal change.

FROM OTHER EYES

SKILLS: Characterization/Point of View/Retelling/Expressive Language/Written Expression

As readers, we learn about a character from what the character says and does and by what others say about the character. We gain greater understanding of a character by trying to see the world from that character's point of view. Join your child to see the world From Other Eyes.

Share a book such as *The True Story of the 3 Little Pigs by A. Wolf* as told to Jon Scieszka. Demonstrate concretely that the perception we have of a character often depends on who is telling the tale. When A. Wolf has the opportunity to tell the story of the little pigs from his point of view, your second grader sees that the wolf isn't really as big and bad as the pigs would have us believe!

Step into the role of any book character. Make one pair of pig's feet and one pair of wolf's feet out of construction paper. Step on a pair of feet and retell the tale from that character's point of view. Take on the persona of Aesop's Tortoise or Hare, Lion or Mouse, Monkey or Crocodile. Open new eyes to the possibilities for oral or written expression.

REQUIRED:
- A book
- Construction paper
- Paper and pencils
- Safety scissors

OPTIONAL:
- Library/bookstore visit

FLIP A SET

SKILLS: Setting/Imaginative Thinking/Cutting/Drawing

A towering castle, a cozy cottage, a gnarled tree stump, a mushroom house . . . Children are fascinated by the possibilities of what is inside the structures that writers and illustrators create in words and pictures.

As you share a book such as Caldecott winners *The Little House* by Virginia Lee Burton or *Rapunzel* by Paul O. Zelinsky, pay close attention to the details the author-illustrators use. Hold a large sheet of construction paper vertically. Fold in half, top edge to bottom. With the fold at the top, draw the little house or the castle tower. Cut out the structure, leaving the fold intact. Trace the structure on white construction paper. Cut out, fit and paste inside the folded structure

Let imagination take charge. Flip open the structure and, on the white paper, draw the interior. Add stairways, rooms, and furnishings. Work collaboratively as you emphasize the use of detail. When the interior design is complete, decorate the exterior. Cut out three sides of doors and windows to lift up or out and give a peek inside. Flip a Set to view the inner workings of your second grader's imagination.

REQUIRED:
- A book
- Construction paper
- Safety scissors
- Nontoxic glue

OPTIONAL
- Library/bookstore visit

THE TONY GOES TO . . .

SKILLS: Setting/Facts & Details/Cutting/Drawing

For set design, the Tony goes to second grader . . .

While sharing a favorite book, pay close attention to details used by the author to paint a scene. Note location, time of day, characters, and environment. Focus on the language the author employed to create a picture in the reader's eye.

Emphasize the ways in which the senses were sparked by the descriptive words used. Ask, "What do you see, hear, smell, feel, or taste?"

Put your set designer to work. Recycle a large box by cutting away the bottom, top, and one side. Use the remaining tri-fold cardboard structure for your set design. Draft a selected scene on scrap paper before applying any medium to bring the setting to life. Use crayons, markers, paint, fabric, paper, and clay. Recycle wrapping paper, ribbons, and lace. Use pinecones, pebbles, shells, acorns, and twigs. Get out the scissors, glue, and imagination to bring the inside or outside of any scene into your home. Take time and focus on detail. Emphasize quality, not quantity.

When the set design is complete, admire the artistry as you reread the author's description. Then take visitors on a tour of the book scene brought to life.

REQUIRED:
- A book
- Box
- Safety scissors
- Nontoxic glue
- Art supplies

FOUR W SPIN

SKILLS: Reading Comprehension/Facts & Details

Facts are pieces of information that are true. All reading material is bound to include one or more of the four *w* facts, information that tells about the *who, what, where,* or *when* of the story.

Just before you read together, talk about facts. Remind your second grader that in order to find facts, you need to know what to look for in the text. The *who* names a character; the *what,* an event or thing; the *where,* a place; the *when,* a time.

Make a spinner from cardboard. Cut a 5″ square and a 3″ × ½″ arrow. Divide the square into four sections by drawing diagonal lines from corner to corner. Label each section with one of the four *w*'s. Punch a small hole in the center of the square and arrow. Loosely attach the arrow to the square with a paper fastener.

After reading a paragraph, page, or chapter, alternate turns to spin the spinner. If the arrow lands on *who,* create a *who* question for your reading partner to answer. Return to the text just read to find or confirm the answer. Repeat the process so that both readers have several opportunities to ask and answer factual questions.

REQUIRED:
- A book
- Cardboard
- Marker
- Safety scissors
- Paper fastener

A+ ACTIVITIES FOR SECOND GRADE

IN THE MAIN

Main Street is the most important or central street in a town or city. The mainsail is the most important or central sail on a sailboat. In the same way, the main idea is the most important idea. It tells what the whole story, chapter, or paragraph is about without giving extended details.

When you share a story, jot down, on an index card, the main idea of the material. Don't show the index card to your child. While reading, jot down, one per index card, four supporting details taken directly from the text.

After reading, show your child the cards in random order. Ask your young reader to find the main idea card. Place it on a working surface with the four supporting details beneath it. Invite your child to explain why the card chosen is the main idea and why the others provide support.

To begin, try the paragraph below. The main idea is italicized for you.

Our dog Bailey is smart and playful. When he sees one of us go into the pantry, Bailey waits by the door for a biscuit. Bailey follows commands to sit, speak, lie down, and roll over. He loves to go ice-skating and play Frisbee and tag!

REQUIRED:
• A book
• Index cards
• Pencil/pen

HOOK, LINE, AND SINKER

To tell what a whole story, chapter, or paragraph is about in a few words is the difficult and challenging job of the main idea. Chapter titles reveal the main idea. They give a hint of what is to come. In so doing, chapter titles hook the reader, pull the line in, and, if effective, sink the reader, too! Once immersed, the reader proceeds with eagerness and interest.

Choose a chapter book such as *Horrible Harry and the Dungeon* by Suzy Kline, *Camp Ghost-Away* by Judy Delton, or *Second-Grade Friends* by Miriam Cohen. Be sure that the chapters in the book have titles. Read the title of the first chapter. Use it to predict the contents of the chapter. Read the chapter to confirm your prediction. Was the title effective? Did it include the main idea? Repeat the process for each chapter to enhance your second grader's ability to recognize and work with the main idea.

REQUIRED:
• Chapter book

OPTIONAL:
• Library/bookstore visit

REMEMBER THE MAIN

SKILLS: Main Idea/Brainstorming/Supporting Details/Sequencing/Retelling

Generate chapter titles to enhance your child's ability to determine the main idea, find supporting details, and sequence and retell a story.

Choose a chapter book without chapter titles such as *Cam Jansen and the Mystery of Flight 54* by David A. Adler, *Monster Rabbit Runs Amuck* by Patricia Reilly Giff, or *The Littles and the Trash Tinies* by John Peterson.

Point out to your second grader that the chapters in the book do not have titles. Read the first chapter together. Talk about what the chapter was mostly about, and brainstorm two or three possible chapter titles. Choose one from the ideas generated and write it on an index card. Repeat this process as each chapter is read, recognizing that the title chosen states the main idea of the chapter by telling what the chapter is mostly about.

REQUIRED:
• Chapter book
• Index cards
• Pencil/pen

OPTIONAL:
• Library/bookstore visit

After every few chapters, review the chapter titles and scramble the cards. Then, sequence the cards by focusing on the main ideas as you retell the story. Work your way to sequencing and retelling the complete book as you Remember the Main.

BIO-VIEW

SKILLS: Reading Comprehension/Facts & Details/Inferential Thinking/Expressive Language

During second grade, as children begin to enjoy learning factual information about people of interest, share a biography, a true story about the life and times of the person selected.

Read about a famous sports figure, president, inventor, or musician. For example, your budding pianist is interested in learning about Ludwig Van Beethoven or your star on the Little League team really wants to know more about Jackie Robinson. Read and discuss a biography such as *Beethoven* by Ann Rachin or *A Picture Book of Jackie Robinson* by David A. Adler.

Upon completion of the biography, ask your child to step into the shoes of the famous figure as you conduct a Bio-View. You ask the questions; your child answers from the point of view of the figure. Questions should be both factual, "Where and when were you born? How old were you when you started playing the piano?" and inferential, "How did you feel when you were signed by the Brooklyn Dodgers? What was the greatest accomplishment of your career?"

As an option, trade places. Invite your child to conduct interviews of other famous figures you read about, including Helen Keller, Amelia Earhart, Thomas Edison, or John F. Kennedy.

REQUIRED:
• Library/bookstore visit

READ BETWEEN THE LINES

SKILLS: Reading Comprehension/Inferential Thinking

You have probably heard the expression, "Read between the lines." That is exactly what readers must do in order to make inferences. Authors don't tell readers everything. Rather, they trust that readers will apply background knowledge to catch the meaning suggested or written "between the lines'."

Consider this passage:

Grandma and Grandpa are coming to visit for the weekend. They plan to leave their house at noon on Friday. They'll arrive at our house at 1:00 on Friday afternoon.

Although the paragraph doesn't tell the reader that Grandma and Grandpa live close by and are driving from their house to yours, readers make that inference.

Whenever you share a story or book with your second grader, ask questions that require inferential thinking. Encourage your child to Read Between the Lines. Build a strong foundation for higher-level thinking skills right from the start.

REQUIRED:
• A book

REALITY CHECK

SKILLS: Reading Comprehension/Fantasy vs. Reality/Drawing/Written Expression

Hogwash! Moonshine! Flumadiddle! The words are fun and so are the books that demonstrate concretely the difference between fantasy and reality.

Share a book such as 1967 Caldecott winner *Sam, Bangs and Moonshine* by Evaline Ness. While reading, talk about what could really happen. Then talk about how fantasy causes near disaster for Sam's friend Thomas and Sam's cat, Bangs. Work together to discriminate between what can really happen and what can't.

Upon completion of the book, fold a 12″ × 18″ piece of construction paper in half to open like a book. On the cover, draw a picture representative of the story and write the title and author. Label the inside left page, "Reality," and the inside right page, "Fantasy." Then challenge each other to a Reality Check. Alternate turns as you recall and write what can really happen on the left, and hogwash, moonshine, and flumadiddle on the right. "A girl can live by the sea and have a cat named Bangs" on the left. "A girl can't own a tiny kangaroo and have a mermaid mother" on the right.

Finally, on the back page of the booklet, write an original story that incorporates fantasy and reality.

REQUIRED:
• Crayons/markers
• Construction paper
• Pencil

OPTIONAL:
• Library/bookstore visit

CONCLUSION CLUES

You show up at a party dressed in a lion costume. Your hosts open the door dressed elegantly in formal attire. What conclusion do you draw? It is not a costume party!

A conclusion is a judgment made based on the clues provided. Since authors don't always tell readers all they need to know, readers need to search for clues. When the clues are gathered, readers put them together in order to draw a conclusion.

Choose any book from your child's library. Select a passage that gives factual information without reaching a conclusion. Read the passage together. Ask your child to gather the clues in order to come to a conclusion about the material read. Here's an example from *Dancing with Manatees* by Faith McNulty.

A baby manatee is born underwater and swims to the surface for its first breath. It makes squeaky sounds, and its mother answers. If it is frightened, it screams. Mother and baby know each other's voices and constantly "talk." The baby follows its mother closely for two years.

REQUIRED:
• A book

OPTIONAL:
• Library/bookstore visit

Gather the clues in the story to draw a conclusion about manatees. Conclude that mother manatees take good care of their young, manatees communicate, and baby manatees depend on their mothers.

WE'RE BAKING COOKIES!

SKILLS: Reading Comprehension/Drawing Conclusions

It's a cold, rainy Saturday, too wet to play outside. Your second grader is looking for something fun to do. Use this opportunity to enhance your child's ability to draw conclusions.

Write numbered clue cards and leave them around the house for your young sleuth to find in order, read, and put together to draw a conclusion. A sample follows.

REQUIRED:
• Index cards
• Pencil

OPTIONAL:
• Cookie ingredients

Clue One: I went to the grocery store this morning.
Clue Two: First I found all the dry goods we'll need. I got granulated sugar, brown sugar, flour, baking soda, and salt.
Clue Three: Next I went to the dairy case for butter and eggs.
Clue Four: Finally, I got vanilla extract and chocolate chips.
Clue Five: At the checkout, the clerk said, "The kids in your house are in for a surprise today!"
Clue Six: We're going to have lots of fun in the kitchen this afternoon!

Draw the conclusion that, "We're baking chocolate chip cookies!"

BECAUSE, BECAUSE ◆ ◆ ◆

SKILLS: Reading Comprehension/Cause & Effect/Drawing

"Because, because, because, because, because . . . because of the wonderful things he does. We're off to see the wizard . . ."

In Frank L. Baum's *Wizard of Oz,* Dorothy follows the yellow brick road to see the wizard because she wants to return to Kansas. In Steven Kellogg's *Jack and the Beanstalk,* Jack climbs the beanstalk a second time because he wants more treasure.

Make a cause-and-effect gameboard to match a story. Hold a file folder vertically. Draw, for example, Dorothy or Jack in the bottom left-hand corner. Draw a wizard or ogre in the top right-hand corner. Connect Dorothy to the wizard or Jack to the ogre with a path of 30 circles. In every other circle, write a message: "Met the good witch: Go ahead two." "Stop to water beanstalk: Go back two."

Alternate turns. Roll the die and move that number of spaces. If you land on a message, read the message. Before following the directions, tell which part of the message is the cause and which part is the effect, the part that tells what happens. "Because I hear the ogre, I go back two." The first player to reach the wizard or ogre wins.

REQUIRED:
- File folder
- Crayons/markers
- Pencil
- Game markers
- Die

OPTIONAL:
- Library/bookstore visit

F/O SCAN

SKILLS: Reading Comprehension/Fact vs. Opinion/Recording Data/Making Comparisons

"Smart and funny!" "Marvelous!" "You won't stop laughing!" Opinions. "Starts Friday in Los Angeles." "Now playing at theaters everywhere." Facts.

Even though most of the movies today are not rated for young children, second graders can learn to discriminate between fact and opinion by reading newspaper ads for entertainment, stores, businesses, and products.

Talk with your child about the difference between a fact—a bit of information that is true—and an opinion—a statement of what someone thinks or believes to be true. Next do an F/O Scan.

Provision each participant with a sheet of paper and a pencil. Divide the sheet in half, one side labeled "Facts"; the other, "Opinions." Open a newspaper to a page of advertisements. Set a timer to five minutes. Scan the newspaper for facts and opinions. Record facts in the "Facts" column and opinions in the "Opinions" column.

When time is up, compare and discuss the results. Fact: Your child will have good understanding of fact versus opinion. Opinion: You'll have lots of fun!

REQUIRED:
- Newspaper
- Paper and pencils

THE ROOM TEST

SKILLS: Sentence Structure/Imaginative Thinking

In second grade, children learn that a sentence has four essential components. A sentence requires an uppercase letter at the beginning; a subject that names the person, place, thing, or idea that the whole sentence is about; a verb or predicate that is the action of the subject; and a stop sign at the end—a period, question mark, or exclamation point.

To reinforce your child's awareness of the complete sentence, try the Room Test. Simply walk out of the room, return, and say a complete sentence or an incomplete sentence. Your second grader listens, then tells you whether the sentence is complete or incomplete. If incomplete, your child provides the missing subject or predicate. Follow the model below to get started.

Walk in and say: ran across the yard
Listener response: Incomplete! You forgot the subject. The dog ran across the yard.
Walk in and say: A big green lizard
Listener response: Incomplete! You forgot the predicate. A big green lizard crawled under the rock.
Walk in and say: We ate pancakes for breakfast today.
Listener response: Complete sentence!

Alternate turns, giving your child the opportunity to try the Room Test on you!

REQUIRED:
• Your time

SENTENCE BUFFET

SKILLS: Sentence Structure/Brainstorming/Written Expression

A sentence is a group of words that conveys a complete thought. Second graders recognize the naming part of a sentence and call it the subject. They also recognize the action part and call it either the verb or predicate. They learn that the sentence is complete when it includes a subject and predicate.

Set the table with a Sentence Buffet to help your young writer stretch the predicate. Brainstorm and write 10 plural subjects on index cards, one subject per card: "cats," "girls." Place the subjects facedown on a plate labeled "Subjects." Do the same for 10 verbs: "run," "jump." Place on a plate labeled "Verbs/Predicates." Label a third plate "Where." Brainstorm and write 10 phrases that tell where something happened: "in the kitchen," "at the circus."

Sit beside your child. Randomly choose a subject and predicate. Place faceup on the table and read. Stretch the predicate by choosing a card from the "Where" plate. Place the card after the predicate. "Girls jump at the circus." Now the reader knows where the action happened.

Vary the buffet by trying a "How," "When," or "Why" plate. Then read *Up, Up and Away: A Book About Adverbs* by Ruth Heller.

REQUIRED:
• Index cards
• Pencil
• Plates

OPTIONAL:
• Library/bookstore visit

A+ ACTIVITIES FOR SECOND GRADE

FLOWER POWER

SKILLS: Writing Process/Cutting

In second grade, children become more adept at following the five essential steps of the writing process. To enhance your child's organizational skills any time writing is done at home, provide Flower Power.

Cut a 4″ circle from yellow construction paper. In the center of the circle, write "The Writing Process." Cut five 6″ oval petals, each from a different color. Arrange around the yellow circle and attach. Label the petals as follows, starting at the top and working clockwise:

1. Prepare: Brainstorm, Story Map, Story Web, Story Star
2. First Draft: Weave ideas into sentences.
3. Revise: Change ideas, add details, remove information.
4. Proofread/Edit: Check capitalization, punctuation, spelling.
5. Publish: Make final copy in any format.

REQUIRED:
- Construction paper
- Safety scissors
- Fine point marker
- Tape/nontoxic glue

Add a stem and leaves to the writing process flower and post in your child's homework spot for easy reference.

WRITING ROSTER

SKILLS: Written Expression/Preparation/Drawing

One antidote to the "I don't know what to write about" syndrome is to generate an ongoing Writing Roster with your second grader.

Since personal interests spark story ideas for fact and fantasy, encourage your child to decorate the front of a notebook or journal to reflect favorite hobbies, sports, colors, places, foods, animals, or interests. Begin the Writing Roster by asking, at the end of a busy day, "What is one special thing that happened today either at school or at home?" Tell your child to write the date at the top of the first page of the roster and jot down a note or two about something that happened during the day. Suggest a quick sketch, too. For example: "September 14—We watched our butterfly emerge from its chrysalis." "October 2—I did a cartwheel at recess!"

Make entries often to record ideas, thoughts, and events. When it is time to write, remind your child to check the Writing Roster. Select a topic or idea and decide whether to write a story, letter, poem, play, song, report, recipe, or advertisement. Pick up a pencil, get out the paper, and write!

REQUIRED:
- Notebook/journal
- Paper and pencil
- Crayons/markers

PLAN A PIECE

SKILLS: Writing Process/Organization/Preparation/Story Form

Beginning	Middle	End
Character(s)	events	Resolution
Setting		
Wish/problem		

The first step in the writing process is to Plan a Piece. In first grade your child may have had the opportunity to work with you to create a story map from beginning to middle to end. Your child dictated the elements as you wrote them on the chart. In second grade, your child should continue to use this kind of graphic organizer. While generating and discussing ideas with you, your young author now does the writing.

Work together to design a story map. For example, create a three-column chart to organize the sequence and ideas of a story. Hold a piece of paper vertically or horizontally. Divide into three equal columns labeled "Beginning," "Middle," and "End." In the "Beginning" column, write the headings "Character(s)," "Setting," "Wish/Problem." In the "Middle" column, write "Events" (steps taken by the main character to make the wish come true or solve the problem). In the "End" column, write "Resolution" (wish granted, problem solved). Vary the format if you wish, but include these elements.

Discuss your child's plans for a story as your child fills in the map. Be sure that your child has ready access to this kind of graphic organizer for all writing endeavors.

REQUIRED:
- Paper and pencil
- Ruler

LADDERS, WEBS, AND STARS

SKILLS: Writing Process/Organization/Preparation

Preparation or prewriting, the first step in the writing process, can occur in a number of ways. Prepare graphic organizers to use with your child as stories are generated and move to completion.

Brainstorm ideas about the chosen topic. Ask your child to write these ideas on a story ladder. Draw a ladder and, on each rung, jot ideas in sequential order from bottom to top.

Try a story web. Encourage your child to write the subject in a circle drawn in the center of a sheet of paper. Attach spokes with a circle at the end of each. In these outer circles, your child writes ideas about the subject to weave into the story. Depending on the topic, write short questions inside each circle—"Where did the story take place?" "What did the creature look like?"—to spark response.

Finally, try a five-point story star. Invite your child to write the topic in the center of the star and the *who, what, where, when,* and *how* in each of the five points.

Whatever the format, guide your child in the use of graphic organizers. They are invaluable tools in the generation of both fiction and nonfiction writing and are certain to facilitate the completion of homework assignments.

REQUIRED:
- Paper and pencil
- Ruler

SKIP A LINE

SKILLS: Organization/Drafting/Revising/Proofreading/Editing

Something as simple as skipping a line between each line of print is a powerful strategy that makes a huge and positive impact on the effectiveness of a child's writing.

Whenever your child works on a first draft of a school assignment or independent piece of writing, remind your young author to write on every other line. The extra space heightens organization. Your youngster will be able to reread the work in process with greater ease with text well spaced on the page.

The space between each line facilitates revising. Your child will have room to make changes without compromising the ability to read the material. Between the lines is room to make changes by adding information, descriptive adjectives, or supportive phrases.

The extra space also facilitates proofreading and editing the draft. Recognition and correction of mechanical errors are easier for a young writer when the text and revisions aren't crammed into single lines and spaces.

Skip a Line to enhance all the steps your child follows in the production of a "published" piece of writing.

REQUIRED:
• Your time

STORY BUFFET

SKILLS: Story Form/Brainstorming/Written Expression/Drawing/Oral Reading Fluency

In Kate Duke's masterful book, *Aunt Isabel Tells A Good One,* an eccentric mouse engages her niece Penelope in storytelling. By asking Penelope to provide the essential pieces—the main characters (who), the setting (where and when), and the problem— Aunt Isabel sets the stage for the captivating story that follows.

Just as Aunt Isabel sets the stage for storytelling, set the table for story writing. Place four plates on the table, one labeled "Who," another "Where," a third "When," and the last, "Problem/Wish." Brainstorm characters and write each on an index card. Place facedown on the "Who" plate. Do the same for "Where," "When," and "Problem/Wish."

Invite your second grader to select a card from each plate. Discuss all story components selected. Remind your child to introduce the main character, setting, and problem/wish at the beginning; to relate what the character does to solve the problem or make the wish come true in the middle; and to resolve the problem or grant the wish (or not) at the end. Then write collaboratively or independently.

Illustrate and bind the story upon completion. At a family buffet, share the stories over dessert.

REQUIRED:
• Four plates
• Index cards
• Paper and pencil
• Crayons/markers
• Stapler

OPTIONAL:
• Library/bookstore visit

LANGUAGE ARTS ACTIVITIES

ERROR CHECKER

SKILL: Proofreading

☑ uppercase
☑ punctuation
☑ spelling

One essential step in the writing process is proofreading. As writers, we need to check our written work for errors before making a final copy. Here are a few handy tips to share with your second-grade writer.

- Read all written work orally. Look and listen for errors.
- While reading, point to each word across the line and down the page. Focusing on each word enhances recognition of spelling errors.
- Remind your child to ask you to proofread the paper, too.

Make multiple copies of a basic proofreader's checklist that your second grader can use with each piece of written work. Write four simple reminders, each followed by a box to check when the task is accomplished.

- Check for uppercase letter at the start of each sentence. ❑
- Check for uppercase letter at the start of a proper noun. ❑
- Check for end-mark punctuation: period, question mark, exclamation point. ❑
- Check spelling. ❑

Keep the checklists easily accessible in your child's homework spot. Get in the Error Checker habit early so that your second grader automatically includes proofreading in the writing process.

REQUIRED:
- Paper and pencil

CAPPUNC!

SKILLS: Proofreading/Editing

Ready, set, Cappunc! When your child has completed a piece of writing, enjoy a quick and easy check for an uppercase letter at the start of each sentence and end-mark punctuation—period, question mark, or exclamation point—at the end of each sentence.

By combining the first syllable of "capitalize" and the first syllable of "punctuate," create the reminder message, Cappunc! Ask your second grader to reread a piece of writing aloud, carefully checking for correct application of initial capital letter and final punctuation. Simply repeat the word "cappunc" as each sentence is read. Encourage your child to confirm that both the capital letter and end-mark punctuation have been appropriately applied in each sentence.

Write Cappunc! clearly on a strip of construction paper to post in your child's homework spot as a regular reminder to proofread.

REQUIRED:
- First draft
- Pencil
- Construction paper
- Marker

FIND-IT AND FIX-IT

SKILLS: Proofreading/Editing

When your child completes a piece of writing and asks, "Are there any mistakes?" show your young writer how to Find-It and Fix-It.

As you read through a completed draft, sit beside your child. Comment on content in a positive way. Say things such as, "I like the action word you used here," or "This describing word is perfect!" Let your youngster know that you are excited about and proud of the work done. Weave into your comments, in a fun and motivating way, remarks such as, "I see one word that needs a spelling fix-it on this line." Using a colored pencil, draw a circle to the right of the line. Inside the circle write "sp." If you see two spelling errors, put a little "2" just outside the circle.

Do the same as you read through each line of the piece. Write "cap" inside a circle beside a line with an uppercase error. Put a period, question mark, or exclamation point inside a circle beside a line that has a punctuation error. Return the paper to your child to find and fix the errors.

By making the finding and fixing of errors fun, you motivate your child to proofread and edit all written work automatically.

REQUIRED:
- First draft
- Colored pencil
- Pencil

PEANUT BUTTER PARAGRAPH

SKILL: Paragraphing

Use a concrete demonstration to enhance your child's understanding of the construction of a paragraph. As you make a sandwich for lunch, tell your child that, like a sandwich, every paragraph must have three parts. The base or bottom slice on which all else rests, the good stuff in the middle, and the top slice to close the sandwich.

Show your child that the first sentence in a paragraph, called the topic sentence, tells the subject of the paragraph. It is like the base of the sandwich. The middle sentence(s), called the body, gives details about the subject. It is like the peanut butter and jelly in the middle. The final sentence of the paragraph, called the closing sentence, sums up the information given about the subject. It is like the top slice of bread.

REQUIRED:
- Sandwich ingredients

The next time your child writes a paragraph on any subject, remind your young author to check for the bottom slice, the filling inside, and the slice on the top.

PURPOSEFUL PARAGRAPHS

SKILLS: Written Expression/Paragraphing

What's in a name? *Par* means "same." *Graph* means "write." A paragraph is made from three or more sentences written about the same subject. As early as second grade, children are exposed to the paragraph in writing and reading instruction.

Enhance your child's recognition of the purpose of the paragraph whenever you write at home. Enjoy a delicious dessert. Pass out paper and pencils to all family members to write a three-sentence paragraph to describe the dessert. Remind everyone to indent the first word of the first sentence and to include a topic sentence, body, and closing idea. Share the completed paragraphs that describe dessert.

After a family gathering or party, take time for each family member to write a paragraph to tell about the special event. Share the completed paragraphs that tell the story of the event.

Choose a favorite place and write a paragraph to tell why that place is special. Share the completed paragraphs that give reasons why the place is special.

Finally, after visiting a museum or reading a nonfiction book, write a paragraph that tells about something you've learned. Share the completed paragraphs that give information.

Everyone in the family will benefit from writing and sharing Purposeful Paragraphs.

REQUIRED:
• Paper and pencils

EXTRA, EXTRA . . .

SKILLS: Facts & Details/Main Idea/Brainstorming/Written Expression/Drawing/Oral Reading Fluency

Follow up your reading of any book or chapter by writing an article for the newspaper in the town, city, forest, or kingdom where the story occurred.

Read a book such as *Appelemando's Dreams* by Patricia Polacco, a story set in a drab village. A young boy, Appelemando, brings joy and excitement to his friends when his dreams appear in the air above his head. One rainy day, Appelemando's colorful dreams stick to everything wet, causing problems in his village.

Invite your news reporter to write the feature story for a headline such as "Boy Paints Town With Dreams." Brainstorm a headline to reinforce your child's ability to determine the main idea.

Record the facts inside a five-point star organizer labeled "who," "what," "where," "when," and "how." Weave the facts into a news report that describes the astounding event.

Finally, create a banner for the front page of the paper, *The Drab Daily*, for example. Glue the banner onto your local front-page banner. Attach your child's article directly onto the front page, including an illustration if desired.

Surprise the family by reading the story aloud at breakfast or dinner.

REQUIRED:
• A book
• Paper and pencil

OPTIONAL:
• Newspaper
• Nontoxic glue
• Crayons/markers
• Safety scissors
• Library/bookstore visit

HEAR YE! HEAR YE!

SKILLS: Written Expression/News Reporting/Facts & Details

Hear Ye! Hear Ye! Queen devises plan to discover princess! A great follow-up to reading any fairy tale or tale of old is to take on the role of Town Crier to report the news from a story scroll.

After enjoying an old favorite such as *The Princess and the Pea* by Hans Christian Anderson, adapted and illustrated by Janet Stevens, or a tale of old such as *Jethro and Joel Were a Troll* by Bill Peet, work with your child to draft the proclamation that the prince has finally found his princess or that a two-headed troll is causing panic in the kingdom! When you have completed the *who, what, where, when,* and *how* of the proclamation, write the proclamation on any kind of paper roll: a brown grocery bag, cut and rolled; the back of a sheet of wrapping paper; a sheet of rolled construction paper.

Unroll the paper. Begin writing at the top of the scroll and work your way down the page. Decorate the borders, roll up, and tie. At the next family gathering, invite your town crier to proclaim the news!

REQUIRED:
- A book
- Roll of paper
- Pencil
- Crayons/markers
- Yarn/ribbon/string
- Safety scissors

OPTIONAL:
- Library/bookstore visit

TWO THUMBS UP

SKILLS: Written Expression/Making Comparisons

Give your child the opportunity to say, "Thumbs up" or "Thumbs Down," after viewing a television program or movie.

Congratulate your second grader on being "hired" as the entertainment critic for your family. To train for the job, read a few television or movie reviews in a newspaper or magazine. Note the kinds of remarks reviewers include. Then, pop the popcorn and view a developmentally appropriate program or movie together. Talk about the pros and cons. Was the story clearly told? Did the actors portray their parts in a believable way? Was the setting well created? Did you like the ending? Why or why not?

After discussion, write your reviews independently. Then share and compare the results. Were your opinions "Two thumbs up," "One thumb up, one down," or "Two thumbs down"?

REQUIRED:
- Newspaper/magazine reviews
- Television program or movie
- Paper and pencils

OPTIONAL:
- Popcorn

BOOK BALLAD

SKILLS: Written Expression/Sequencing/Main Idea

A ballad is a song or poem that tells a story in short stanzas. After sharing a book with your second grader, integrate the arts as you create a ballad to retell the tale.

Determine and list, in sequential order, the main events of a book such as Bill Peet's *The Whingdingdilly,* the story of a farm dog named Scamp who wishes he could be a horse. When the list is complete, work to weave two or more of the main events into a ballad to tell the tale of Scamp. Put your ballad to a favorite tune or make up a tune of your own. Entertain the whole family by performing your Book Ballad for all to enjoy.

REQUIRED:
- A book
- Paper and pencil

OPTIONAL:
- Library/bookstore visit
- Musical accompaniment

SING A SEA CHANTEY

SKILLS: Written Expression/Sequencing/Main Idea/Story Form

A sea chantey is a song that tells of adventures on the high seas. After sharing a seagoing story with your second grader, create a chantey to retell the tale.

Recall the beginning, middle, and end of the story, focusing on the main character, the setting, the wish or problem, the actions taken to make the wish come true or solve the problem, and the resolution. List the main events in sequential order. Write a sea chantey to tell the tale of, for example, Barbara Cooney's *Island Boy,* Steven Kellogg's *Island of the Skog,* or Bill Peet's *Cyrus the Unsinkable Sea Serpent.* Weave in two or more main events.

REQUIRED:
- A book
- Paper and pencil

OPTIONAL:
- Library/bookstore visit
- Musical accompaniment

Put your chantey to a favorite tune or make up a tune of your own. Then hoist the mainsail and Sing a Sea Chantey to the delight of the whole family.

SPOTS AND HUMPS

SKILLS: Brainstorming/Written Expression/Imaginative Thinking/Drawing

For a century, children the world over have delighted in hearing or reading about how the leopard got his spots, the camel got his hump, and the rhinoceros got his skin. Enjoy one of Rudyard Kipling's beloved tales by sharing *How the Leopard Got His Spots and Other Just So Stories*.

Use any of the *Just So Stories* as a model for creating your own story. Perhaps your second grader wonders how the cat got its purr, how the turtle got its shell, how the raccoon got its mask, how the giraffe got its neck, or how the rose got its thorns. Work together to brainstorm ideas to explain any natural phenomenon that interests your child.

Make a map, web, or ladder to plan the story. Be sure to introduce the characters, setting, and wish or problem at the beginning; present a sequence of events in the middle; and reach a resolution at the end. Follow the writing process through the stages of preparation, first draft, revision, proofread/edit, and publish. Make the final copy in any format. Include illustrations to complement the writing. Add a construction paper cover, punch a hole in the upper left-hand corner of each page, and bind with yarn, ribbon, or string. Share the completed story and add to your family's treasury of favorite books.

REQUIRED:
- Library/bookstore visit
- Paper and pencil
- Crayons/markers

OPTIONAL:
- Yarn/ribbon/string
- Hole punch

JUST FOR ME JOURNAL

SKILL: Written Expression

A journal is a mirror of you, a place to write about feelings and thoughts, a place to record the events of each day. Provide your second grader with a personal journal and the encouragement to make an entry every day.

To begin, set the example. Make two journals, one for your child, one for you. Punch holes along the left margin of inviting colored paper. Tie with ribbon or yarn. Decorate and label the cover to reflect personal interests. As an alternative, use notebooks, pads, or store-bought journals or diaries.

Encourage your child to give the journal a name. Addressing a journal or diary by a name personifies the journal and adds to the book's viability as a "listener." On the day and at the time your child makes the first entry, you do the same.

Anything goes! Remind your child to write as neatly as possible and to draw pictures at any time. Emphasize that any idea is a good idea and that there is no need to worry about spelling and mechanics.

Read your journals often to remember and reflect.

REQUIRED:
- Paper and pencils
- Safety scissors
- Yarn/ribbon/string
- Hole punch
- Art supplies

OPTIONAL:
- Purchased journal

QUICK NOTES

SKILL: Written Expression

Just as we try to keep a memo pad and pencil by the telephone at work to write a quick note or message, keep a memo pad and pencil in an accessible place at home so that family members can write each other Quick Notes.

Jot a message such as "Dear Leigh, Enjoy your lunch and have fun at your gymnastics class!" and slip it into your child's lunch box. Write "Sweet dreams! See you at breakfast!" and slide it under your child's pillow.

Imagine the smile on your child's face upon discovering your note. Imagine a moment of relaxed calm at work when you find a note from your child.

REQUIRED:
• Memo pad
• Pencil

DEAR GRANDPA

SKILLS: Written Expression/Friendly Letter/Handwriting/Spelling/Capitalization/Punctuation

In our fast-paced world of e-mail and voice mail, reserve space for snail mail. A handwritten letter from your second grader is sure to bring a smile to the recipient.

When your child celebrates a birthday, sings in a class performance, or runs in a race, take time to write a friendly letter to a relative or friend.

Take your child to the stationery store to select a package of appealing stationery. At home, review the five parts of a friendly letter: the date, greeting, body, closing, and signature. Talk about the news your child wishes to share.

Model letter-writing format. Encourage your child to use neatly and correctly formed handwriting so that the letter is pleasing to the eye as well as to the mind. Write the date in the upper right-hand corner. Skip a space and write the greeting, "Dear Grandpa," at the left margin. Skip a space, indent, and write the body. Skip a space, move to the right, and write the closing, "Love,." Beneath the closing, write the signature.

Reread the letter, proofreading for spelling, capitalization, and punctuation. Help your second-grade correspondent address the envelope. Add a stamp and send the news!

REQUIRED:
• Stationery
• Pencil
• Envelope
• Stamp

POWER OF PERSUASION

SKILLS: Written Expression/Reading Comprehension/Inferential Thinking/
Expressive Language/Friendly Letter/Persuasive Writing/Proofreading

Children can enhance expressive and persuasive writing abilities as they state their opinions and share their values in friendly letters to book characters.

Share a story such as *The Legend of Scarface* by Robert D. San Souci or *Chicken Sunday* by Patricia Polacco. Talk about the interpersonal relationships you witness in the story. If you read about an injustice, as in *Scarface,* discuss your feelings. If you read about a cooperative effort, as in *Chicken Sunday,* examine the actions of all involved.

Imagine that you travel in time or space to the setting of the story. Write a letter to the children of the Blackfeet Village of *Scarface.* Persuade them not to make fun of Scarface because he is poor and scarred. Write a letter to Trisha, Stewart, and Winston of *Chicken Sunday*. Persuade them to work together to earn money for the hat they want to buy for Miss Eula.

Encourage your child to include the date, greeting, body, closing, and signature in each letter. Proofread together, checking for spelling, initial letter capitalization, and end-mark punctuation.

As a special surprise, respond to your child from the point of view of the character.

REQUIRED:
• A book
• Pencil
• Stationery

OPTIONAL:
• Library/bookstore visit

A POEM A DAY

SKILLS: Poetry Appreciation/Oral Reading Fluency/Vocabulary Development/
Expressive Language/Figurative Language

Take the rush from morning routines and the hustle from evening commitments. Find a few minutes to relax with your child to share a poem.

Read a poem aloud to your second grader or invite your second grader to read the poem to you. Read the poem together or alternate lines or verses. Listen to the language used by the poet. Ask, "What do you like about the poem? What do you notice about the words used? Is there a sound you like, a word that makes you laugh, a thought that makes you smile?"

Look for examples of *alliteration* and talk about the effect of the repeated sound. Let *onomatopoeia* tickle your tongues as you articulate the sounds of *clicks, splashes,* or *growls.* Wonder about words you've never seen or used and learn their meanings from context. Close your eyes. Picture the images created by the poet's language. See, hear, feel, taste, and touch with the words of poetry.

Enjoy a collection of poems, one a day, such as those presented in *Turtle in July* by Marilyn Singer and Jerry Pinkney. Invite all family members to join in as you enjoy A Poem a Day.

REQUIRED:
• Poems

OPTIONAL:
• Library/bookstore visit

LANGUAGE ARTS ACTIVITIES

PICTURE IN A POEM

SKILLS: Written Expression/Poetry

The world around us is rich with sights that can be captured in a poem. All you need are simple tools, a subject, a thought, a feeling, and freedom to express ideas. An anonymous seven-year-old once wrote:

Stars, stars
 Why do people wish on stars?
 Why not the sun
Or the moon?
Do stars take messages?

Join your child and watch the world. See a butterfly alight on a flower. Watch clouds race across the sky. Notice an old sneaker tossed in a corner and wonder why. Then pick up a pencil, pen, marker, or crayon and capture the Picture in a Poem. All conventions are off! Imagination is on! Put away concerns about complete sentences, spelling, uppercase letters, and punctuation. Let the words flow as you feel and see them. Then, one afternoon or evening, find a cozy spot to gather the family. Light candles, play relaxing music, serve a snack, and share your poetry.

REQUIRED:
• Paper and pencils/pens
• Crayons/markers

OPTIONAL:
• Candlelight
• Music
• Snacks

PICNIC AND POETRY

SKILLS: Written Expression/Poetry/Imaginative Thinking/Oral Reading Fluency

Be on the lookout for unusual pictures in magazine articles and advertisements. When you find a photo that captures your fancy, cut it out and store it in a "Poetry Pictures" envelope or folder. Get the whole family involved in stocking the envelope.

When an array of pictures has been collected, plan a family picnic at which you take time for poetry. Distribute paper, pencils, crayons, or markers. Then pass the "Poetry Pictures" envelope around so that all participants can randomly pick a picture and write a poem. Encourage everyone to use the picture to generate ideas. Choose a picture of laughing chimpanzees and write about them. Choose a picture of a mountain sunset and describe it. Choose a picture of a huge ice cream sundae and capture it in a poem. When everyone has written, sit back, relax, and share.

REQUIRED:
• Pictures
• Safety scissors
• Envelope/file folder
• Paper and pencils
• Crayons/markers

OPTIONAL:
• Picnic

INSIDE OR ALL AROUND

SKILLS: Written Expression/Poetry/Drawing/Painting

You don't need a camera to remember a special day!

Imagine this. You are sitting on the beach. A boat sails by, a kite flies over, a gull soars aloft, a pail and shovel rest by your feet. A seal surfaces, a dolphin leaps.

You are sitting at the ballpark. A fly ball arches, a hot dog sizzles. The pitcher winds up, the batter swings, the fans cheer.

Find a few moments to capture an image from a special day in a shape poem. Draw a picture of whatever comes to mind and write a poem Inside or All Around the shape. Focus on what you see, feel, hear, taste, or smell as you weave your recollections together. Color or paint the completed shape poem. Draw the sailboat you saw and write a poem in the sail. Draw the hot dog you enjoyed and write a poem around the roll.

Make an album of shape poems. Punch holes in the left margin of each one written. Tie together with ribbon. As an option, glue poems into an album or scrapbook for all to read, admire, and enjoy.

REQUIRED:
- Paper and pencil
- Crayons/markers/paint/ paintbrush
- Hole punch
- Yarn/ribbon/string

OPTIONAL:
- Nontoxic glue
- Album/scrapbook

HOMEWORK SLOT AND SPOT

SKILLS: Study Skills/Organization

Has your second grader ever asked, "Do I have to do my homework?" Has your second grader ever said, just before bedtime, "I forgot to do my spelling sentences"?

Be a homework helper to enhance your child's organizational skills, self-direction, and love of learning. Designate a time as the Homework Slot. Choose a time that is convenient and relaxed for all, one that is free from the pressure of wanting and needing to do something else. Next, set up a Homework Spot, one that is well lit, quiet, and equipped with necessary tools, including lined paper, pencils, crayons, a ruler, and manipulatives to assist with reading, written expression, spelling, and math. These may include a line marker for reading, sticky tags and graphic organizers for writing, letter tiles for spelling, and countable items for math.

At the Homework Slot, set the example. As your second grader sits in the Homework Spot to work on a report or study the weekly words for spelling, sit nearby in your Homework Spot to balance your checkbook or catch up on correspondence. Be available to answer questions and lend a hand as needed. Establish a routine and lay the foundation early for productive and enjoyable learning time at home.

REQUIRED:
- Quiet space
- Homework tools

LANGUAGE ARTS ACTIVITIES

STEP BY STEP

SKILLS: Following Directions/Listening Comprehension/Literal Recall/Drawing/Making Comparisons

Enhance your child's ability to follow oral and written directions with Step by Step.

Before inviting your second grader and any other family member to participate, write a set of directions, such as the one that follows, on a piece of paper.

Draw a blue lake. Draw two boats on the lake. In one boat, draw a boy in brown shorts. In the other boat, draw a girl with a green hat. Put a flower on the hat. Draw four fish in the lake. Beside the lake, draw a tree. Draw a nest in the tree. Put a red bird in the nest. Under the tree, draw a rock. On top of the rock, draw a frog. Put the sun in the sky.

Provide all participants with paper and crayons. Then dictate the directions, one sentence at a time, giving ample time for listeners to respond by drawing. Continue until all sentences have been read and all pictures drawn. Then compare the results.

Write a second set of directions. This time ask participants to read all the directions aloud. Then work independently to read the sentences one at a time and, Step by Step, follow the directions. Again compare the results.

REQUIRED:
• Paper and pencil
• Crayons/markers

SCRAMBLED SPELLING EGGS

SKILLS: Spelling/Researching/Recording Data/Sentence Construction

Plastic eggs are a fabulous incentive for practicing spelling words, challenging thinking, and sparking curiosity for research of any topic.

Retrieve a dozen or more plastic eggs from your holiday supplies or, in the spring, purchase a bag for $.99. Without your second grader's knowledge, copy any or all of his or her weekly spelling words on 1″ graph paper, writing one letter per square. Cut out the letters for a word, scramble them, and put them inside an egg. Do the same for each word on the list.

When it is time to practice spelling words, present your child with a dozen eggs to open, one at a time, and unscramble. Provide assistance as needed. Then ask your child to read the word, spell the word, and use it in a sentence.

For added fun, challenge your child to unscramble the name of a dinosaur, insect, favorite sports figure, president, or planet. Then research the unscrambled word. Write three sentences to tell three facts about whatever was inside the egg. Get the whole family involved, one egg per person, on a specific topic, so that you can work together while unscrambling, researching, writing, sharing, and learning.

REQUIRED:
• Paper and pencils
• Graph paper
• Plastic eggs
• Safety scissors

OPTIONAL:
• Library visit

QUICK-CHECK SPELLING

SKILLS: Spelling/Visual Memory/Homonyms/Proofreading

While second graders can use a children's dictionary to confirm spelling, they also benefit from maintaining a personal spelling dictionary of high-frequency words. Because a Quick-Check Spelling dictionary is manageable and easy to use, your child is more likely to check for unfamiliar words.

Use a loose-leaf binder or spiral notebook as a personal spelling dictionary. Allow two pages for each letter in the alphabet. Label the top of each page with both the uppercase and lowercase letter, "Aa Words," "Bb Words," for example. Fill the pages as words occur in writing that are troublesome. If your child asks, "How do you spell 'who'?" provide the correct spelling so that your child can make the entry on the *Ww* page.

Specialized pages are also helpful. Work together to make a Homonym section. Write "to, too, two" and include a sentence for each for verification. Do the same for "there, their, they're"; "one, won"; "hear, here"; "your, you're"; and any other words that sound the same, are spelled differently, and have different meanings. Also include theme pages such as Months of the Year, Days of the Week, Foods, and Animals.

REQUIRED:
- Notebook
- Pencil

Keep Quick-Check Spelling handy as a helpful writing tool to enhance proofreading and self-correction skills.

DOWN WITH DEMONS

SKILLS: Spelling/Visual Memory

The "Monsters," "Outlaws," "Ogres," or, most commonly, "Demons" are those spelling words that give children the most trouble. These are the words that break the rules, calling upon youngsters to spell by applying visual memory skills rather than by combining visual memory skills and spelling rules. Put an end to the havoc these demons cause by creating a Down with Demons chart or poster to display in your child's homework spot.

Encourage your second grader to decorate the corners and borders of the chart with colorful creatures and monsters. Then, neatly print the words provided on lined paper. Attach to the center of the chart. Add personal spelling demons to the list as they present themselves. Remind your child to refer to the chart whenever one of the demons occurs in writing. Before long, the spelling demons will take a back seat to standard spelling.

WORD BANK: about, again, all right, a lot, already, among, because, been, bought, buy, could, couldn't, country, didn't, does, enough, every, first, forty, friend, goes, guess, haven't, here, hour, knew, know, little, minute, none, off, often, once, people, please, pretty, quite, ready, rough, said, sure, their, there, they, though, thought, through, too, when, where, which, would, wouldn't, your, you're

REQUIRED
- Construction paper
- Crayons/markers
- Lined paper
- Nontoxic glue

MATH

A group of children, heads down in studied concentration, stretches rubber bands from peg to peg to create geometric designs on a geoboard. A child lies on the floor with arms stretched above his head while another carefully places her ruler to measure his length from fingertips to toes. Two pals drop a handful of dominoes on a tabletop then race to add or subtract the visible dots. A few children group pretzels into six sets of eight while a few others record survey results on a graph. It is math time in second grade.

Children come to second grade equipped with math skills acquired from previous years in school and at home, skills they use as the foundation for new learning. While second graders continue to require manipulative materials, number tiles, counters, tangrams, attribute blocks, and dice, they come to second grade prepared to move from concrete exploration to abstract thinking. With eagerness and curiosity, they begin to "talk math," to develop and share problem-solving strategies with peers, teachers, and parents. They diligently work to master addition and subtraction facts and cautiously tackle the basics of multiplication and division.

Second-grade mathematicians measure with rulers, yardsticks, scales, thermometers, and clocks. They manipulate coins and dollars to estimate costs, spend, save, and make change. They move clock hands to tell time to the nearest hour, half hour, quarter hour, and minute. They maintain math journals to write, draw, and discover problem-solving strategies, to validate and confirm mathematical notions, to stretch thinking and challenge discovery.

Use the range of activities provided to encourage and celebrate math exploration at home. Bowl your way to mastery of subtraction facts or appoint your child Certified Family Accountant and grocery manager. Ask Ten Questions to find the secret number or Rock Around the Clock to tell time. Problem solve with cucumbers and carrots or Bake and Divvy a batch of cookies to enhance understanding of fractions.

Let the dominoes fall, the dice roll, the coins flip, and the noodles group as you encourage excitement, confidence, and willingness in all mathematical exploration.

TEN QUESTIONS

SKILL: Number Awareness

This fast-paced question-and-answer game is sure to keep all participants on their toes! Ask Ten Questions to reveal the identity of a secret number.

Tell your second grader to think of a secret number. Inform your child that you will try to guess the number by asking no more than 10 *yes* or *no* questions.

Ask your child, "Is the number higher than 100?" Your child responds, "No." Ask, "Is the number between 0 and 50?" Your second grader responds, "Yes." Ask, "Is the number lower than 25?" Your child responds, "Yes." Ask, "Is the number odd?" Your child responds, "No." Continue in this fashion until you have asked 10 *yes* or *no* questions or have guessed the secret number. Then, switch roles so your child can ask you Ten Questions.

Play anytime and anywhere. Vary the number of questions asked and use large numbers as appropriate.

REQUIRED:
• Your time

MATHEMATICIAN KIT

SKILLS: Math Awareness/Study Skills/Organization/Brainstorming

As homework demands on your second grader increase, you may hear, "Mom, I can't find a ruler!" or "Dad, where is the calculator?" Organize a Mathematician Kit to enhance your child's organizational skills and increase independence during homework time.

Remove the cover from an empty shoebox. Label the shoebox, "Mathematician Kit." Provide your child with materials to decorate the kit. Brainstorm a list of math tools and materials to gather and include in the kit. Include a ruler, tape measure, calculator, counters, coins, number chart, compass, dice, dominoes, scratch pad, pencils, and anything else your young mathematician can use to assist with homework and other math explorations.

Store your child's Mathematician Kit in the Homework Spot so that tools are easily accessible for efficient application of concepts learned.

REQUIRED:
• Shoebox
• Paper and pencil
• Math tools
• Art supplies

OUTDOOR MATH MURAL

SKILLS: Math Awareness/Number Awareness/Math Appreciation/Drawing

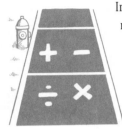

Invite everyone on your street to demonstrate math appreciation by using colorful chalk to make an Outdoor Math Mural.

Find a safe, clear section of asphalt. Your driveway and the sidewalk in front of your home make good spots. Work together to make a border around the selected area.

Provide chalk to all participants. Use vivid colors to fill the area with anything related to math. Watch artistic ability meet with math as neighborhood artists draw big and bold shape and color patterns, detailed calendars, and thermometers. Provide positive reinforcement to all as they draw scenes that generate addition, subtraction, multiplication, and division problems. Witness the drawing of large rulers, tape measures, and calculators. Compliment the appearance of large, decorative numbers. Participants may include number patterns, money notation, and word problems for others to solve.

Use the work in progress as a springboard for rich math discussion. When all have had the opportunity to admire the mural, clean the surface with water or wait for rain to do the job!

REQUIRED:
• Colored chalk

OPTIONAL:
• Water

METAPHORIC MATH

SKILLS: Math Awareness/Number Awareness/Math Appreciation/
Brainstorming/Metaphor/Poetry/Written Expression

A metaphor is a figure of speech that uses one noun (person, place, or thing) to describe another. Second graders don't need to define "metaphor" in order to use metaphors to write Metaphoric Math poems.

Share a poem such as "Calculator," by Rebecca Kai Dotlich, found in *Marvelous Math, A Book of Poems* selected by Lee Bennett Hopkins.

Pocket-size tutor.
Mathematician.
Genius with fractions.
Mini-magician.

REQUIRED:
• Paper and pencil

OPTIONAL:
• Library/bookstore visit

Talk about the way the poet described a calculator as a tutor, mathematician, genius, and mini-magician.

Make a list of math-related items; such a list might include a ruler, coin, clock, circle, square, domino, calendar. Choose one item and brainstorm nouns that could describe the item. Weave the ideas together into a mathematical metaphor to paint a picture of the role, purpose, or use of the item. The poem that results can be as simple as a single line.

SEVENS AND EIGHTS

SKILLS: Number Awareness/Written Expression/Imaginative Thinking/Counting/Cutting/Shape Recognition

Make your child's second-grade birthday party a memorable celebration of seven or eight. If you plan a party, invite seven friends for a seventh birthday, eight friends for an eighth. Work together to create, address, and mail invitations decorated with 7s or 8s. Greet your child in the morning with seven or eight hugs. Share a story such as *The Seven Chinese Brothers* by Margaret Mahy or *Be Ready at Eight* by Peggy Parish. Cut your child's waffles, pancakes, or French toast into sevenths or eighths before serving.

Throughout the day, celebrate seven or eight in all you do! Cut 7s or 8s, heptagons or octagons from construction paper for decorations. Group seven or eight candles on the cake, keeping the one for good luck to the side. Open seven or eight gifts. Play games such as Seven Musical Chairs or Eight Questions. Have partygoers make hats decorated with 7s or 8s. Use glitter glue to decorate goodie bags with 7s or 8s and put seven or eight goodies inside.

REQUIRED:
• Party supplies

OPTIONAL:
• Library/bookstore visit

The celebration of seven or eight is sure to be special for all!

NEWSPAPER MATH

SKILLS: Math Awareness/Number Awareness/Expressive Language

What do movie times, weather forecasts, maps, page numbers, indexes, tables, graphs, charts, dates, times, telephone numbers, advertisements, coupons, schedules, scores, and statistics have in common? Each is found daily in a newspaper! Engage in Newspaper Math exploration to enhance your second grader's awareness that math and numbers are everywhere.

Sit beside your child to peruse the front page. Encourage your second grader to find and discuss math-related items. Then, read the index, noting that page numbers guide the reader to each section.

Turn to the arts and films section. Alternate turns to locate a math-related item to discuss. Note movie times at 4:20 and 7:15. Discuss ticket prices at $4.00 for the first show and $7.25 for the second. Ask which show is a better value.

Continue in this fashion, noting theater phone numbers and address numbers. Then move to another section of the paper to continue the exploration. Check the cost of items advertised at the hardware store, the results of yesterday's sports events, the closing values on the stock market, and the high and low temperatures predicted for the day. By the time your exploration is complete, your second grader will recognize the importance of numbers.

REQUIRED:
• A newspaper

SCORES, STATS, AND STANDINGS

SKILLS: Math Awareness/Number Awareness

A gymnast scored a 10 on the uneven bars. The Stars are in first place. The 76ers beat the Spurs by 12 points. A sprinter ran the 40-yard dash in 4.8 seconds. The pitcher gave up six runs in four innings. Sports scores, statistics, and standings motivate authentic discussion of numbers.

Open the sports section of a daily newspaper. Notice that the local football team won 24–14 and determine the difference in the score. Point out the list of homerun leaders. Calculate the total number of homeruns hit by the top two homerun hitters.

Find and discuss other Scores, Stats, and Standings. Talk about the swimmers' times in the last swim meet and the average number of points your favorite basketball player scores per game. Marvel at the number of consecutive games the local college volleyball or field hockey team has won.

If possible, enjoy a day at a sporting event. Connect sports and numbers as you examine ticket stubs; section, row, and seat numbers; scoreboards; concession stand prices; and numbers on the back of a team member's jersey.

REQUIRED:
- Sports section

OPTIONAL:
- Sporting event

MATH INTERVIEWS

SKILLS: Math Awareness/Brainstorming/Expressive Language/Recording Data/Making Comparisons

How do the members of your family use math every day? Encourage your child to hold Math Interviews to find out!

Brainstorm questions that focus on how family members apply math processes and tools. Number and record each question on an interviewer's question sheet.

1. Do you use addition at work? How?
2. Do you use subtraction in your job? How?
3. How do you use a ruler each day?
4. Is there a calculator in your office? Why do you use it?
5. Do you work with money? How?

Be sure to generate questions that are applicable to both children and adults.

Hold five to eight sheets of paper horizontally. Fold the sheets in half and staple on the left edge to make a book. Label the front cover "Family Math Interviews." Tuck the interviewer's question sheet inside the booklet.

Now your second grader is ready to conduct interviews. Remind your child to label each page with the name of the interviewee and to record the answer given to each numbered question.

Take time when the family is together to review the interviews and make comparisons of the results.

REQUIRED:
- Paper and pencil
- Stapler

MATHERATURE

SKILLS: Math Awareness/Number Awareness/Connecting Math & Literature

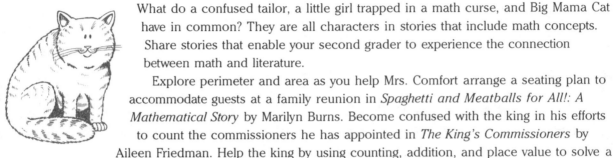

What do a confused tailor, a little girl trapped in a math curse, and Big Mama Cat have in common? They are all characters in stories that include math concepts. Share stories that enable your second grader to experience the connection between math and literature.

Explore perimeter and area as you help Mrs. Comfort arrange a seating plan to accommodate guests at a family reunion in *Spaghetti and Meatballs for All!: A Mathematical Story* by Marilyn Burns. Become confused with the king in his efforts to count the commissioners he has appointed in *The King's Commissioners* by Aileen Friedman. Help the king by using counting, addition, and place value to solve a problem. Help a brother and sister understand fractions in *Give Me Half!* by Stuart J. Murphy.

Other stories that lead to rich discussion about math concepts include *A Cloak for the Dreamer* by Aileen Friedman, *Amanda Bean's Amazing Dream* by Cindy Neuschwander and Marilyn Burns, *Telling Time with Big Mama Cat* by Dan Harper, and *Math Curse* by Jon Scieszka.

REQUIRED:
• Math stories

OPTIONAL:
• Library/bookstore visit

TALK MATH

SKILLS: Math Awareness/Number Awareness/Expressive Language/
Visual Patterns/Estimating/Making Comparisons/Counting

Just as reading to your child enhances reading development, engaging your child in meaningful discussions about math helps your second grader become a confident, strong, and well-rounded mathematician. After a year of formal math instruction in grade one, your second grader will be eager to Talk Math.

Daily activities provide opportunities to talk about math. On the way to school, discuss visual patterns you see in gardens and windows. Estimate how long it takes to drive to school or how many steps it is to walk to school. At the shoe store, compare the size and price of new shoes to those of old shoes. At the supermarket, talk about the prices of the items selected and the weight or volume noted on packages. Count the number of items in your cart as you place them on the checkout counter. Tally the value of coupons to determine your savings. Estimate the cost of your order.

Whenever and wherever the opportunity arises, engage your second grader in talking about math. In this way, you continue to build awareness of the powerful presence of math and numbers in our world.

REQUIRED:
• Your time

SUPERMARKET MATH

SKILLS: Math Awareness/Money/Measurement

One dozen eggs, $1.59. Swiss cheese, $4.79 per pound. Buy two boxes, get the third free. 10–ounce bag of pretzels, $.20 off. The supermarket is a mecca for building awareness of money and measurement!

Invite your second grader to join you on your next visit to the supermarket. En route, discuss Supermarket Math. Explain that some items are sold individually, some in a package of six, by the dozen, or by weight. Talk about different types of sales and other promotions: 20 percent off, two for the price of one, and $1.00 off.

At the supermarket, read and discuss advertising signs, posters, and flyers. Notice that fresh fruits and vegetables, meat, fish, and poultry are priced by the pound. Look at spring scales in the produce department and electronic scales at the deli counter. Whenever possible, have your child read the scale to determine weight. View cash registers at the checkout counter. Read the display. Note the amount of money owed. Let your child assist as you pay the bill and receive change. You'll come home from the supermarket with bags of groceries and a second grader who is more aware of money and measurement.

REQUIRED:
• Supermarket visit

WHAT IS MATH?

SKILLS: Math Awareness/Number Awareness/Brainstorming/Drawing/Expressive Language

Ask your second grader to create a What Is Math? poster to show that math is more than numbers.

Provide a sheet of construction paper and a marker. Encourage your child to fill the poster with calendars, thermometers, shapes, rulers, tape measures, calculators, tables, number grids, graphs, and patterns of shape, color, and size. Your second grader may choose to write number patterns, addition and subtraction facts, money notation, information about place value, and solutions to word problems.

As your child works on the What Is Math? poster, ask questions about items included. Encourage your second grader and other family members to add to the poster often and talk about math.

REQUIRED:
• Construction paper
• Pencil/marker

BOX O' MATH

Create a Box o' Math from a shoebox to reinforce and authenticate your second grader's awareness of math and numbers.

Provide your child with supplies to decorate the box with anything—numbers, shapes, patterns—representative of math. Clearly label the box, "Ben's Box o' Math," for example.

Encourage your second grader to collect and save math-related items in the box. Include ticket stubs, maps, pictures of shapes, receipts, coins, and special math papers from school. Surprise your child by adding interactive items to the math box. Enclose secret envelopes with math problems for your child to solve or notes about math that require a response.

Add to the box often and share the items included. Be amazed by the array of math-related items collected and saved.

REQUIRED:
- Shoebox
- Safety scissors
- Tape or nontoxic glue
- Recyclable print materials
- Crayons/markers/colored pencils
- Construction paper
- Math-related items

UP AND DOWN

Second graders benefit from and enjoy counting games. Play Up and Down to sharpen your child's skill in counting by any number—ones, twos, fives, tens, hundreds.

Set a timer to 10 seconds. Ask your child to count by twos as high as possible. Say, "Go!" and let the counting begin. At the end of 10 seconds, congratulate your second grader on a job well done. Then, without imposing a time limit, ask your child to start at the number that was reached and count down to zero, by twos. Continue in this fashion, letting your child choose the numbers by which to count.

Variation: Increase the amount of time given for counting up, and time the counting down. Your child will also get a kick out of timing you, when you choose a number to count Up and Down.

REQUIRED:
- Timer

COUNT AND CLAP

SKILL: Counting

Try a fast, fun-filled counting game that keeps you and your child on your toes.

In this counting game, clap for the multiples of five. Start off the game by saying, "One!" Your child says, "Two!" You say, "Three!" Your child says, "Four!" Instead of responding, "Five!" you clap. Your child then continues, "Six!" Continue counting in this manner. When you get to ten, your child claps. Alternate calling numbers, clapping at multiples of five.

Play often, varying the game by counting faster. When your child is comfortable with the rules, change the multiples. Clap at 3, 6, 9, 12, 15. Clap at 7, 14, 21, 28.

Increase the challenge by counting down as well as up and by inviting other family members to participate. Remember, when you play this game, Count and Clap!

REQUIRED:
• Your time

YELLOW PAGE COUNT

SKILLS: Counting/Alphabetical Order/Recording Data/Addition/Subtraction/Making Comparisons

Young children enjoy counting. They love to see how high they can count by ones, twos, fives, and tens. They relish opportunities to count money, pieces of gum, and trading cards. Use the Yellow Pages to count, add, subtract, and compare.

Together, find the restaurant section in the Yellow Pages. Ask your second grader to find and count the pizza shops in the section. Record this number on a sheet of paper.

Then, find the ice cream section in the Yellow Pages. Ask your second grader to count the ice cream shops in the section. Record this number. Compare the number of pizza shops to the number of ice cream shops.

Continue the Yellow Page Count as your child counts and compares the number of hardware stores, supermarkets, toy stores, and movie theaters. No matter what you choose to count, you'll find it in the Yellow Pages.

REQUIRED:
• Yellow Pages
• Paper and pencil

MULTIPURPOSE HELPER

SKILLS: Number Writing/Number Recognition/Number Sequence/Counting/
Number Patterns/Number Relations/Addition/Subtraction

Make a number chart to give your second grader a Multipurpose Helper for working on a range of math skills.

Work together to draw a 10 × 10 grid on a horizontal sheet of construction paper. Use one color for odd numbers and one for even numbers to write numbers 1 to 100, in sequence, one number per box, left to right, top to bottom. Work together to confirm that numbers are in sequence and that odd and even numbers are color-coded appropriately.

Use the chart to help with homework; practice an array of skills; identify odd or even number patterns; and support counting, skip counting, number relations, addition, and subtraction.

Store the Multipurpose Helper in the Homework Spot for easy access.

REQUIRED:
• Construction paper
• Ruler
• Markers

ADDITION BINGO

SKILL: Addition

B	i	N	G	O
5	10	3	6
9	16	8	12
14	1	13	17
11	7	4	15

Everyone loves a game of Bingo! Help your child reach mastery of addition facts with sums from 0 to 18 by playing Addition Bingo.

Each participant draws a four-by-four grid. On the grid, write numbers randomly, choosing numbers from 0 to 18, one number per box. Players can use any given number in no more than two boxes.

After creating the Bingo grids, make 20 number cards. Clearly print "0" on two cards, "1" on two cards, and "2" on two cards. Continue in this fashion up to and including 9. Shuffle the cards. Place facedown between participants. Supply each player with game markers.

Alternate turns drawing the top two cards from the deck. Each player adds the two numbers together. If the sum of the numbers matches a number on a player's grid, the player puts a game marker on that number. If that number is already covered with a game marker, cover it again.

Continue until a player gets four game markers in a row, column, or diagonal and shouts, "Addition Bingo!" If all the cards are used before a winner is determined, the player with the most game markers on the grid is the winner.

REQUIRED:
• Paper and pencils
• Game markers

VICE VERSA

SKILL: Addition

Use your telephone number to generate addition facts. Demonstrate that 4 + 2 = 6 and, Vice Versa, 2 + 4 = 6.

Make a Vice Versa record sheet for each player. Write your telephone number, 473-2931, across the top of each sheet. Set a time limit for finding and recording addition facts using the digits of your telephone number. When time expires, players search for and circle all pairs of Vice

Versa facts, 7 + 9 = 16 and 9 + 7 = 16. Receive two points for each pair circled. The player with the most points is the winner.

REQUIRED:
- Paper and pencils
- Timer

ADDITION AUTHOR

SKILLS: Addition/Written Expression/Oral Reading Fluency

Your second grader can expand his or her understanding of addition as an Addition Author.

Find a picture or photograph that shows lots of activity. Use the picture to generate ideas for an addition story, a story that includes an addition problem for readers to solve.

For example, select a picture of children flying kites in a park. As Addition Author, your child writes:

One breezy morning, eight children flew kites in the park. They had a great time. Soon, four children with kites joined them. How many children flew kites in the park that day?

Your second grader then reads the addition story to another family member. That family member solves the problem, saying, "8 children + 4 children = 12 children flew kites in the park."

You may want to collect all the photos and addition stories in a journal or notebook. Add to the notebook whenever a new addition story is written.

REQUIRED:
- Picture/photograph
- Paper and pencil

OPTIONAL:
- Journal/notebook
- Stapler
- Nontoxic glue
- Safety scissors

ICE CREAM TONIGHT!

Strengthen addition skills by assigning letters to the sums of addition problems. Use the letter/sum chart below to write a secret message for your child to decode. For example, if the sum of an addition problem is seven, the corresponding letter is *g;* if the sum is thirteen, the corresponding letter is *m.*

a=1, *b*=2, *c*=3, *d*=4, *e*=5, *f*=6, *g*=7, *h*=8, *i*=9, *j*=10, *k*=11, *l*=12, *m*=13, *n*=14, *o*=15, *p*=16, *q*=17, *r*=18, *s*=19, *t*=20, *u*=21, *v*=22, *w*=23, *x*=24, *y*=25, *z*=26

To write the first word of the secret message, "Ice Cream Tonight," write the addition problems 5 + 4, 0 + 3, 3 + 2. Your second grader solves the problems in order, finds the corresponding letters—*i, c, e*—and reads the word. Continue in this fashion until your child has discovered the treat planned for dessert.

To work with larger numbers, provide a calculator as needed. As an option, ask your child to write a secret message for you to decode.

REQUIRED:
- Paper and pencil
- Ice cream

OPTIONAL:
- Calculator

THREE DICE ROLL

SKILL: Addition

Three dice are better than two! Help your child get a firm grasp on the concept of adding three numbers by playing Three Dice Roll.

Prepare a scorecard by drawing a line down the center of a sheet of paper. Label one side "Dad," the other, "Lisa," for example. Alternate turns rolling three dice, adding the digits together, and recording the sum on the scorecard.

Go first to demonstrate the steps. Roll a 2, 5, 3 and say, "Two plus five plus three equals ten!" Record "10" in the "Dad" column. Give your child the dice and continue. After each turn, calculate the cumulative score for each player. The first to reach 100 wins the game.

REQUIRED:
- Three dice
- Paper and pencil

TRIPLE TROUBLE

SKILL: Addition

Challenge your child to stay out of Triple Trouble while practicing addition with three addends. Make a Triple Trouble gameboard from a file folder opened horizontally. In the upper left-hand corner, draw a 1″ square. Label it "Start." Do the same in the lower right-hand corner. Label this square "Finish." Draw 30 connecting squares between Start and Finish. Print "TT," short for Triple Trouble, in every other square, beginning in the third square from the start. Next, cut 10 index cards in half. Print addition problems, such as 2 + 3 + 1 or 5 + 4 + 3, one per card. Shuffle and place facedown in a pile. Use one die and buttons or plastic chips as game markers. Keep paper, pencils, and counters on hand for calculating sums.

The first player rolls the die and moves that number of spaces. If the player lands on a blank square, play continues. If the player lands on a "TT" square, the player picks the top card, reads the three addends, and uses whatever means necessary to find the sum.

Move ahead three spaces for a correct answer. Go back three for an incorrect answer. Alternate turns. The first to the finish is the winner.

REQUIRED:
- File folder
- Marker
- Index cards
- Die
- Game markers
- Paper and pencils
- Counters
- Safety scissors

SUM UP THE JERSEYS

SKILLS: Addition/Calculator/Making Comparisons

Are you a Red Sox fan, Vikings fan, Maple Leafs fan, Comets fan, or Nuggets fan? Use the jersey numbers of the players on your favorite sports team to practice addition problems with multiple addends, the numbers you add together.

Work with your second grader to find a roster of your favorite sports team in a newspaper, game program, or team yearbook. Provide paper, pencil, and, if necessary, a calculator. Challenge your child to determine the total of all team jersey numbers. Record the sum. For example, total the jersey numbers of the Seattle Seahawks.

Find a roster of another team within the same sport, the Tampa Bay Buccaneers. Again, challenge your second grader to determine the total of all team jersey numbers for the Bucs. Record the sum and compare to the Seahawks total.

Sum Up the Jerseys to enhance addition skills in a fun-filled and sporty way!

REQUIRED
- Team rosters
- Paper and pencil
- Calculator

MAGIC SQUARE

SKILL: Addition

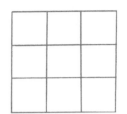

Challenge your child with Magic Square, a three-by-three grid in which the digits in each row, column, and diagonal add up to 15. Use the square to practice addition with three addends.

Each participant draws a three-by-three grid on a sheet of paper. Write the numbers 1 through 9 on slips of paper, one number per slip. Make the slips the same size as the squares on the grid. Arrange the number slips on the grid to cover all squares. Add the numbers in each row and record the sum. Add the numbers in each column and record the sum. Finally, add the numbers on each diagonal and record the sum. Be sure there is plenty of scrap paper on hand for computation. Were all of the sums equal to 15? If not, rearrange the number slips and start again. Work to get the sum of the numbers from each row, column, and diagonal to equal 15. You may need to involve the whole family in your efforts to conquer this challenging addition puzzle.

REQUIRED:
• Paper and pencils
• Safety scissors

SUBTRACTION BINGO

SKILL: Subtraction

Help your child reach mastery of subtraction facts with differences from 0 to 12 by playing Subtraction Bingo.

Each participant draws a three-by-three grid. On the grid, write numbers randomly, choosing from 0 to 12, one number per box. Players can use any given number in no more than two boxes.

After creating the Bingo grids, make 24 number cards. Clearly print "0" on two cards, "1" on two cards, and "2" on two cards. Continue in this fashion up to and including 12. Shuffle the cards. Place facedown between participants. Supply each player with game markers.

Alternate turns drawing the top two cards from the deck. Each player subtracts the smaller number from the larger number. If the difference of the numbers matches a number on a player's grid, the player puts a game marker on that number. If that number is already covered with a game marker, cover it again.

Continue until a player gets three game markers in a row, column, or diagonal and shouts, "Subtraction Bingo!" If all the cards are used before a winner is determined, the player with the most game markers on the grid is the winner.

REQUIRED:
• Paper and pencils
• Game markers

SUBTRACTION AUTHOR

SKILLS: Subtraction/Written Expression

Encourage your child to write a subtraction story to expand his or her understanding of subtraction.

Find a picture or photograph that shows lots of activity. Use the picture to generate ideas for a subtraction story, a story that includes a subtraction problem for readers to solve.

For example, select a picture of cars parked in a lot. As Subtraction Author, your child writes:

I saw nine shiny cars parked in the lot outside the mall. Three people came out of the department store, got into their cars, and drove away. How many cars were left in the lot?

Your second grader reads the subtraction story to another family member. That family member solves the problem, saying "9 cars – 3 cars = 6 cars were left in the lot."

You may want to collect all the photos and subtraction stories in a journal or notebook. Add to the notebook whenever a new subtraction story is written.

REQUIRED:
- Picture/photograph
- Paper and pencil

OPTIONAL:
- Journal/notebook
- Stapler
- Nontoxic glue
- Safety scissors

YOUR ROYAL MINUS

SKILL: Subtraction

0	1	2	3
4	5	6	7
8	9	10	11
12	13	14	15

Help your child reach mastery of subtraction facts with differences from 0 to 15.

Divide a large piece of construction paper into 16 equal boxes. In bold print that can be seen from several feet away, write the numbers 0 through 15, one number per box. Prepare a score sheet split into equal sections, one for each player.

Place the gameboard on the floor, three to five feet before you. Take turns pitching two coins or plastic chips so that they land in any of the number squares. If the coins or chips land on 13 and 4, the pitcher says, "13 – 4 = 9!"

The pitcher retrieves the coins or chips and records nine points for the toss. If the coin or chip lands on a line or misses the board, the pitcher tosses again. Alternate turns. The first player to reach 30 is the winner and dubbed, Your Royal Minus.

REQUIRED:
- Construction paper
- Marker
- Coins or plastic chips
- Paper and pencils

BOWL, SUBTRACT, BOWL

SKILL: Subtraction

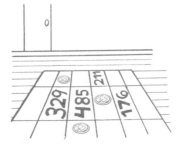

The next time your second grader asks to go bowling, set up an alley right in your own home!

Save paper towel and toilet paper tubes until you have a set of 10. Free an area of obstacles. Stand the pins at one end of the "alley," arranging them in rows from back to front, four, three, two, one. Roll two socks together for each bowling ball. Give each player two "balls." Provide bowlers with a score sheet and a pencil. Write "100" across the top of each score sheet. Stand six to eight feet away from the pins.

The first player bowls two consecutive balls, counts the number of pins knocked over, subtracts that number from 100, and records the difference on the appropriate score sheet. When a player gets a strike by knocking all pins over with one ball, subtract 10 from 100 and take another turn, again rolling two balls. Alternate turns. The first player to Bowl, Subtract, Bowl to zero is the winner.

REQUIRED:
- 10 paper towel or toilet paper tubes
- Two socks
- Paper and pencils

THREE-FOOT DROP

SKILL: Subtraction

Enjoy exploring and developing strategies to solve subtraction problems with large numbers. Play Three-Foot Drop to facilitate this exploration.

Draw a six-by-six grid on a sheet of paper. Write numbers randomly, choosing numbers from 100 to 500, one number per box. Player one uses two pennies as game markers. Player two uses two dimes as game markers.

Place the grid on the floor. Alternate turns. A player holds the markers approximately three feet above the grid. The player drops the penny or dime markers onto the grid, one at a time, reads each number, uses any strategy to subtract the smaller number from the larger number, and records the difference on a sheet of paper. The player with the greater difference at the end of the first round gets a point. For example, player one lands on 329 and 120 for a difference of 209. Player two lands on 485 and 440 for a difference of 45. Player one earns one point.

Decide on the number of rounds to play or play to an agreed-upon score.

REQUIRED:
- Paper and pencils
- Two pennies
- Two dimes

CLOSELY RELATED

SKILLS: Addition/Subtraction

Create a family of addition and subtraction facts from a single domino to demonstrate that addition and subtraction are Closely Related.

Place a handful of dominoes in a paper lunch bag. If you don't have dominoes, draw them on cardboard. Provision all players with paper and pencil.

Ask your child to reach into the bag and pull out one domino. Your second grader records the number of dots on the left side of the domino, the number of dots on the right side of the domino, and the total number of dots.

Work together to create a family of facts, two addition facts and two subtraction facts, from the numbers recorded. For example, if the numbers are 4, 5, and 9, create a family of 4 + 5 = 9, 5 + 4 = 9, 9 – 5 = 4, and 9 – 4 = 5. Alternate turns picking dominoes. Share the fact family for each, and play until the bag is empty.

REQUIRED:
- Dominoes
- Bag
- Paper and pencils

OPTIONAL:
- Cardboard
- Safety scissors
- Marker

NUMBER MYSTERY

SKILLS: Addition/Subtraction

Put on a detective hat to play Number Mystery, a fast-paced game that focuses on addition and subtraction.

Write any number on a piece of paper. Show the number to your child. Take the paper back, cross out the number, and write a new number beneath the original number. Show the new number to your child. Your second grader determines what was done to the original number to create the new one.

For example, write "13." Show it to your child. Cross out 13 and write a new number below it, "8." Show the new number to your second grader. Your child solves the Number Mystery by exclaiming, "You changed 13 to 8 by subtracting 5!" Provision your detective with paper, pencil, and counters if needed.

Continue play, alternating turns to solve each mystery. Incorporate both addition and subtraction into the game. For extra fun, invite other family members to participate.

REQUIRED:
- Paper and pencils

OPTIONAL:
- Counters

NINE IS FINE

SKILLS: Addition/Subtraction/Equivalent Names/Making Comparisons

Reinforce understanding that there are many ways to arrive at the same answer. Nine Is Fine challenges you and your child to discover all the different ways to arrive at 9.

Provide each player with a record sheet. On the top of each sheet, write "9." Set a timer to an agreed-upon limit. Say, "Go!" Each player writes different ways to arrive at 9: 5 + 4, 2 + 7, 9 + 0, 3 + 3 + 3, 10 – 1, 12 – 3, 19 – 10, 27 – 18, 79 – 70, 100 – 91.

When time is up, compare record sheets. Receive one point for each fact you have that no other player has. The player with the most points wins.

Play often, changing the activity to Four Galore, Five Jive, Seven Heaven, or Great Eight.

REQUIRED:
- Paper and pencils
- Timer

UNHAPPY CALCULATOR

SKILLS: Addition/Subtraction/Equivalent Names/Calculator/Multiplication/Division

A calculator with a broken key may be an Unhappy Calculator, but it is a terrific teaching tool for addition and subtraction.

Sit beside your child. Place a calculator before you and cover the [4] key with a small piece of tape. Tell your second grader that the [4] key is broken.

Say any number, 8, for example. Your child uses the calculator to find ways to show 8 in the display without using the broken key. On a sheet of paper, record all findings, 5 + 3, 1 + 7, 3 + 3 + 2, 9 – 1, and 11 – 3. When possibilities for 8 have been exhausted, remove the tape, place over another "broken" key and repeat the process. For each number tried, discuss the different ways used to arrive at the same answer.

As an option, invite your second grader to choose the broken key so that you can find alternate ways to display a number.

For extra challenge, place tape over the [+] key or [–] key. Ask your child to display any number, 9, 16, 24, using the [×] key or [÷] key.

REQUIRED:
- Calculator
- Tape
- Paper and pencil

EXTEND-A-FACT

SKILLS: Addition/Subtraction

When your child has mastered addition facts with sums to 18 and subtraction facts with differences to 12, Extend-a-Fact to help your second grader become more confident while adding and subtracting larger numbers.

Ask your child to write "5 + 3 = 8" across the top of a sheet of paper. Beneath this addition fact, line up the digits as you write "15 + 3 = 18." Point out and discuss that when either addend increases by 10, the sum also increases by 10.

Ask your child to write "25 + 3 = 28" directly beneath the other two facts. Highlight the change to the first addend and the resultant sum. Continue down the page, discussing the pattern in the first addends and the sum of each fact.

Recognize that 5 + 3 = 8 extends to 15 + 3 = 18, 25 + 3 = 28, 35 + 3 = 38, 45 + 3 = 48, all the way to 95 + 3 = 98.

Variation: Extend-a-Fact with subtraction. Write "9 – 6 = 3" across the top of a sheet of paper. Directly below it, write "19 – 6 = 13, 29 – 6 = 23, 39 – 6 = 33, 49 – 6 = 43," all the way to "99 – 6 = 93."

REQUIRED:
• Paper and pencil

RECORD BREAKER

SKILLS: Addition/Subtraction/Calculator/Making Comparisons

As your second grader becomes more automatic with addition and subtraction facts, challenge your child to set a record and work to break it!

Provide your child with pencil and paper. Set a timer to three minutes. Say, "Go!" Your child writes as many addition and subtraction facts as possible within the allotted time. When time is up, ask your second grader to check the work with a calculator, circling each correct fact. When all answers are checked, count and record the total number of addition and subtraction facts circled, and write the date.

Every few weeks, challenge your child to break the record. Always record the date and total number of correct addition and subtraction facts written. Compare the second trial to the first, the third to the second, always congratulating your child on efforts to break the record.

REQUIRED:
• Paper and pencil
• Timer
• Calculator

FAST FLASH

SKILLS: Addition/Subtraction

We have all heard the saying "Practice makes perfect." Can you imagine a musician or an actress who does not rehearse? How good can a tennis player be without practicing serves and backhands? Can an artist paint a masterpiece without hard work? Can a second grader master addition and subtraction facts without practice? *No!* To master the facts, your second grader must drill, drill, and drill some more!

Fast Flash is a quick and easy way to support your child in efforts to master addition facts and subtraction facts. Make a set of 20 to 30 flash cards. Write problems such as "2 + 6," "7 + 9," "5 – 4," and " 12 – 8," one problem per card. Keep the cards in a small box. As facts are mastered, add more flash cards to the collection. Provide Fast Flash drill often, selecting cards at random from the box. Make and use flash cards at any time for any skill.

REQUIRED:
- Index cards
- Marker
- Small box

FACT MIX

SKILLS: Addition/Subtraction/Calculator

Play Fact Mix to enhance your child's ability to solve problems that include both addition and subtraction.

On index cards, write the numbers 0 through 9, one number per card. Place these cards in a paper lunch bag. Make a card for each symbol, +, –, =.

Sit beside your child. Choose three cards from the bag. Place the cards before you. Ask your child to plug in the "+" card, the "–" card, and the "=" card to form a number sentence. For example, select 3, 7, 5. Make a number sentence such as 3 + 7 – 5 =. Encourage your child to solve the problem in any way possible. Use counters or a calculator as needed.

Challenge your child to manipulate the numbers and symbols to form and solve as many number sentences as possible from the three digits.

Return the number cards to the bag and choose again, each time heightening your child's facility with two-operation problems.

REQUIRED:
- Index cards
- Marker
- Paper lunch bag

OPTIONAL:
- Calculator
- Counters

PARENTHESES PUZZLES

SKILLS: Addition/Subtraction/Calculator

Use M&Ms and licorice strings to show that there can be two answers to the problem 20 – 6 + 7. Do the subtraction portion first, 20 – 6, and add the difference, 14, to 7. The answer is 21. Do the addition portion first, 6 + 7, and subtract the sum, 13, from 20. The answer is 7. Show your second grader that the answer to a problem depends on which portion of the problem is solved first.

Concretely demonstrate this abstract concept with countable candies. Use licorice strings to form the opening and closing parentheses. Use candies to represent numbers. When your child grasps the concept, move to the abstract.

Write the problem "12 – 4 + 5" on a sheet of paper. Add parentheses to make the problem "(12 – 4) + 5 = 13." Now write the problem as "12 – (4 + 5) = 3." Remind your child to solve the problem in the parentheses first.

Finally, write the problems "22 – 6 + 5 = 21" and "22 – 6 + 5 = 11." Challenge your second grader to place parentheses appropriately within each problem so that the answers are indeed correct,

"(22 – 6) + 5 = 21" and "22 – (6 + 5) = 11." Use a calculator to confirm answers. Gobble up the parentheses and counters when problems are complete.

REQUIRED:
- Paper and pencil
- Candy counters
- Licorice strings

OPTIONAL:
- Calculator

THREE TIMES AS MANY

SKILLS: Multiplication/Addition

Multiplication can be used to find the number that is Three Times As Many as another number. Concrete experiences provide your child with a basic understanding of this concept.

Sit beside your child. Place a group of five uncooked pasta shells before you. Place a larger supply of pasta shells to the side. Ask your child to count the number of pasta shells in the group: five. Next manipulate the shells to determine the number that is three times as many. Make three groups of five pasta shells. Ask your child to count the total number of pasta shells to determine the number that is Three Times As Many.

Reinforce that $5 \times 3 = 15$ is the same as $5 + 5 + 5 = 15$. Repeat the process to find twice as many, four times as many, up to ten times as many.

REQUIRED:
- Uncooked pasta shells

MARSHMALLOW MULTIPLICATION

SKILL: Multiplication

Your second grader may know the term "multiplication," one mathematical operation that can be applied to find the total number of items in several equal groups. Move from the concrete to the abstract to enhance your child's understanding of basic multiplication.

Place four paper cups before you. Put six mini-marshmallows in each cup. Ask your child to count the number of paper cups. Write the number, "4," on a sheet of paper. To the right of 4, write the multiplication symbol, "×." Ask your second grader to count the number of mini-marshmallows in each cup. Write this number, "6," to the right of ×. To the right of 6, write the equal symbol, "=."

Ask your child to use any means to determine the total number of mini-marshmallows. Write the total, the *product,* to the right of =. Finally, ask your second grader to read the multiplication problem, "Four times six equals twenty-four."

Try three cups with four raisins in each or seven cups with two toothpicks in each. Vary the number and contents of cups as your child builds skill in multiplication.

REQUIRED:
- Mini-marshmallows
- Paper cups
- Paper and pencil

OPTIONAL:
- Countable items

HANDS-ON DIVISION

SKILL: Division

Your second grader may know the term "division," the mathematical operation that is used to separate a total amount into several equal groups. Move from the concrete to the abstract to enhance your child's understanding of basic division.

Place a pile of 20 pretzels before you. Ask your second grader to count the number of pretzels. Write "20" on a sheet of paper. To the right of 20, write the division symbol, "÷."

Ask your child to divide the pretzels into four equal groups. Record this number, "4," to the right of ÷. To the right of 4, write the equal symbol, "=."

Ask your child to manipulate the pretzels to determine the total number of pretzels in each group, 5. Write "5" to the right of =. Finally, ask your second grader to read the division problem, "Twenty divided by four equals five."

Divide a group of 12 cookies into three equal groups, 25 stickers into five equal groups, and 40 trading cards into eight equal groups. Vary the number and items as your child builds skill in division.

REQUIRED:
- Pretzels
- Paper and pencil

OPTIONAL:
- Countable items

GIANT STEPS

SKILLS: Addition/Subtraction/Multiplication/Division

Invite the whole family to play the sidewalk game Giant Steps, a great way to practice mental math problems in addition, subtraction, multiplication, and division.

Select one person to be the caller. Sit on the front porch or at one end of the sidewalk in front of your home. All other players stand at the opposite end of the sidewalk, allowing at least 25 feet between ends.

Players wait their turns as the caller says, "Dad, you can take 3 + 2 + 1 giant steps."

Dad asks, "May I?"

The caller responds either, "Yes, you may," or "No, you may not!"

If the caller responds in the negative, the player doesn't move.

Continue play, varying the kinds of commands made. "Elana, you may take 4 × 2 baby steps."

"May I?"

"Yes, you may!"

Elana moves 8 baby steps.

The first person to reach the caller is the winner and assumes the role of caller for the next round.

REQUIRED:
• Your time

BATTER UP!

SKILLS: Addition/Subtraction/Multiplication/Division

All you need is baseball, paper, and a pencil to solve math problems using addition, subtraction, multiplication, and division.

Start with an addition problem such as, "The Braves scored three runs in the first inning, two runs in the second, and three runs in the third. How many runs did the Braves score in the first three innings?" Your child adds the runs scored in the three innings for a total of eight runs.

For subtraction, present a problem such as, "The Marlins beat the Reds, 11 to 4. By how many runs did the Marlins win?" Your child subtracts 4 from 11 for a difference of 7.

For multiplication, present a problem such as, "The Dodgers scored six runs in each of the last five games. How many runs have the Dodgers scored in the last five games?" Your second grader multiplies 6 × 5 for a total of 30 runs.

For division, try, "The Cubs got 12 hits in the first four innings of the game, the same number of hits per inning. How many hits did the Cubs get in each of the first four innings?" Your child divides 12 by 4 for an answer of 3 hits in each of the first four innings.

Batter Up for fun-filled facts practice!

REQUIRED:
• Paper and pencil

BAR, LINE, PICTURE, AND PIE

SKILLS: Graphs/Charts

Bar, Line, Picture, and Pie are kinds of graphs and charts. A bar graph uses bars to organize and display information. A line graph uses lines to organize and display information. A picture graph uses pictures to organize and display information. A pie chart uses a circle to organize and display information.

Along with your second grader, be on the lookout for graphs and charts. Find and interpret a bar graph in a book or magazine. Find and read a line graph in an almanac or encyclopedia. Find and interpret a picture graph in your library or school. Find and read a pie chart in a newspaper or at the bookstore.

When an example of each graph and chart is found, encourage your second grader to gather information on any topic. Make a graph or chart of any kind to display the information.

REQUIRED:
• Paper and pencil
• Markers
• Ruler
• Graphs/charts

OPTIONAL:
• Library/bookstore visit

GRID GRAPH MESSAGE

SKILL: Graphs

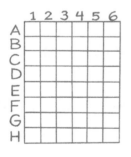

Send your child a secret message and practice graphing coordinates on a grid at the same time.

Make a six-column, eight-row graph. Number the columns "1" to "6" from left to right. Label the rows "A" to "H" from top to bottom.

Give your child a list of coordinates to find and color. Select coordinates that form a single letter, for example, the first letter of your child's name; spell a short message; or make a shape.

Provide your child with crayons or markers. Show your child how to find and fill in the grid for each set of coordinates. To spell "Hi," start with the following coordinates:

B1, C3, D5, E3, F3, G1, G5, B3, C1, D2, E1, E5, F1, C5, B5, D1, D3, F5, G3, E2

Vary the activity by inviting your child to send you a secret message by giving you a set of coordinates to find and color.

REQUIRED:
• Graph paper
• Pencil
• Crayons/markers

SNEAKY SORT

SKILLS: Attributes/Sorting

Second graders know that objects can be sorted in several ways: by shape, size, color, texture, use, number of letters or syllables in the name of the object. Hold a Sneaky Sort to reinforce awareness of attributes.

Gather a set of objects: a cookie, book, pencil, baseball cap, pair of socks, lollipop, banana, ball. Sort the items into two groups. Place the socks and baseball cap to the left and the remaining items to the right. Ask your child to examine the two groups. Determine one way the objects are sorted. *The objects on the left are things you wear; the objects on the right are not. The objects on the left are made of cloth; those on the right are not.*

Ask your second grader to turn around as you sort the objects again. Place the cookie, lollipop, and banana to the left and the remaining objects to the right. Your child examines the two groups and determines how the objects are sorted. *The objects on the left are edible; the objects on the right are not.*

Increase the difficulty of each Sneaky Sort to challenge your child's thinking.

REQUIRED:
• Objects

COIN COMBOS

SKILLS: Coin Recognition/Coin Value/Sorting

There is more than one way to pay for a 35¢ item. Use a quarter and a dime or seven nickels. Try two dimes, two nickels, and five pennies.

Provide your child with a supply of pennies, nickels, dimes, and quarters. As your second grader sorts the coins by value, place a piece of fruit on the table. Tell your child that the piece of fruit costs 40¢. Challenge your second grader to make at least five Coin Combos that equal 40¢.

Change the item, raise the price, and tally the number of combinations created for each item offered.

REQUIRED:
• Coins
• Variety of items
• Paper and pencil

OODLES OF ZOODLES

SKILLS: Money/Imaginative Thinking

Coins go in wallets, pockets, cash registers, and piggy banks, circulating from one to the next without anyone stopping to notice anything other than color and size. Pennies, nickels, dimes, and quarters get little notice! Take a few minutes to examine coins with your second grader. Study a quarter. Talk about the portrait of George Washington and note the words and numbers used to designate the country and value of the coin.

Invite your second grader to create a new coin, a *zoodle,* for example, while you create a new coin, too. Be sure that each coin has a value different from that of our existing coins.

Choose a value for your coin. Draw two circles, one for heads and one for tails. Work independently on your designs, including the name and value on the coin.

Challenge each other with problems based on your new coins. "If a zoodle is worth 20¢, how many zoodles are in a dollar?" "How much is one zoodle plus one nickel?" "How many zoodles do you need to buy a ball that costs $1.40?"

For extra fun, etch your new coins into aluminum foil and use them for solving problems.

> **REQUIRED:**
> • Coins
> • Paper and pencil
> • Crayons/markers
>
> **OPTIONAL:**
> • Safety scissors
> • Aluminum foil

SPIN FOR A BUCK

SKILLS: Coin Recognition/Coin Value/Addition

Spin for a Buck to practice totaling the value of coin combinations.

Cut an 8″ square from a piece of cardboard. Draw diagonal lines to make four equal sections. Place a quarter and dime in one section; two nickels and a dime in another; three nickels and six pennies in another; and a quarter, dime, and penny in the remaining section. Have an ample supply of coins to serve as the bank. Provide paper and a pencil for each player. Write the numbers "1" through "5" down the left edge of each sheet.

Hold a paper clip at the center of the square with a pencil. Alternate turns to spin the paper clip by flicking it with a finger. Wherever the clip stops, the player counts the total value of the coins, records the value on the record sheet, takes the coins, and places a new coin combination in that section. Alternate turns. After five rounds, each player determines the total value of the coins taken. The player with the total closest to $1.00 wins.

Vary the activity by placing more coins in each section and playing to reach $2.00, $3.00, $4.00, or $5.00.

> **REQUIRED:**
> • Cardboard
> • Coins
> • Paper and pencil
> • Paper clip
> • Safety scissors

WHAT'S THE WORD WORTH?

SKILLS: Money/Addition/Spelling

Practice adding monetary amounts by assigning a monetary value to each letter of the alphabet. Write the alphabet on a sheet of paper. Write a monetary value next to each letter. For example, "a=1¢," "b=2¢," "c=3¢," "d=4¢."

Make a record sheet by folding a piece of paper into three equal columns. Label column one, "1¢ to 50¢," column two, "51¢ to $1.00," and column three, "Greater than $1.00."

Say, spell, and write a word. Determine the word's total value by adding the monetary value of each letter in the word. For example, spell "cake," determine its value, and record "cake = 20¢" in column one on the record sheet. Spell "school," determine its value, and record "school = 72¢" in column two. Spell "blueberry," determine its value, and record "blueberry = $1.08" in column three.

Work independently or cooperatively. When two or more people play, make a record sheet for each one. Set a time limit for spelling and determining the monetary value of each word. When time expires, each player determines the total value of all words on the record sheet. The player with the highest total wins.

REQUIRED:
- Paper and pencil

COIN COURT

SKILLS: Coin Recognition/Coin Value/Addition

Travel down Coin Court to review and reinforce your child's skill in recognizing coins and knowing the value of each.

Open a file folder horizontally. In the upper left-hand corner, draw a 1″ square. Label it "¢¢¢." Do the same in the lower right-hand corner. Label this square "$$$." Build Coin Court by drawing 20 to 30 connecting squares between ¢¢¢ and $$$. In random squares along the court, write messages such as, "Rescue kittens, 20¢ reward." "Buy bubble gum, pay 5¢." "Find a quarter." and "Tough luck, lose 15¢ at the movies." Provide a supply of ten pennies, five nickels, five dimes, and four quarters for each participant's bank and for the game bank. Use one die and buttons or plastic chips as game pieces.

To start, a player rolls the die and moves ahead that number of spaces. Land on a blank square, pass the die to the next player. Land on a message, read the message and act accordingly. "Spend 40¢ on lemonade," deposit money into the game bank. "Allowance Day, collect 75¢," withdraw money from the game bank. Play continues until both players reach the $$$ square. The player with the most money wins. Fold game for storage.

REQUIRED:
- File folder
- Marker
- One die
- Coins
- Buttons or plastic chips

DIME DATES

SKILLS: Coin Recognition/Number Recognition/Recording Data/Coin Values/
Addition/Sorting/Graphing/Number Sequence

Your second grader can gain experience recognizing, reading, and writing four-digit numbers by examining dates on coins.

Together examine both sides of a dime. Heads up, find the year the dime was made. Ask your child to read the year, 1994, for example. Examine pennies, nickels, and quarters, too. Find and read the year in which each coin was made. If needed, use a magnifying glass on old coins.

Provision your child with a supply of coins, a pencil, and a recording sheet. Ask your second grader to examine each coin and record the date on the recording sheet. When a date repeats, make a tally mark to the right of the year. Repeat the process for the remaining coins. Count the tally marks to discover how many coins from your supply were made each year. Sort the coins by year to confirm totals on the recording sheet.

REQUIRED:
• Coins
• Paper and pencil
OPTIONAL:
• Magnifying glass

For extension, sequence coins from earliest date to latest date or vice versa. Determine the total value of coins from each year. Challenge your second grader to use the data gathered to make a graph that displays the years in which different coins were made.

CERTIFIED FAMILY ACCOUNTANT

SKILLS: Money Notation/Calculator/Addition/Making Comparisons/Subtraction

The next time you go grocery shopping, ask your child to be Certified Family Accountant. In so doing, you provide your second grader with authentic experience entering and adding costs on a calculator.

At the store, call out the cost of each item as you put it into your cart. Say, "$1.15." Your child presses 1, [.], 1, 5, [+]. Say, "$2.99." Press 2, [.], 9, 9, [+]. The total, $4.14, is now in the display. Repeat the process for all items you select. Enter the cost of the final item into the calculator and press the [=] key to determine the total.

At the checkout, compare the amount owed to the amount in the calculator's display. Point out that the amounts may differ because of the tax that is applied to certain items. Determine the tax by subtracting the amount in the calculator's display from the amount owed.

As Certified Family Accountant, your child will experience the importance of calculators in real-world transactions.

REQUIRED:
• Calculator
• Grocery store visit

A+ ACTIVITIES FOR SECOND GRADE

OPEN FOR BUSINESS

SKILLS: Coin Recognition/Making Change/Coin Value/Counting/Recording Data/Calculator

Concrete experiences provide your child with better understanding of making change. Divide a sheet of paper into four equal sections. Label the sections, left to right, "Item," "Cost," "Amount Paid," and "Change Due."

Set up a household store with your child as clerk, you as customer. Place a pencil, eraser, pad of paper, pen, and paper clips on a table. Write the cost of each item on a slip of paper and place it next to the item. Label the pencil 15¢, the eraser 25¢, the pad of paper 45¢, the pen 27¢, and the paper clips 8¢ each. Provision yourself, as customer, with a supply of coins. Provide your child with pennies to make change.

Ask, "How much is a pencil?" Your child answers, "15¢." Ask to buy one pencil. Pay with two dimes. Your child, using pennies, says, "15," the price, then counts out change, "16, 17, 18, 19, 20 cents," while giving you five pennies. Record all data in the appropriate columns on the record sheet. Confirm change due with a calculator.

Role-play other transactions as your clerk practices counting up to make change. Add challenge by increasing the cost of each item.

REQUIRED:
- Paper and pencil
- Five household items
- Coins
- Marker
- Calculator

MENU SEARCH

SKILLS: Money/Estimation

When dining out, productively fill the time between ordering and eating. Use prices on the menu to generate math problems with money.

Open a menu. Challenge your child to find and read the name and cost of the least expensive item. Your second grader then challenges you to find the most expensive item on the menu. Name this item and its cost. Alternate turns challenging family members to take part in the Menu Search.

Search for all items with a cost less than $10. Look for all items with a cost between $5 and $15. Find three items whose estimated total cost is no less than $9 but no more than $20.

Hold a Menu Search to whet your appetite not only for food but also for solving money problems.

REQUIRED:
- Restaurant visit
- Menu

HOW MUCH IS THE MILK?

SKILLS: Money Recognition/Money Value/Estimating Costs/Recording Data/Calculator/Making Comparisons

How Much Is the Milk? Ask your child this question and make an estimate. A visit to the grocery store provides your second grader with authentic use of estimation and money.

Divide a sheet of paper into three columns. Label the left column, "Item," the middle, "Estimate," and the right, "Actual Cost."

List six items from your weekly grocery list in the "Item" column. Ask your child to estimate the cost of each item. Record estimates in the "Estimate" column. Use a calculator to determine total estimated cost of the groceries. Record this amount at the bottom of the column.

Take the recording sheet with you to the market. Locate each item from the list. Note the cost and record it in the "Actual Cost" column. While shopping, compare the actual cost to the estimated cost of each item. At the checkout, ask your second grader to pay the clerk and count the change. At home, use a calculator to total the actual cost of the six estimated items. Compare the actual total cost with the estimated total cost and discuss your findings.

REQUIRED:
- Paper and pencil
- Calculator
- Supermarket visit

MONEY READ AND WRITE

SKILLS: Money/Connecting Math & Literature/Brainstorming/Written Expression/Drawing

Several books for second graders focus on money concepts. Choose one to share and use the story to generate ideas to write an original story about money.

Share *Sam and the Lucky Money* by Karen Chinn. Sympathize with Sam, a youngster who discovers that the lucky money he received for Chinese New Year won't buy as much as he had hoped. In *The Monster Money Book* by Loreen Leedy, discuss how the members of the Monster Club manage their money.

Finally, be a private eye to discover what has happened to P. B.'s allowance in *The Case of the Shrunken Allowance* by Joanne Rocklin.

After reading, brainstorm ideas for another money story. Choose a main character and invent a money-related wish or problem. Provide your child with writing and drawing materials and let the creativity flow! When complete, bind the story with yarn, ribbon, or string. Read aloud to family members before adding to your child's personal library.

REQUIRED:
- Library visit
- Paper and pencil
- Crayons/markers
- Hole punch
- Yarn/ribbon/string

YEAR AT A GLANCE

SKILLS: Calendar/Sequencing/Number Writing/Drawing

Juanita's birthday is January 21st! Father's Day is Sunday the 20th! Steven's swim meet is on Saturday, October 14th! Remember special occasions by making a year-long calendar.

Hold a sheet of 8½″ × 11″ paper horizontally. Make five rows of seven 1½″ squares, creating a grid of a calendar month. Label each column, at the top, with the appropriate day of the week, starting with Sunday. Photocopy the grid 12 times, one copy for each month. Next, hold a white sheet of 12″ × 18″ construction paper vertically. Glue or staple a grid to the bottom half of the paper. Using a premade calendar as a guide, your child writes the dates in the top right corner of each square on the grid.

When the days and dates are complete, work together to record birthdays of family members and friends, holidays, and events that are important to your child and family.

Use the top half of the construction paper to print the month in bold letters and to illustrate a scene particular to the month. Repeat the process for all months. Display in a prominent place for all to use and admire.

REQUIRED:
- Paper
- White construction paper
- Ruler
- Markers/crayons
- Nontoxic glue/stapler

OPTIONAL:
- Premade calendar

FROM JANUARY TO DECEMBER

SKILLS: Calendar/Months of the Year/Written Expression/Drawing/Sequencing

Celebrate the uniqueness of each month by writing a personal From January to December book.

Make the book from seven sheets of folded construction paper. Tape the right edge of the first folded sheet to the left edge of the second, and the second to the third. Continue in this fashion for all pages. Fold accordion style, front to back.

Print the title, "From January to December," and the author on the cover.

Open the accordion book, page by page, sequentially saying the names of the months as you do so.

Begin in any month of the year. Throughout that month, choose special events or occasions to describe on the appropriate page. On the January page, for example, your child writes, "In January, we celebrated the first day of the new year and the first snowfall." Your second grader may also include a picture of Martin Luther King, Jr., to note the celebration of the civil rights leader's birthday.

Use a variety of materials along with your writing to make a collage that depicts events and characteristics particular to January. At the end of each month, enjoy the month in review.

REQUIRED:
- Construction paper
- Tape
- Pencil
- Crayons/markers

OPTIONAL:
- Art supplies
- Safety scissors
- Nontoxic glue

ROCK AROUND THE CLOCK

SKILL: Time

Help your second grader tell the time on the hour, quarter past the hour, half past the hour, and quarter to the hour.

On four index cards, write times as they appear on a digital clock, one time per card: "1:00," "1:15," "1:30," "1:45." On a second set of cards, write the phrases for those times—"one o'clock," "quarter past one," "half past one," "quarter to two"—one phrase per card. On a third set of cards, draw clocks with clock hands indicating the same times, one clock per card.

Divide the table into two areas. Choose one set of cards and spread, facedown, in one area. Choose a second set to spread, facedown, in the second area.

Choose and read one card from each area. Do the cards match? If they do, keep the cards. If they don't, return the cards facedown to their original positions. Alternate turns. Play until no cards remain on the playing surface. The player with the most pairs at the end is the winner. Play again, substituting the unused set of cards for one that has been tried. Add cards and times as your child becomes adept at reading all notations.

REQUIRED:
- Index cards
- Marker

TWO HANDS

SKILL: Time

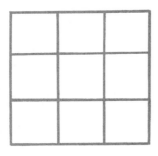

Play Two Hands, a variation of Bingo, for reading clocks and telling time.

Ask each participant to draw a three-by-three grid on a sheet of paper. In each square of each grid, write a random digital time, "8:10," "12:25," "4:40," "6:50." Distribute nine index cards to each participant. On each index card, draw one clock face to match one digital time from the grid.

Shuffle the cards. Place facedown between participants. Supply each player with game markers. Alternate turns drawing the top card from the deck. Each player reads the clock. If the time on the clock matches a time on a player's grid, the player puts a game marker in that square.

REQUIRED:
- Paper and pencils
- Index cards
- Game markers

Continue until a player gets three game markers in a row, column, or diagonal and shouts, "Two Hands!"

PERSONAL TIMELINE

SKILLS: Timelines/Sequencing

A timeline is a tool that documents the chronology of events. Work with your second grader to create a Personal Timeline.

Hold a large sheet of construction paper horizontally. Across the top of the paper, write, for example, "Pedro's Personal Timeline." Leave approximately 1″ at each edge. Draw a line from the left side of the paper to the right. Start at the far left and draw equidistant 1″ vertical lines on the timeline, one for each year of your child's life.

Next, on sticky tags, write special events from each year of your child's life, one event per tag. For example, "1993: Born at 5:00 A.M. on May 3rd." "1994: Took first steps in early summer." "1995: Started pre-school in the fall."

Ask your second grader to read the year and event on each tag. Place the tags on the timeline in the correct sequence. Invite your second grader to add events to the timeline.

Vary the activity a number of ways. Collaborate to make a family timeline. Make a timeline to document the chronology of any topic of interest. Make a timeline of the life and events of a favorite book character.

REQUIRED:
- Construction paper
- Marker
- Ruler
- Pencil
- Sticky tags

OPTIONAL:
- Book

TIME FRAME TEASERS

SKILLS: Calendar/Time

Play this fast-paced game anywhere and anytime. Sharpen calendar skills and work toward mastery of time concepts by asking and answering Time Frame Teasers. Use the teasers provided to get started.

- Today is Tuesday. What day will it be in five days?
- This month is April. What month will it be in four months?
- It is 1:15 P.M. What time was it fifteen minutes ago?
- Today is July 6. What will the date be one week from today?

Continue in this fashion, alternating turns to ask teasers. Keep the action quick and vary the types of questions asked. Incorporate questions that focus on minutes, hours, days, weeks, months, and years.

REQUIRED:
- Your time

MEMORY MEASURE

SKILLS: Measurement/Nonstandard Linear Measure/Visual Memory/Making Comparisons

Short-term visual memory, string, scissors, and measurable household objects are all you need for Memory Measure.

Place a pencil on the table before you. Look at the pencil, focusing on its length. After a few seconds, remove the pencil from sight. Then, from memory, players each cut a length of string to match the length of the pencil. When cutting is complete, view the pencil again. Align the strings to the pencil. Compare the length of the pencil with the lengths of the string. The player whose length is closest gets the pieces of string.

Repeat the process. View the height of a lamp. Turn around and, from memory, cut a length of string to match the height of the lamp. Do the same for the distance across a tabletop or the distance around the cookie jar. After several rounds, players take turns lining up their winning strings end to end across the floor. The player whose strings make the longest line wins.

Witness measurement at work in *The Biggest Fish* by Sheila Keenan and *Jim and the Beanstalk* by Raymond Briggs.

REQUIRED:
• Objects to measure
• String
• Safety scissors

OPTIONAL:
• Library/bookstore visit

HOW FAR CAN YOU • • • ?

SKILLS: Measurement/Linear Measure/Estimating/Recording Data/Making Comparisons/Elapsed Time

How far can you run in five seconds? How far can you jump? Estimate the results of different activities and get practice measuring in inches, feet, and meters.

Ask your second grader to estimate how far a tennis ball can be thrown. Record the estimate. After your child throws the ball, work together to determine the length of the throw. Use a tape measure or count strides. Compare the measurement with the estimate.

Repeat this process with other activities. Ask, "How far can you hop (run, skip, walk) in ten seconds?" or "How far can you spit a watermelon seed or cherry pit?" Invite other family members to join the fun.

REQUIRED:
• Paper and pencil
• Tape measure
• Tennis ball
• Stopwatch

OPTIONAL:
• Seeds/pits

A+ ACTIVITIES FOR SECOND GRADE

FEET, INCHES, AND POUNDS

SKILLS: Measurement/Linear Measure/Weight/Recording Data/Making Comparisons

Work together to record changes in your child's height and weight for a year.

Hold a large sheet of construction paper vertically. Write the heading, "Todd's Height and Weight," across the top of the paper. Just below the heading, draw a horizontal line from the left edge of the paper to the right. From the horizontal line, draw two lines to the bottom of the paper to make three equal columns. Label the left column, "Date," the middle, "Height," and the right, "Weight." To accommodate 12 months of measurement, draw 12 equidistant horizontal lines to the bottom of the paper.

Record the date in the "Date" column. Use a tape measure to determine your child's height. Ask your child to record the measurement, in feet and inches, in the "Height" column.

Next ask your child to step on a scale and read the weight register. Your second grader records the figure in the "Weight" column. Follow this routine once a month for a year.

Review the data periodically. Discuss changes in height and weight. Is there a connection between height and weight? After a year, determine how much your child grew.

REQUIRED:
- Construction paper
- Marker
- Tape measure
- Scale

FULL O' MACARONI

SKILLS: Measurement/Capacity/Predicting/Making Comparisons

Your second grader won't be Full o' Macaroni when you use uncooked macaroni to demonstrate the amount a container can hold, its capacity.

Hold one sheet of 12″ × 18″ construction paper horizontally. Use tape to attach the bottom edge to the top edge, to form a long cylinder. Attach the long cylinder, standing upright, to a cardboard base.

Hold a second sheet of 12″ × 18″ construction paper vertically. Use tape to attach the bottom edge to the top edge, to form a short cylinder. Attach the short cylinder, standing upright, to a second cardboard base.

Ask your second grader to examine the cylinders. Ask questions such as, "Will the cylinders hold the same amount of macaroni? Why? Why not? Will one cylinder hold more macaroni than the other? Which one will hold less macaroni?" Record predictions. Carefully fill the long cylinder with macaroni. Then, pour the macaroni from the long cylinder into the short cylinder. Do they hold the same amount of macaroni? Compare the actual result to the prediction.

REQUIRED:
- Construction paper
- Tape
- Cardboard
- Paper and pencil
- Uncooked macaroni

MATH ACTIVITIES

POT OF YUM

SKILLS: Measurement/Fractions/Following Directions

Second graders love to mix and measure. Give your child the opportunity to create a version of a Kraft General Foods unique kitchen confection by applying knowledge of standard measurement and fractions to authentic practice.

Shop for necessary ingredients, encouraging your second grader to find the weight information on the packages required.

At home, put on the aprons, line up the ingredients, and follow directions, step by step.

1. Crush 1¼ pounds of chocolate sandwich cookies to crumb consistency.
2. Blend 8 ounces of cream cheese, ½ stick of margarine, and 1 cup of powdered sugar.
3. Mix together 3¼ cups of milk, two 3.4-ounce packages of instant vanilla pudding and 8 ounces of Cool Whip.
4. Blend the milk mixture with the cream cheese mixture.
5. Line the bottom of a clean plastic planter or clay pot with foil. Spoon in a layer of crumbs.
6. Spoon on a layer of pudding mixture.
7. Continue layering, ending with cookie crumbs.
8. Chill for 24 hours.
9. Weave in gummy worms on top and stick a plastic flower in the center.

Surprise the family at dessert when you use a trowel or spade to serve the Pot of Yum.

REQUIRED:
• Ingredients listed

OPTIONAL:
• Flowerpot
• Trowel/spade

RULER, SCALE, OR TEASPOON?

SKILLS: Measurement/Linear Measure/Weight/Capacity/Brainstorming/Categorizing

In first grade your child learned about length, height, weight, and capacity. In second grade, your child continues to work with these measures and recognizes their differences.

Make a set of playing cards, each labeled with a phrase that identifies a measure of length, height, weight, or capacity. Use the following phrases to get started and have fun brainstorming others.

Length/Height: 15-foot giraffe, 3-inch mouse, mile-high city, 40-yard dash, 4-centimeter noodle
Weight: 20-pound watermelon, 85-gram candy bar, 103-pound porpoise, 65-pound child, 12-ounce bag of pretzels
Capacity: 12 cups of popcorn, 6 teaspoons of sugar, 2 gallons of lemonade, 7 tablespoons of flour, 1 liter of juice

Shuffle the cards and set aside, facedown. Put a ruler, scale, and teaspoon, or a sign representing each, on the table.

Sit beside your child. Alternate turns. Draw a card from the pile, read the phrase, and state whether the item is a measure of length/height, weight, or capacity. Place the card directly below the ruler for length and height, the scale for weight, or the teaspoon for capacity. The game ends when all cards have been drawn and categorized.

REQUIRED:
- Index cards
- Pencil/pen
- Measuring tools

ROAD MAP ROMP

SKILLS: Measurement/Distance/Map Skills/Recording Data/Addition/
Subtraction/Calculator/Making Comparisons

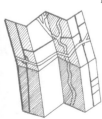

How many miles from Philadelphia, Pennsylvania, to Baltimore, Maryland? Use a road map or atlas to expose your second grader to measuring long distances. Be sure that the map indicates the distance in miles between cities.

Work together to find Miami, Florida, on a map. Ask your child to put a finger on Miami. Find Orlando, Florida, to the north. Trace the mile line from Miami to Orlando. Point out the distance noted between the two cities and record. Find and record the distance between other cities: Boston, Massachusetts, and New York, New York; Cleveland, Ohio, and Chicago, Illinois; Seattle, Washington, and San Francisco, California.

REQUIRED:
- Road map or atlas
- Paper and pencil

OPTIONAL:
- Library visit
- Calculator

Alternate turns asking Road Map Romp questions. "Is the distance between Boston and New York greater than, less than, or equal to the distance between Cleveland and Chicago? How much greater? How much less?" Use a calculator if needed.

MATH ACTIVITIES

ALL THE WAY AROUND

Perimeter is the distance around an area with a boundary. Explore perimeter using squares and rectangles you find in and around your home.

Make a recording sheet for each room visited and one for outside. Start in the kitchen. Write the name and perimeter of each object measured. Begin with a cabinet door. Use a ruler, yardstick, or tape measure to find and record the length of each side. Add the four lengths to determine the perimeter of the door. Do the same for a dishtowel, floor tile, baking pan, or pot holder.

In the bedroom, find the perimeter of a bed, pillow, windowpane, or mirror.

In the bathroom, find the perimeter of a bar of soap, area rug, or bath mat. In the living room or den, find the perimeter of a videocassette box, magazine, picture frame, or book. Outside, find the perimeter of a square on the sidewalk, the seat of a swing, a mailbox, a brick, or a shingle.

By measuring All the Way Around, your second grader enhances awareness of perimeter.

REQUIRED:
- Paper and pencil
- Ruler/yardstick
- Tape measure

BREAKFAST SQUARES

The concept of area, the measure of a bounded surface, is a difficult one for second graders to grasp. Breakfast time is the perfect time to use concrete examples to guide your child in area explorations.

Fill two bowls with any brand of cereal squares, one bowl for eating, one for measuring. Place a 6″ × 6″ paper napkin on the table. Ask your child to cover the napkin with cereal squares. When the napkin is covered, count the cereal squares to determine area. The area of the napkin equals the number of cereal squares that it takes to cover the napkin. Discover that the area of the napkin is approximately 72 cereal squares.

Try the same procedure covering a square piece of toast with cereal squares. Again, count the squares to determine the area of the toast in cereal squares. If waffles are on the morning menu, count the squares on the surface of a waffle to determine the area of the waffle.

Enjoy your cereal, toast, and waffles over a game of chess or checkers. Count the number of squares on the board to determine the area of the playing surface.

REQUIRED:
- Square cereal
- Napkin
- Bowls

OPTIONAL:
- Checkerboard
- Toast
- Waffle

MEASURE MATCH

SKILLS: Measurement/Linear Measure/Weight/Capacity/Time/Equivalents

How many feet in a yard? How many weeks in a year? Your second grader will know the answers to these and other measurement questions by playing Measure Match.

Cut 16 index cards in half to make a deck of 32 cards. Work together to write all the measures below, one per card.

foot	=	12 inches
yard	=	3 feet
mile	=	5,280 feet
pound	=	16 ounces
cup	=	½ pint
pint	=	2 cups
quart	=	2 pints
gallon	=	4 quarts
year	=	365/366 days
year	=	52 weeks
year	=	12 months
month	=	28 to 31 days
week	=	7 days
day	=	24 hours
hour	=	60 minutes
minute	=	60 seconds

Scramble the cards faceup on the table. Alternate turns as you match a measure to its equivalent. Match "hour" to "60 minutes." Match "pound" to "16 ounces."

Try a game of Concentration. Place all the cards facedown on the table in four rows of eight. Alternate turns as you work to make a match from memory. Turn over one card; turn over a second. If it's a match, keep the cards and go again. If not, return the cards to their original position. The winner is the one with the most pairs at the end.

REQUIRED:
• Index cards
• Safety scissors
• Pencils

TWO SCALE TEMPERATURE

SKILLS: Temperature/Making Comparisons/Recording Data/Predicting

Your second grader has heard the term "Fahrenheit," the temperature scale on which water freezes at 32°. Your child may also recognize the term "Celsius," the temperature scale on which water freezes at 0°. Establish a daily outdoor temperature routine, keeping a record of the temperature in both Fahrenheit and Celsius.

Review the proper way to read an outdoor thermometer. Compare and discuss the differences between the two scales.

Select a time for your child to read the thermometer each day. Post a recording sheet with three equal columns, labeled "Date," "Degrees Fahrenheit," and "Degrees Celsius" in an easily accessible location. If you do not have an outdoor thermometer, show your child how to find the daily temperature in the newspaper. Be consistent as you record either the high or low temperature reported each day.

Encourage your child to use the information gathered to observe temperature trends, looking for warm or cold spells. Additionally, predict the next day's temperature. Compare predictions with a local meteorologist's predictions and with the actual temperature.

REQUIRED:
- Outdoor thermometer
- Paper and pencil

OPTIONAL:
- Daily newspaper

ROLL, RECORD, ROLL

SKILLS: Frequency Distribution/Tables & Graphs/Predicting/Addition/Recording Data/Making Comparisons

When two six-sided dice are rolled, the smallest possible outcome is 2; the largest, 12. Roll, Record, Roll to discover the most frequent outcome of 30 rolls.

Make an 11-column, 20-row grid to serve as the Roll, Record, Roll chart. At the top of the chart write the title, "30 Rolls." At the base of the first column on the left, write "2." At the base of the next column, write "3." Continue to "12."

Predict the most frequent outcome of 30 rolls. Record the prediction on paper. Then, roll the dice!

Roll 5, color a square in the "5" column. Roll 10, color a square in the "10" column. Be sure your child works from the bottom of each column to the top.

After 30 rolls, examine the data. What was the most frequent outcome after 30 rolls? Was your prediction correct? What was the second most frequent outcome? Why do you think certain outcomes were rolled more often than others?

After discussion, try again with 50, 75, or 100 rolls!

REQUIRED:
- Construction paper
- Ruler
- Marker
- Paper and pencil
- Dice

CANDYMATION

SKILLS: Estimating/Making Comparisons/Counting

Estimate the number of candies in a bag. Divide two sheets of paper into three equal columns. Label the left column, "Candy Brand," the middle column, "Estimate," and the right column, "Actual Number."

Place a small bag of M&Ms and a small bag of Skittles on the table. Direct your child to pick up the bag of M&Ms, note the size of the bag, and manipulate the candies inside. Estimate and record the number of M&Ms in the bag on one recording sheet. You do the same with the bag of Skittles. Keep your estimates a secret from each other. Exchange bags and repeat the process.

When ready, share the estimates. Were the estimates close? Who made the higher estimate for each bag? What is the difference between the estimates your child made and the estimates you made?

Open the bags. Count the candies in each. Record the actual number on both record sheets. Compare the actual number of M&Ms and Skittles to both estimates. Who was closest? Finally, enjoy your tasty treat!

REQUIRED:
- Candy
- Paper and pencil

QUENCH AND COUNT

SKILLS: Recording Data/Counting/Estimating/Making Comparisons/Multiplication/Calculator

How many glasses of milk or juice does your second grader drink in a week, a month, a year? Place a tally sheet on the front of your refrigerator with a magnet. Make a tally mark on the sheet each time a glass of milk or juice is enjoyed.

At the end of the week, count the tally marks and use that information and the knowledge that there are four weeks in a month to estimate the total number of glasses of milk or juice enjoyed in one month.

Challenge your child to maintain the tally through the month. Compare the actual number of glasses of milk or juice consumed to the estimated number of glasses of milk or juice enjoyed in a month.

Use the knowledge that there are 12 months in a year to determine the number of glasses of milk or juice that are likely to be consumed in a year. Calculate the number of glasses of milk or juice likely to be consumed in one year by multiplying the actual number of glasses of milk or juice consumed in one month by 12.

REQUIRED:
- Paper and pencil
- Calculator
- Milk/juice

SLIP AND SLIDE

SKILLS: Using a Straightedge/Imaginative Thinking/Drawing/Making Comparisons

Young children can get frustrated when using a ruler to draw a straight line. The reason is simple. If the ruler is not held properly with a free hand, it will Slip and Slide. This movement could prevent your child from making the straight line that is needed to complete a drawing, polygon, or bar graph. Practice this skill by using a straightedge to create imaginative drawings with lines.

Supply your child with a ruler, paper, and pencil. To facilitate placement and use of the straightedge, free the workspace of obstructions. Be sure that your child holds the straightedge firmly to the paper with his or her free hand while making the first line of an imaginative line drawing. Use only straight lines to draw a winter scene, a house, or even a family portrait. Encourage your child to color the drawing when complete. With this type of practice, your child's ruler will never Slip and Slide.

Variation: Choose a theme for your straight-line drawing. While your child draws, you draw, too. Then enjoy comparing two versions of the same straight-line theme.

REQUIRED:
- Paper and pencil
- Ruler

OPTIONAL:
- Crayons/markers

PUSHPIN POLYGONS

SKILLS: Making Polygons/Recognizing Polygons/Dictionary Skills

Pushpin your way into greater familiarity with polygons. Polygons are closed, two-dimensional figures made from line segments (sides) that join three or more points (corners). A triangle is a three-sided polygon. A pentagon is a five-sided polygon. A hexagon is a six-sided polygon.

Provide your child with a piece of corkboard and a supply of pushpins and rubber bands. Work together to make a triangle by arranging three pushpins in the cork for the corners of the triangle. Fit the rubber band around the three pushpins to make the sides of the polygon.

After discussion, remove the pushpins and rubber band. Tell your second grader to make a four-sided polygon: square, rectangle, rhombus (leaning square), parallelogram (leaning rectangle), trapezoid (a shape that looks like a triangle with a flat top), or diamond. Use more than one rubber band as needed. Discuss the characteristics of four-sided polygons and look up the definitions for each in the dictionary. Move on to make pentagons (five sides), hexagons (six sides), heptagons (seven sides), octagons (eight sides), nonagons (nine sides), and decagons (ten sides).

REQUIRED:
- Bulletin board or corkboard
- Pushpins
- Rubber bands
- Dictionary

BUDGET BUILD

Combine geometry, money, and addition as your second grader builds a house from shapes.

Cut a variety of shapes from construction paper. Assign a cost to each shape. For example, a triangle may cost 15¢; a square, 20¢; a rectangle, 40¢; a circle, 50¢. Prepare a tally sheet by drawing a triangle, square, rectangle, and circle down the left side of a piece of paper.

Invite your second grader to plan and build a house by gluing shapes on a large sheet of construction paper. For each shape used, put a tally mark next to that shape on the tally sheet. When the house is complete, count the tally marks to determine the total number of each shape used. Use a calculator to find the total cost of each shape used. Finally, ask your child to determine the total cost of the house. Display the house for all to admire.

Variation: Put your second grader on a budget. Limit your house builder to $8, $10, or $12.

REQUIRED:
- Construction paper
- Safety scissors
- Paper and pencil
- Nontoxic glue
- Calculator

FRIENDSHIP BRACELETS

SKILL: Visual Patterns

We don't need to look far to find patterns! We see patterns in our linens, in the butterflies overhead, and on our shirts and shorts. Create more patterns by making Friendship Bracelets.

Cut a 10″ length of plastic lacing (gimp), available at craft stores. Tie a double knot at one end of the lacing and tape that end to the table. Provide your child with a supply of plastic beads. Include seven colors in the supply.

Ask your child to create a pattern for the bracelet using all seven colors. Be sure to repeat the pattern of colors across seven inches of gimp, leaving sufficient slack for tying. Encourage complex design. Tie a double knot at the free end of the bracelet. Repeat the process to create an exact copy of the bracelet.

Remove the tape from both bracelets. Tie one to your child's wrist. Present the matching bracelet to a special friend as a gift of friendship.

REQUIRED:
- Beads
- Lacing/gimp
- Tape
- Ruler
- Safety scissors

PATTERN GREETINGS

SKILLS: Visual Patterns/Painting/Shape Recognition/Written Expression

With a splash of color, make Pattern Greetings to commemorate birthdays, anniversaries, and other special occasions.

Ahead of time, cut sponges into a variety of shapes. On paper plates, spread thin layers of paint, one color per plate. Fold construction paper in half, greeting-card style.

Make patterns along the border of each card. Dip a round sponge into paint and press to the paper. Repeat the process using an array of shapes and colors to make a patterned border: a green circle, blue square, yellow diamond, green circle, blue square, yellow diamond. When the paint is dry, decorate the interior of the card in the same fashion.

To celebrate important occasions or milestones, write poems, expressions, or messages on the cover and inside each card.

REQUIRED:
- Sponges
- Safety scissors
- Paper plates
- Construction paper
- Tempera/finger paint
- Pencil/pen

CUTTING CORNERS

SKILLS: Shape Recognition/Cutting/Counting

Turn a square sheet of paper into a variety of shapes by Cutting Corners.

Cut a sheet of construction paper or cardboard into a square. Count the four sides of the square. Ask your second grader to cut one corner from the square. Discover that the new shape has five sides and is a pentagon.

Continue in this fashion. Cut the opposite corner from the same square and count the six sides of a hexagon. Cut a third corner and count the seven sides of a heptagon. Cut a fourth corner and count the sides of an octagon.

For variation, cut corners from triangles, rectangles, or trapezoids. This is one time that Cutting Corners makes sense.

REQUIRED:
- Construction paper/cardboard
- Safety scissors

TRIANGLE PLAY

SKILLS: Manipulating Shapes/Shape Recognition/Cutting

Manipulate and combine triangles to see that different shapes can be made from two or more of the same shape.

Cut a bunch of 2″ triangles from a sheet of construction paper. Ask your child to manipulate and combine two triangles to create a diamond. Challenge your child to manipulate the two triangles to create a rhombus, a polygon that looks like a leaning square. Encourage your second grader to use different numbers of triangles to create a square, rectangle, trapezoid, parallelogram, pentagon, hexagon, or octagon.

Manipulate and explore other shapes.

As an extension, visit with a triangle who longs for more sides and angles in *The Greedy Triangle* by Marilyn Burns or learn about tangrams, an ancient Chinese puzzle consisting of seven shapes cut from a square by reading *Three Pigs, One Wolf, and Seven Magic Shapes* by Grace Maccarone and Marilyn Burns.

REQUIRED:
- Construction paper
- Ruler
- Marker
- Safety scissors

OPTIONAL:
- Library/bookstore visit

CONES AND PYRAMIDS

SKILLS: Three-Dimensional Shapes/Drawing/Categorizing

How many three-dimensional shapes can you find in your home or on a short walk outside? Equipped with a notepad or clipboard, paper, and a pencil, find examples of cones: an ice cream cone, a party hat, and the top half of a funnel. Locate pyramids: the roof of a birdhouse and pictures of the pyramids of Egypt. Point out spheres: a soccer ball, a globe, and an orange. Note cylinders: a tree trunk, a can, and a sign post. Discover prisms: a box, a triangular hunk of cheese, and a book.

Encourage your second grader to record all observations. Draw each object observed. Below each drawing, write the name of the object and its three-dimensional shape. Categorize the objects found into five groups: cones, pyramids, spheres, cylinders, and prisms. Add to the list as examples of three-dimensional shapes are found.

REQUIRED:
- Notepad/clipboard with paper
- Pencil

MIRROR IMAGE

SKILLS: Symmetry/Cutting/Observation

Symmetrical objects have the same characteristics on both sides of a center dividing line; what is on the left of the dividing line is a Mirror Image of what is on the right.

Talk about things that are or can be symmetrical: a butterfly, a double domino, a design on a tablecloth, and windowpanes.

Draw a line down the center of a large sheet of construction paper. Cut a variety of different colored shapes from construction paper. Ask your child to create a design to the left of the dividing line by arranging and gluing the shapes.

When the design is complete, take a moment to focus on the details of placement, shape, and color. Recreate the design on the right side of the dividing line so that it mirrors the left. Display your young artist's symmetrical work of art.

Variation: You create a design to the left of a dividing line. Challenge your child to recreate the design to the right of the line. Again, display your collaborative symmetry.

REQUIRED:
- Construction paper
- Safety scissors
- Nontoxic glue

CENTS FOR DOLLARS

SKILLS: Place Value/Coin Recognition/Coin Value

Gather your loose change and play Cents for Dollars, an exchange game of place value and money.

Make a three-column game sheet for each player. On each sheet, label the left column "$1.00/Hundreds," the middle column "$.10/Tens," and the third column "$.01/Ones." Provision the game bank with pennies, dimes, and two $1 bills. Place the bank between players.

Players take turns rolling a die and collecting pennies from the bank. For example, if a player rolls a 6, that player takes six pennies and places them in the "$.01/Ones" column of the game sheet. When a player acquires 10 or more pennies, the player calls, "Exchange," and exchanges 10 pennies for a dime. That player places the dime in the "$.10/Tens" column of the game sheet. Continue in this fashion. The game ends when a player exchanges 10 dimes for a $1 bill.

Vary the activity in several ways. Play with two or three dice. Add a fourth column labeled "$10.00/Thousands" and add a $10 bill to the bank.

REQUIRED:
- Paper and pencil
- Die
- Pennies and dimes
- $1 bills

OPTIONAL:
- Dice
- $10 bill

GUMDROP GOBBLE

SKILL: Place Value

Expand your child's facility with place value by manipulating gumdrops.

Divide a sheet of paper into four equal sections. Ask your child to use markers to label each section, from left to right, "Thousands" in orange, "Hundreds" in yellow, "Tens" in green, "Ones" in red.

Put four red gumdrops in the "Ones" column. Ask your child to determine the value of the four gumdrops in the "Ones" column, 4. Put two green gumdrops in the "Tens" column. Ask your second grader to determine the value of the two gumdrops in the "Tens" column, 20, and the total value thus far, 24. Put six yellow gumdrops in the "Hundreds" column, 600, and three orange gumdrops in the "Thousands" column, 3,000. Ask your child to determine the value of the gumdrops in their respective columns. Finally, name the number represented by all gumdrops, 3,624.

Challenge your second grader to make the biggest (9,999) and smallest (1,000) four-digit numbers possible by manipulating groups of gumdrops from place to place. When your child has met the challenge, gobble up the gumdrops that have enhanced awareness of place value.

REQUIRED:
- Paper
- Markers
- Gumdrops

DIGIT SHIFT

SKILLS: Place Value/Number Recognition/Number Writing/Making Comparisons

Expand place value skills to ten thousands by playing Digit Shift. Write the digits "1," "4," "3," "2," and "8" on index cards, one digit per card. Arrange the cards on the table to form the number 14,328. Discuss the value of the digit in the ones place, 8; the tens place, 20; the hundreds place, 300; the thousands place, 4,000; and the ten thousands place, 10,000.

Use 14,328 to make new numbers by shifting the order of the digits. For example, use and shift two digits to make 84, three digits to make 412, four digits to make 2,481, and five digits to make 31,284. Record all numbers made on a record sheet.

When two or more people play, make a Digit Shift record sheet for each. Set a time limit for finding and recording numbers. Then compare number lists. Receive one point for each number you have written that no other player has made. Play to an agreed-upon score. Continue play, starting with any five-digit number you choose.

REQUIRED:
- Paper and pencils
- Index cards

CUKES AND CARROTS

SKILLS: Problem Solving/Organization

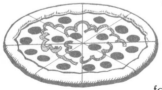

How many different ways can your child arrange a carrot, celery stick, green bean, and cucumber? Find out while your child strengthens problem solving and organizational skills. Provide your second grader with a sheet of paper and a pencil. Sit beside your child and place a carrot, celery stick, green bean, and cucumber on the table before you. Ask your child to arrange the vegetables on the table, from left to right. For example, place the carrot to the left, followed by the celery stick, green bean, and cucumber. Record the order of the vegetables on the sheet of paper.

Ask your child to reorder the vegetables. Place the celery stick to the left, followed by the carrot, cucumber, and green bean. Again, record the order of the vegetables on the sheet of paper.

Challenge your second grader to reorder the vegetables in as many ways as possible. Record all arrangements on the sheet of paper. When all arrangements have been exhausted, add a fifth vegetable and repeat the process.

REQUIRED:
• Vegetables
• Paper and pencil

PIZZA PROBLEMS

SKILL: Problem Solving

To strengthen your second grader's problem-solving skills, include math as one topping on your homemade pizza.

Provision yourself with dough or premade crust, tomato sauce, and cheese, or buy a plain frozen pizza. Agree on three additional toppings, perhaps mushrooms, pepperoni, and olives. Ask your young chef to place four mushroom slices on the pizza. Next tell your child to place twice as many olives as mushrooms on the pizza. Provide paper, a pencil, and counters as needed. Now request that your child place six more pepperoni slices than olive slices on the pizza. Finally, with just four mushroom slices on the pizza, ask your child to add half as many mushroom slices as pepperoni slices. Bake your 11-mushroom, 8-olive, and 14-pepperoni-slices pizza. Discuss strategies used to solve the problems. Bon appetit!

REQUIRED:
• Pizza ingredients

OPTIONAL:
• Paper and pencil
• Counters

LONG STEMS

SKILLS: Problem Solving/Drawing/Cutting

Two dozen eye-pleasing roses will strengthen your second grader's problem-solving skills. Present your child with a Long Stems problem. For example, "I saw two people carrying long-stem roses. Each person had six roses in each hand. How many roses did the people have in all?"

Provide your child with a sheet of construction paper and crayons or markers to draw the way to a solution. Your child might draw two people, each holding six roses in each hand. Your child might draw four groups of six roses. Finally, your second grader might complement the drawing by writing "6 + 6 + 6 + 6 = 24" or "6 × 4 = 24." Ask your child to share the strategy used to solve the problem. Ask what other strategies could be used. Explore possibilities together.

Variation: Make roses together to use as manipulatives. Use pipe cleaners for the stems and construction paper or tissue paper for the blossoms.

REQUIRED:
• Construction paper
• Crayons/markers

OPTIONAL:
• Pipe cleaners
• Tissue paper
• Safety scissors
• Nontoxic glue/tape/stapler

COOKIE SOLVERS

SKILLS: Problem Solving/Recording Data/Cutting

Cut 24 circles—12 brown, 12 white—from construction paper. Use the circles as cookies to enhance your child's problem-solving skills.

Give your child the following problem: "I have 12 cookies. Some are chocolate and some are sugar. How many of each cookie do I have?"

Encourage your second grader to use the paper cookies to provide all possible solutions to the problem. Your child may split the cookies into groups of six and say, "There are six chocolate cookies and six sugar cookies," or into a group of four chocolate cookies and a group of eight sugar cookies. Give your child the opportunity to share the strategies used to solve the problem. Give assistance as necessary.

Provide paper and a pencil for recording all solutions. When complete, celebrate a job well done with chocolate cookies, sugar cookies, and a glass of milk.

REQUIRED:
• Construction paper
• Safety scissors
• Paper and pencil

OPTIONAL:
• Cookies
• Milk

RUBBER BAND FRACTIONS

SKILLS: Fractions/Making Polygons/Recognizing Polygons

Pushpins, rubber bands, and a piece of corkboard are all that are needed for concrete exploration with fractions.

Make a rectangle by arranging four pushpins in the cork for the corners of the rectangle. Fit a rubber band around the four pushpins to make the sides of the rectangle. Ask your child to use two additional pushpins and another rubber band to divide the rectangle in half. Discuss the fact that the rectangle has two equal sections, halves. Remove the pushpins and rubber bands. Make a square by arranging four pushpins in the cork for the corners of the square. Fit a rubber band around the four pushpins to make the sides of the square. Ask your child to use four additional pushpins and two additional rubber bands to divide the square into thirds. Discuss the fact that the square has three equal parts, thirds.

Continue working with Rubber Band Fractions. Provide your child the opportunity to make a shape for you to divide. Make and divide a parallelogram, trapezoid, diamond, pentagon, hexagon, and octagon.

In addition, encourage your second grader to be on the lookout for objects divided into fractional parts.

REQUIRED:
- Bulletin board or corkboard
- Pushpins
- Rubber bands

TALKING FRACTIONS

SKILLS: Fractions/Recording Data

We often use the words "quarter" and "half" in our everyday conversation. "We have to leave at quarter past four." "We went through a half gallon of milk in a day and a half." "Peter! You only ate half your vegetables." "Mom, can I borrow a quarter?"

Make a tally sheet of Talking Fractions by dividing a piece of paper into two sections. Label one section "Quarter" and the other "Half." Post the tally sheet on the refrigerator.

Ask your child to listen for the word "quarter" or "half." Each time your second grader hears a family member use the word "quarter" or "half," make a tally mark in the appropriate column. As your child makes a tally mark, discuss the context in which the word "quarter" or "half" was used. Tally the results for a week.

As an extension, listen and record other math terms heard in daily conversation.

REQUIRED:
- Paper and pencil

A+ ACTIVITIES FOR SECOND GRADE

BAKE AND DIVVY

SKILL: Fractions

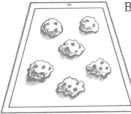

Bake and Divvy to provide your second grader with concrete experiences with fractions. Use slice-and-bake dough or a favorite cookie recipe to make cookies to share equally among family members. If there are four members in your family, bake 12, 16, 20, or 24 cookies.

When the cookies have cooled, use them as manipulatives. Invite your second grader to divvy up the cookies so that each family member gets an equal share.

As family members munch and crunch, encourage your child to articulate the strategies used to solve the problem.

Whenever your second grader is assisting with baking and cooking, point out and discuss how fractions and other math concepts are involved in the process.

REQUIRED:
• Cookie dough

FRACTION MATCHIN'

SKILL: Fractions

$$\frac{2}{3}$$

Fractions are represented in different ways. We write them with numerators and denominators, $\frac{3}{4}$; we draw them by dividing shapes into equal parts and shading parts. Match the two to build skill with fractions.

On 10 index cards, write the fractions "$\frac{3}{10}$," "$\frac{1}{8}$," "$\frac{3}{8}$," "$\frac{5}{6}$," "$\frac{4}{5}$," "$\frac{1}{4}$," "$\frac{3}{4}$," "$\frac{1}{3}$," "$\frac{2}{3}$," and "$\frac{1}{2}$," one fraction per card. On a second set of cards, draw shapes with lightly shaded areas to match the fractions. For example, draw a rectangle with 10 equal sections, 3 of them lightly shaded, to match $\frac{3}{10}$. Draw a square with 8 equal sections, 1 of them lightly shaded, to match $\frac{1}{8}$. Continue until you have a shaded shape card to match each fraction card.

Spread the fraction cards facedown on one area of the playing surface and the shaded shape cards facedown on another.

Choose one card from each area. Do the cards match? If they do, keep the cards. If they don't, return the cards facedown to their original positions. Alternate turns. Play until no cards remain. The player with the most pairs at the end wins. Add new pairs of cards as your child becomes more adept with fractions.

REQUIRED:
• Index cards
• Crayons/colored pencils

FRACTION CUPS

SKILLS: Fractions/Measurement/Capacity/Estimating/Recording Data/Making Comparisons

Your second grader may know that a fraction is an equal part of a whole. Use a set of measuring cups to give your child concrete experience with fractions.

Sit beside your child with a set of measuring cups, a recording sheet, a pencil, and a canister of sugar. Ask your second grader to read the notation on the $\frac{1}{4}$ cup, $\frac{1}{2}$ cup, and one cup. Estimate how many $\frac{1}{4}$ cups of sugar fit into the $\frac{1}{2}$ cup. Record the estimate. Then, use the $\frac{1}{4}$ cup as a scoop to check the estimate. Compare the actual number with the estimated number.

Continue exploration as you estimate and determine how many $\frac{1}{4}$ cups of sugar fit into one cup and how many $\frac{1}{2}$ cups fit into one cup.

Extend the activity by exploring with the $\frac{1}{3}$ cup, $\frac{2}{3}$ cup, and $\frac{3}{4}$ cup measures. How many $\frac{1}{3}$ cups fit into the $\frac{2}{3}$ cup? How may $\frac{1}{4}$ cups fit into the $\frac{3}{4}$ cup?

REQUIRED:
- Measuring cups
- Sugar
- Paper and pencil

PIECE OF CAKE

SKILL: Fractions

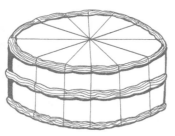

Concrete experiences reinforce the concept that a fraction is an equal part of a whole.

Open a file folder horizontally. In the upper left-hand corner, draw a 1″ square labeled "Start." Do the same in the lower right-hand corner. Label this square "Finish." Draw 30 circles between Start and Finish. In random circles, write messages such as: "Collect $\frac{4}{12}$ from the bakery," "Collect $\frac{7}{12}$ from the bakery," "Return $\frac{2}{12}$ to the bakery," "Give your opponent $\frac{5}{12}$," "Take $\frac{4}{12}$ from your opponent."

Cut two equivalent cakes from construction paper. Cut each cake into 12 equal pieces, label each "$\frac{1}{12}$," and put the 24 pieces into a draw pile called "bakery." Give each player a game marker.

Player one rolls a die and moves that number of spaces. Land on a blank circle, pass the die to player two. Land on a message, read the message and act accordingly, if possible. If the message says, "Return $\frac{3}{12}$ to the bakery," do so. If you don't have three pieces, give what you have.

Continue play, alternating turns, until one player reaches Finish or makes a cake of 12 pieces.

REQUIRED:
- File folder
- Marker
- Construction paper
- Safety scissors
- Die
- Game markers

 # SCIENCE

A butterfly flits from blossom to blossom. The warm sun filters light between gently rustling leaves. Tiny stones sparkle beside a path, and beads of dew drip from blades of grass. The air is crispy clean, the sky is cerulean blue, the clouds are fluffy white. Stop. Take notice. Science!

Second grade is a time of inquiry and discovery. It is a time when children are fascinated by the wonders of nature, eager and willing to explore. It is a time to observe with focus, pose questions with curiosity and purpose, form hypotheses with commitment, keep records with precision, and share discoveries with excitement, pride, and awe.

The science activities that follow invite, encourage, and stimulate interest. Across a range of topics, you and your child brainstorm, ask questions, and investigate the natural world through observation, comparison, theory, prediction, experimentation, and conclusion. You'll have the opportunity to view a cross section of the Earth, construct mountains from simulated granite, go Kitchen Spelunking, gauge wind speed and direction, grow avocado trees and pineapple plants, make metamorphosis mobiles and migration maps, discover a dinosaur, unearth fragile fossils, save a whale, conserve energy, filter water, balance a diet, create a constellation, meet the Man in the Moon, and wonder at a sunset.

From the age of dinosaurs to observation and inquiry about our solar system, we have provided you with basic factual information to enhance discussion and discovery. Find a moment to write science poetry, simulate a volcano, create salt crystals, or calculate your weight on the moon. Keep your explanations appropriate, providing your young scientist with information that matches a second grader's level of understanding. Above all, take time to notice the butterfly, to let real-life experiences kindle the curiosity and wonder of scientific investigation.

SCIENCE SACK

SKILLS: Study Skills/Organization/Brainstorming

As homework demands increase and your second grader's curiosity about science continues to blossom, you may hear, "Dad, I can't find my magnifying glass!" or "Mom, where is the bug house I made?" Organize a Science Sack to enhance your child's organizational skills and increase independence during homework time and exploration.

Label a canvas tote bag, "Science Sack." Provide your child with art supplies to decorate the sack. Brainstorm a list of science tools and materials to include in the sack: a magnifying glass, timer or stopwatch, homemade bug house, trowel, ruler, tape measure, journal, pencils, crayons, markers, containers with lids, labels, and anything else your young scientist needs to assist with homework and other science explorations.

REQUIRED:
- Bag
- Art supplies
- Science tools

Store your second grader's Science Sack in the Homework Spot so that tools are easily accessible for explorations and experimentation.

VERSATILE VENN

SKILLS: Brainstorming/Recording Data/Study Skills/Organization/Making Comparisons

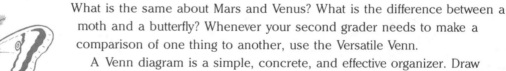

What is the same about Mars and Venus? What is the difference between a moth and a butterfly? Whenever your second grader needs to make a comparison of one thing to another, use the Versatile Venn.

A Venn diagram is a simple, concrete, and effective organizer. Draw two intersecting circles. For comparing a toad and a frog, write "Toad" in the left section and "Frog" in the right. Label the intersection, "Both." Before reading about toads and frogs, brainstorm and record phrases that tell what you know or believe to be true about toads in the "Toad" section and frogs in the "Frog" section. Write facts specific to both animals in the section labeled "Both."

As you share nonfiction books about topics of interest, continue to record information in the appropriate section of the diagram. Confirm correct facts and adjust inaccurate facts. Add new learning.

Use the completed diagram for making comparisons of the topics researched. If your child is interested in comparing and contrasting three topics, make a third circle and follow the same procedure. You are sure to find the Venn diagram a helpful study tool not only in second grade but also in the grades that follow.

REQUIRED:
- Paper and pencil
- Nonfiction books

OPTIONAL:
- Library/bookstore visit

A+ ACTIVITIES FOR SECOND GRADE

KWL REVISITED

SKILLS: Brainstorming/Recording Data/Study Skills/Organization

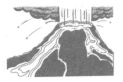

During your child's year in grade one and now again in grade two, you may have heard reference to *KWL,* an acronym for what you *K*now, what you *W*ant to know, and what you have *L*earned. Whenever your second grader researches material for a science report or for the sake of learning, revisit *KWL,* a concrete study guide that enhances new learning in all areas of the curriculum.

Ask your child to fold or rule a piece of paper into three columns. Label the first column, "Know," the middle, "Want to Know," the third, "Learned." Before reading about a topic of choice, record phrases in the first column of facts you know or believe to be true. In the second column, record questions to guide your research of what you want to know. Finally, while reading, look for information to confirm the facts recorded in column one and to answer the questions recorded in column two. Record new learning in column three.

REQUIRED:
• Paper and pencil
• Nonfiction books

OPTIONAL:
• Library/bookstore visit

Use the information gathered as a springboard for learning more. Give your child the opportunity to share knowledge about a topic of interest and be amazed by the enthusiasm, motivation, and learning that follow.

I AM A MOUNTAIN

SKILLS: Facts & Details/Researching/Note Taking/Metaphor/Written Expression/Poetry/Drawing

Combine scientific knowledge, poetry, and art to create science poetry.

Start with a simple metaphor, a figure of speech that compares two nouns by stating that one is the other. Encourage your second grader, along with other family members, to choose any element or aspect of nature—an animal, tree, flower, rock, or natural phenomenon. Research the topic to gather and record basic facts.

Begin and end the poem with the statement, "I am a mountain (river, volcano, hippopotamus, cactus, cloud, the world)." From the point of view of the mountain, for example, introduce yourself, weaving facts about the mountain with descriptive language. Emphasize quality, not quantity.

When all participants have completed a poem, take time to create an illustration. Gather for a poetry reading, sharing and celebrating scientific knowledge, poetry, and art.

I am
A mighty mountain.
A mass of rock. A guard of land around me.
Born slowly over millions of years, by the moving and bumping of
Huge plates of rock that form the earth's crust. I am a mighty mountain.

REQUIRED:
• Paper and pencils
• Crayons/markers

OPTIONAL:
• Library/bookstore visit

Enjoy reading science poems in *101 Science Poems & Songs for Young Learners: With Hands-On Activities* by Meish Goldish.

SCIENCE ACTIVITIES

ROCK STAR

SKILLS: Observation/Making Comparisons/Note Taking/Drawing

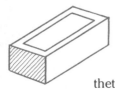

The library building in your city or town might be brick. The steps leading up to the city or town hall might be granite. The floor of the museum might be marble. The sidewalk outside your home might be concrete, and your street might be asphalt.

Invite your second grade geologist to be a Rock Star by identifying the natural and synthetic rocks in your neighborhood.

Before taking your geological walk, you may want to refer to a book such as *Rocks & Minerals* by R. F. Symes. View pictures of granite made of coarse interlocking crystals; marble with its smooth veins and patterns; brick made from red or yellow clay; limestone with its smooth, cream or gray texture.

With pad and pencil in hand, survey the neighborhood. Encourage your child to observe, touch, draw, and write notes about each rock found. Discuss similarities and differences. Focus on appearance and texture. Add information for every rock specimen viewed.

REQUIRED:
- Pad and pencil
- Library/bookstore visit

GEOLOGY BUFF

SKILLS: Vocabulary Development/Collecting/Observation/Sorting/Identifying/Recording Data

Geologists are scientists who study the earth, the earth's forces and rocks.

Gather the tools of a Geology Buff, including a notebook/journal and pencil, small hammer and goggles, magnifying glass, labels, and newspaper. Arrange all tools in a sturdy bag. Head outside to collect specimens of the rocks in your neighborhood. When collecting samples, follow these important rules.

- Be careful near water and on hills, cliffs, mountains.
- Look for samples on the ground.
- Always wear goggles when using the hammer.
- Don't hammer rock faces.
- Never remove samples from private property or local, state, or national parks.

Wrap each sample in newspaper. Affix a label and note the location where the rock was found: on a wooded path, near a lake, on a hilltop.

At home, unwrap the samples. Sort the rocks by the area in which they were found. Use an old toothbrush to wash specimens gently in soapy water. Examine each carefully with the naked eye and with the magnifying glass. Note characteristics such as color, texture, and structure.

Set the rocks aside. Borrow a book from your library on the rocks found in your area. Use the book to identify each sample in your collection.

REQUIRED:
- Geologist's kit
- Old toothbrush
- Soap
- Library visit

ROCK AND ROLL CALL

SKILLS: Vocabulary Development/Observation/Sorting/Classifying/Graphing

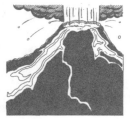

There are three major kinds of rocks, each formed in a different way.

Igneous rocks form when molten materials, magma and lava, cool and harden. These rocks are hard and made from crystals that have merged. An example, granite, is made from quartz, feldspar, and mica.

Sedimentary rocks form from the material (sediment) that erodes from other rocks. The sediment is often carried to a new site, deposited in layers, buried and compressed to form new rocks. These rocks are relatively soft and sometimes contain fossils. Examples include limestone and sandstone.

Metamorphic rocks, usually hard, form when igneous or sedimentary rocks change form over time from heat and/or pressure. Metamorphic rocks, like marble, are often characterized by streaks or bands.

Examine, sort, and classify rocks. Use the descriptions provided and resources such as *Rocks and Minerals* by R. F. Symes to assist in your identification. Record findings on a bar graph. Make three columns of ten segments each. Label one column "Igneous," another "Sedimentary," and the third "Metamorphic." As you classify each rock, fill in one segment of the appropriate column. Determine the type of rock most common in your collection.

REQUIRED:
- Rocks
- Paper and pencil
- Ruler

OPTIONAL:
- Library/bookstore visit

THE SCRATCH TEST

SKILLS: Vocabulary Development/Experimentation/Observation/Classifying

The Scratch Test is an easy experiment that assists in the classification of rocks as igneous, sedimentary, or metamorphic.

Before experimenting, remind your geologist that igneous and metamorphic rocks are usually hard, and sedimentary rocks are soft. Also note that igneous rocks have crystals that have grown together, sedimentary rocks have layers and may contain fossils, and metamorphic rocks have streaks or bands.

Label one area of your work surface, "Very Soft Rocks." Label a second area, "Soft Rocks, and a third, "Hard Rocks." Provision yourselves with a quarter, a nail, and ordinary rocks from your collection.

Scratch the surface of each rock with a fingernail. If a scratch is visible, place the rock in the "Very Soft" section. Scratch the surface of the remaining rocks with a quarter. If a scratch is visible, place the rock in the "Soft" section. Finally, supervise to ensure safety as your child scratches the surface of the remaining rocks with a nail. Place these rocks in the "Hard" section.

Examine the appearance and texture of the rocks. Use all observations to classify each rock as igneous, sedimentary, or metamorphic.

REQUIRED:
- Rocks
- Quarter
- Nail
- Paper and pencil

SCIENCE ACTIVITIES

ROCK GALLERY

SKILLS: Collecting/Sorting/Cataloging/Note Taking/Written Expression/Drawing/Oral Expression

The geological treasures found on beaches, in woodlands, beside lakes and ponds, near streams, on hills, in valleys, or in your backyard are worthy of admiration and display.

Invite your second grader to be curator of a personal Rock Gallery. For each display case of the gallery, remove the top and one side of a shoebox. Line the inside of the box with colored plastic wrap, tissue, or paper. The shoebox display can accommodate six medium-size specimens with labels.

Clear plastic containers make wonderful showcases for up to three specimens. Display specimens, each with a label indicating the kind of rock it is and the location where it was found.

Finally, enhance the viewing of specimens found at the shore by displaying them in jars of water. Place the label on the outside of the jar.

Support your child in efforts to maintain a geological notebook, one page per specimen. Draw a picture of the rock; note location found; describe characteristics of size, shape, texture, and color.

Invite friends and neighbors so that your young curator has the opportunity to guide visitors through the gallery while describing the treasures displayed.

REQUIRED:
- Rock specimens
- Containers
- Colored plastic wrap/tissue/paper liner
- Labels
- Pencil/pen
- Notebook
- Crayons/markers
- Nontoxic glue

ROCK GARDEN WONDERS

SKILL: Map Skills

Experience the wonders of Earth by examining rocks from around the world. Order rock specimens by contacting the Rock Garden, a rock, mineral, and craft store in Branford, Connecticut.

Before your rocks arrive, photocopy or trace a world map from an atlas. Mount the map on posterboard. Extend the posterboard 6 to 12 inches beyond the left and right edges of the map. View the map together. Point to and identify each of the seven continents: Africa, Antarctica, Asia, Australia, Europe, North America, and South America.

When your rocks arrive, note that each is identified by name and place of origin. Carefully examine each rock, focusing on color, texture, and size. Write the name of the rock and its origin on a self-adhesive label. Set the rock on the posterboard, to the left or right of the map. Use the label and tape to secure a piece of yarn or string from the rock to its place of origin. Repeat the process for each rock in the collection. Refer to the atlas as needed.

REQUIRED:
- Rocks
- Atlas
- Posterboard
- Yarn/string
- Labels
- Pencil/marker
- Nontoxic glue/tape

OPTIONAL:
- Tracing paper

The Rock Garden
17 South Main Street
Branford, Connecticut 06405
1-203-488-669

Web site: *www.rockgarden.com*
E-mail: *info@rockgarden.com*

MARILYN AND ANDY'S GRANITE

SKILLS: Measurement/Observation/Making Comparisons/Drawing/Sculpting

You may have a budding Michelangelo or Auguste Rodin living in your home. These famous sculptors worked with marble. Invite your second grade sculptor to work with simulated granite.

Our friends Marilyn and Andy of the Rock Garden in Branford, Connecticut, gave us a foolproof recipe for making granite from art plaster, water, and vermiculite. Join your second grader as you measure, mix, mold, observe, and sculpt.

Mix the art plaster and water according to the directions on the package. Add vermiculite to the plaster mixture. If you add one cup of water, add one cup of vermiculite. Blend thoroughly. Spoon the granite mixture into a recycled carton or plastic container. Allow to dry.

While the granite dries, sketch what you plan to sculpt. Remove the granite from the mold. Observe the external texture, noting its similarity to natural granite. Then, sculpt away, using a plastic knife. Be sure to observe the internal texture of the simulated granite as you work.

Invite other family members to try a hand at sculpting. Display finished masterpieces for all to admire.

REQUIRED:
- Art plaster (available at craft stores)
- Vermiculite (available at garden stores)
- Water
- Recycled containers
- Plastic knives

KITCHEN SPELUNKING

SKILLS: Vocabulary Development/Experimentation/Measurement/
Hypothesizing/Observation/Recording Data/Drawing

You don't have to be a *spelunker,* or cave explorer, to see *stalactites* and *stalagmites.* Go Kitchen Spelunking instead!

Stalactites hang from ceilings of caves along with bats. Stalagmites grow upward from cave floors. Both are formed when limestone dissolved in water drips from the roof of the cave. As the water evaporates, over time, the limestone residue builds, leaving iciclelike rock structures hanging from the ceiling and candlelike structures growing from the floor.

Provision your spelunker with Epsom salts (available at the pharmacy), a spoon, a small dish, two feet of string, and two glasses of warm water. Dissolve as much Epsom salts as possible in each glass.

Place the glasses on the table with the dish between them. Suspend one end of the string into a glass, making sure that the end touches bottom. Suspend the other end into the second glass in the same manner so that the slack portion of string hangs above the dish.

Hypothesize what might happen to the slack portion of string and the dish below it. Observe, draw, and takes notes over several days. Your spelunker will witness the formation of stalactites and stalagmites in the comfort of your kitchen.

REQUIRED:
- Epsom salts
- Spoon
- Glasses
- Water
- Dish
- String
- Paper and pencil

SCIENCE ACTIVITIES

CREATE A CRYSTAL

SKILLS: Vocabulary Development/Experimentation/Measurement/Observation/Recording Data/Drawing

There is something magical about *crystals*. For centuries people have admired their beauty and been intrigued by their "powers." Create a Crystal to give your child the opportunity to view the regular shape of this mineral, or nonliving solid.

At your local pharmacy, purchase a bottle of *alum*, a potassium aluminum silicate, for about $2.00. At home, provision your young geologist with alum, a tablespoon, cup, shallow dish, spoon, and water.

Supervise as your child measures and pours two tablespoons of water into the cup. Use the spoon to dissolve as much alum as possible in the water. Stir after each spoonful of alum is added.

Pour the mixture onto the dish. Keep the dish in the open for two days. Encourage your child to observe the solution regularly. Provide paper and a pencil so that your child can record any changes noted as the solution evaporates and draw the crystals as they form.

After two days, use a magnifying glass to observe the crystals formed.

You may want to contact *The Rock Garden* in Branford, Connecticut, 1-203-488-6699, to purchase a selection of natural crystals to add to your child's rock gallery.

REQUIRED:
- Alum
- Tablespoon
- Cup
- Spoon
- Water
- Dish
- Paper and pencil

JOE'S SALT CRYSTALS

SKILLS: Vocabulary Development/Experimentation/Measurement/Observation/Recording Data/Drawing

Our friend Joe is a Crystal Wizard. Follow his easy recipe to grow salt crystals.

To begin, glue salt grains to the end of a thread. While the glue dries thoroughly, fill the bottom of a pot with water and place on a burner set on low. Supervise as your child fills a glass container with two cups of hot water. Stand the container of hot water in the pot to keep the water hot.

Pour salt into the glass container, stirring constantly. Continue to add about ½ cup of salt until no more dissolves and salt settles on the bottom of the container.

Seed the salt solution by suspending the salt end of the thread in the glass container. Remove the container from the heat. Allow to cool at room temperature. Over the next several hours, see salt crystals form on the thread above the water. Use a magnifying glass to see that the crystals are perfectly square. Record, draw, and date all observations.

To grow bigger crystals, repeat the process with the same thread without removing the crystals. Each time the thread sits in the salt solution and cools, the crystals enlarge.

REQUIRED:
- Salt
- Thread
- Nontoxic glue
- Pot
- Water
- Spoon
- Glass measuring cup
- Paper and pencil

A+ ACTIVITIES FOR SECOND GRADE

GOLD RUSH

In 1849, prospectors raced across the continental United States to California to pan for the precious metal gold. Often, what prospectors discovered was a mineral called pyrite, which, because of its shiny golden crystals, was mistaken for gold. Give your child the opportunity to simulate the experience of panning for gold.

Gather a handful of metal objects such as nails, bolts, or screws. Place them in a flat-bottomed round cake pan or bowl. Select a mixture of two or three ingredients such as popcorn kernels, rice, dried peas, any kind of dried beans, or vermiculite to add to the bowl.

Hold the bowl over a large pot as your second grader slowly pours water over the ingredients. Ask your child to make a hypothesis about what will happen to the materials in the bowl. Observe closely that all of the beans, peas, kernels, and/or vermiculite wash out of the bowl while the heavier metals stay in the pan. Your child will probably draw the conclusion that panning for gold and other minerals works because gold and other metals and minerals are heavy.

REQUIRED:
- Pan/bowl
- Metal objects
- Dry ingredients
- Pitcher of water
- Pot

SOIL AND SAND SAMPLER

Children spend time constructing roadways and tunnels in the soil of the backyard. Children and adults, too, love to play in the sand at the beach or lakeside, building castles and cities.

Sample the soil and sand common to your area. Stick a label on six to eight recycled yogurt containers with covers. Take the containers, a trowel or spoon, and a pencil or marker with you when you go out to gather samples of the ground cover from a garden; beneath a tree; beside a brook, pond, lake, or bay. As you spoon the sample into a container, jot down the origin of the sample on the label.

At home, cover a work surface with protective paper. Work with one sample at a time. Spoon a portion of the sample onto the work surface. Touch and smell the sample. View it with a magnifying glass.

For each sample, make notes of your observations. Look for chips of rock, crystal fragments, plant and animal remains, and small living creatures. Note the color and texture. After thorough examination, scoop the sample back into its container and view another. Compare and contrast the characteristics of all samples collected.

REQUIRED:
- Containers with lids
- Trowel/spoon
- Labels
- Paper and pencil
- Marker
- Magnifying glass

SCIENCE ACTIVITIES

WINDY, RAINY REACTIONS

SKILLS: Vocabulary Development/Experimentation/Measurement/Hypothesizing/Recording
Data/Observation/Making Comparisons/Drawing Conclusions

Erosion is the process by which Earth's surface is worn away.

Do a simple outdoor experiment to demonstrate erosion. In your backyard or courtyard, on your porch step or balcony, tightly pack a small mound of dirt either on the ground itself or in a flowerpot. Use a tape measure to determine the height and circumference of the mound. Record both measurements.

Ask your second grader to make a hypothesis about what will happen to the mound of soil during the coming week. Encourage your child to note weather conditions and observe the mound daily. Talk about the effect that wind or rain, heat or cold can have on the mound. At the end of the week, measure the height and circumference of the mound. Record the results and compare to the first set of measurements. Draw a conclusion based upon your findings. Did it rain? Was it windy? Did the soil freeze? Did the soil become dry? Each of these conditions contributes to erosion.

REQUIRED:
- Soil
- Paper and pencil
- Tape measure

OPTIONAL:
- Flower pot

OUTSIDE IN

SKILLS: Vocabulary Development/Observation

From the Outside In, Earth is divided into four layers. The outside layer is the *crust.* The crust is made of enormous, moving slabs of rock called plates. The plates float on the *mantle,* a layer of hot, liquid rock. Moving in, the third layer is the *outer core,* which is made of hot, liquid metals. Finally, at the center, is the *inner core,* a layer of solid iron.

Concretely demonstrate the four layers of Earth with a kiwifruit. Slice the kiwi in half between its top and bottom. Examine the kiwi from the outside in, likening each visible layer to a layer of Earth. The fuzzy skin is the crust. The green fleshy band is the mantle. The ring of seeds is the outer core and the center circle of yellow is the inner core.

Do the same with a peach, nectarine, or cherry, pointing out that the skin is like Earth's crust, the fleshy fruit like the mantle, the pit like the outer core and the kernel inside the pit like the inner core.

End your observation by eating the fruits of Earth!

REQUIRED:
- Kiwifruit

OPTIONAL:
- Single pit fruit

CROSS SECTION EARTH

SKILLS: Vocabulary Development/Painting

Make a cross section of Earth and view the layers inside. All you need is a slice of sandwich bread; a round cookie cutter or a glass; four colors of vegetable food coloring; a paper bowl or plate; and toothpicks, wooden skewers, or a thin paintbrush.

Freeze a slice of white bread. When frozen, cut a circle from the center of the slice using the cookie cutter or top of the glass. Drip a few drops of green food coloring on the plate. Dip the toothpick in the green and paint a thin line around the perimeter of the circle of bread. This is Earth's surface layer, or crust. Now drip a few drops of red food coloring on the plate. Use another toothpick to paint a ½″ band of red just inside the green crust. This is Earth's mantle, a molten layer. Just inside the mantle, repeat the process with orange to form Earth's outer core, a layer of hot, liquid metal. Finally, paint the center blue to represent Earth's inner core, a layer of solid iron.

This cross section of Earth concretely demonstrates what is just below our feet!

REQUIRED:
- Bread
- Cookie cutter/glass
- Food coloring
- Paper plate/bowl
- Toothpicks/wooden skewers/paintbrush

THAR' SHE BLOWS

SKILLS: Vocabulary Development/Experimentation/Observation

The surface layer of Earth, the crust, is made from enormous moving slabs of rock called plates. These plates are about 62 miles thick. At the site where two plates collide and one plate is forced beneath the other, volcanoes often form. *Magma,* the molten rock inside Earth's mantle, escapes to Earth's surface as lava.

Thanks to Jenny Wood, the author of *Volcanoes,* it is easy to simulate a volcanic eruption. Fill half a small glass with cold water. Make a small hole in the center of a square of cardboard. Set aside. Drip five drops of red food coloring into a small, clean bottle with a narrow opening. Fill the bottle with hot water.

Firmly hold the cardboard, centered, over the glass. Flip the glass quickly, holding the cardboard in place to avoid leakage. Set the cardboard and glass on top of the bottle, press firmly, and, while pressing, if needed, give a little jiggle. Because warm water is lighter than cold water, the warm water rises. Spurts of simulated lava will erupt into the glass.

REQUIRED:
- Glass
- Cardboard
- Pin
- Bottle
- Food coloring
- Water

MIGHTY MOUNTAINS

SKILLS: Vocabulary Development/Experimentation/Sculpting

In 1953, New Zealander Sir Edmund Hillary and Sherpa Tenzing Norgay were the first to reach the 29,028-foot summit of Mount Everest, the world's highest mountain. A mountain like Everest is a mass of rock that rises high above sea level. It forms over millions of years when the plates in Earth's crust bump together. This bumping forces the rock between the plates upward. The rock folds in on itself, creating a mountain.

Use a large sheet of paper as the rock between the plates of Earth's crust. Lay the "rock" horizontally on a hard, flat surface before your second grader. Ask your child to place one hand on the left edge of the "rock" and the other hand on the right edge. Your child's hands are the "plates" of Earth's crust. As the "plates" move slowly together until they bump into each other, the "rock" is forced upward into folds or mountains.

This hands-on demonstration concretely shows how our majestic Mighty Mountains form.

As a follow-up, work together to sculpt your own mountain from simulated granite. Follow the recipe from Marilyn and Andy's Granite (p. 131).

REQUIRED:
- Paper

OPTIONAL:
- Simulated granite recipe

RANGE TO RANGE

SKILLS: Vocabulary Development/Map Skills/Observation/Identifying

A series of mountains similar in form, direction, and origin is called a *range*. Mountain ranges sprawl over enormous areas and contain some of the highest mountains in the world.

Visit your local library to use a topographical globe or map to locate, name, and "touch" the mountain ranges of the world. Ask your second grader to run a hand gently over the map or globe. Observe and discuss the raised surface that depicts a mountain range.

Ask your child to locate and point to North America. Run a hand over the continent to locate the Rocky Mountains, in the western part of the United States, and the Appalachian Mountains, in the eastern part of the United States.

Challenge your child to move from Range to Range while using the same method to find the Andes in South America; the Pyrenees, Alps, and Dolomites in Europe; the East African Mountains in Africa; the Urals and Himalayas in Asia; and the Great Dividing Range in Australia.

REQUIRED:
- Topographical globe/map
- Library visit

ROCK AND READ

SKILLS: Connecting Science & Literature/Imaginative Thinking/Facts
& Details/Written Expression/Drawing

Pebbles, rocks, hills, mountains, and volcanoes are featured in both nonfiction and fiction for children. Rock and Read to learn facts and details about geology and to enjoy stories of tricksters, friendship, wisdom, and sharing.

According to author Nicholas Nirgiotis, people long ago believed that a god of fire lived inside volcanoes. Learn factual information about these phenomena of nature in Nirgiotis's book *Volcanoes, Mountains That Blow Their Tops*. Relive the two-thousand–year-old eruption of Mt. Vesuvius in *Pompeii . . . Buried Alive!* by Edith Kunhardt. Discover the difference between *Hills and Mountains* in the book of the same title by Brenda Williams.

Switch to engaging fantasy as you watch a bird befriend a lonely mountain in *The Mountain That Loved A Bird* by Alice McLerran. Witness the power and magic of a tiny red pebble that miraculously turns a young donkey into a rock in *Sylvester and the Magic Pebble* by William Steig. Finally, visit Ming Lo as he tackles the problem of moving a mountain to satisfy his wife in *Ming Lo Moves a Mountain* by Arnold Lobel.

Use any one of these books as a model for writing and illustrating a geology story of your own.

REQUIRED:
• Paper and pencil
• Library/bookstore visit

WINDBLOWN

SKILLS: Imaginative Thinking/Cutting/Observation/Graphing

Beside an airport runway, a bright orange sock hangs from a pole. The wind blows, and the sock fills with air, lifts, and blows in the wind's direction.

To make a colorful windsock, horizontally spread a white plastic garbage bag on a work surface. Decorate the bag with colored paper or cloth strips. Staple the inside lip of the opening of the bag to a 3′ to 4′ wooden dowel. Be sure to keep the bag open.

Write "north," "east," "south," "west" on four index cards, one direction per card. Seal each card in a sandwich bag. Take all materials outside. Stick the dowel into the ground in an unobstructed area. Point out and mark each direction around the windsock using a toothpick to attach each bag to the ground.

Observe the windsock once a day for a week. Make a seven-row, four-column bar graph, labeling the four columns, "north," "east," "south," and "west." Shade one square each day to indicate wind direction. At the end of the week, determine the wind direction most often observed.

REQUIRED:
• Garbage bag
• Marker
• Construction paper/cloth
• Dowel
• Safety scissors
• Index cards
• Nontoxic glue
• Sandwich bags
• Stapler
• Toothpicks
• Paper and pencil
• Ruler

SCIENCE ACTIVITIES

ANEMOMETER ACTION

SKILLS: Vocabulary Development/Following Directions/Observation

An *anemometer* is an instrument that measures wind speed or *velocity*. Watch the wind work its magic by making an anemometer.

Crisscross two plastic drinking straws. Stick a common pin through the straws at the intersection. Insert the pin into the eraser end of a pencil. Place the pencil structure faceup on a work surface. Hold a two-ounce paper cup sideways with the opening to the left. Staple the inside of the cup to the end of one straw.

Repeat this process three times so that a cup is attached to all straw ends. Be sure that all cups face in the same direction. Finally, make a stand by attaching the bottom of a spool of thread to the top of a cardboard box or wooden block. Stick the pencil point end of the anemometer into the spool.

Place your anemometer outside, in an unobstructed area. Because wind pressure is greater on the inward curving of the cups than on the outward curving of the cups, the wind rotates the cups regardless of wind direction. The greater the wind velocity, the faster the cups rotate. Determine whether the wind is weak or strong by watching your anemometer spin.

REQUIRED:
- Pencil
- Straws
- Pin
- Paper cups
- Stapler
- Spool
- Box/block
- Nontoxic glue

PLASTIC PLATE CONDENSATION

SKILLS: Vocabulary Development/Experimentation/Observation

Water vapor is formed when water from Earth's surface *evaporates* into the air. As air rises, it cools. If the air becomes cold enough, the invisible water vapor turns into tiny drops of water that float in the air to form clouds. This process is called *condensation*. The *dew point* is the temperature at which water vapor begins to *condense*.

Condensation is easy to observe and easy to demonstrate. Show your second grader what happens on a warm day when you pour a cold drink into a glass or remove a soda can from the refrigerator. See water beads form on the outside of the glass or can. The temperature of the air near the surface of the glass or can cools to below the dew point. The water vapor in the air turns to tiny droplets of water.

As an alternative, place a plastic plate in the freezer for five minutes. Remove the plate from the freezer and hold over a cup of hot liquid. As the hot air rises and meets the cold air, see little droplets of water form on the plate. Condensation has occurred and you've witnessed the process by which clouds are formed.

REQUIRED:
- Cold drink
- Plastic plate
- Freezer
- Hot liquid

A+ ACTIVITIES FOR SECOND GRADE

CLOUD CONSTRUCTION

SKILLS: Vocabulary Development/Experimentation/Observation

When water from Earth's surface evaporates, it enters the air as invisible water vapor. Water vapor is carried into the sky by the air. As air rises, it cools. The invisible water vapor condenses or turns into tiny drops of water that float in the air to form clouds. In a rain cloud, the tiny drops of water merge to form bigger drops. Eventually, as the drops become heavy and too big to float, they fall to Earth as rain, sleet, hail, or snow, and the water cycle starts again.

Demonstrate how clouds form with ice and hot water.

Fill a plastic container with ice cubes. Half fill a clear glass container with hot water, supervising your child to ensure safe handling. Carefully place the plastic container of ice cubes atop the glass container of hot water. As the warm air from the water rises and cools, clouds form in the glass container above the water. Note the formation of clouds before removing the plastic container of ice to let the clouds float from the glass container.

REQUIRED:
- Ice
- Plastic container
- Glass container
- Hot water

ONE, TWO, THREE, BOOM!

SKILLS: Observation/Counting/Estimating/Addition/Multiplication/Recording Data/Making Comparisons

Is it true that you can count the seconds between seeing lightning and hearing thunder to determine how far you are from a thunderstorm? Absolutely!

The next time you find yourselves looking out the window at an approaching electrical storm, work with your second-grade meteorologist to determine the distance between you and the storm. Explain that light travels faster than sound. We see the light from lightning instantly. Sound, however, is a slowpoke, traveling at just under 1,100 feet per second. When you see lightning flash, count the seconds until you hear thunder.

If three seconds pass before you hear a boom, the thunderstorm is approximately 3,300 feet away. If five seconds pass before you hear thunder, the storm is approximately 5,500 feet away or just over a mile (5,280 feet).

Continue to count the time elapsed between lightning and thunder. Record each second count to determine whether the storm is coming closer or moving away. Of course, be safe. Observe lightning from indoors.

REQUIRED:
- Paper and pencil

HAIRY LIGHTNING

SKILLS: Experimentation/Observation

In the eyes of a second grader, lightning can be thrilling and scary at the same time. The scary part is eliminated when children know what lightning is and its cause. When the water drops and ice particles of a cumulonimbus storm cloud are blown up and down, static electricity builds. Lightning is static electricity.

Demonstrate static electricity by making Hairy Lightning. Provision yourselves with plastic combs. Make sure your hair is clean and dry. Turn out the lights and pull the shades or draw the blinds so that the room is completely dark. Face each other and comb your hair in even strokes. The rubbing of the comb against your hair causes static electricity. You'll both be amazed to see tiny lightning sparks fly from your hair.

For other demonstrations of static electricity, rub an inflated balloon against your hair, a sweater, or a shirt several times. Place the balloon against the wall and let go. Static electricity holds the balloon to the wall. Finally, get a real shock from static electricity by rubbing the bottoms of leather-soled shoes against a rug. Touch someone with the tip of a finger and get a tiny jolt from static electricity.

REQUIRED:
• Hair combs

OPTIONAL:
• Balloon

WILD AND WOOLLY WEATHER READ

SKILLS: Facts & Details/Written Expression/Oral Expression

No matter what the season, no matter where you live, bring wild and woolly weather to your home. The collection of nonfiction books available for young readers about everything from tornadoes to blizzards is enormous!

Put up your umbrellas and start your weather reading with *Down Comes the Rain* by Franklyn Mansfield Branley. Add a bit of *Flash, Crash, Rumble and Roll* as Branley explains the how and why of thunder and provides safety tips to follow in an electrical storm. Learn more about wind in *Can You See the Wind?* by Allan Fowler.

Be a tornado chaser in *Tornadoes!* or fly into the eye of a hurricane as a storm tracker in *Hurricanes!* both by Lorraine Jean Hopping. Learn about the causes of both storms and get safety tips, too!

Put on your mittens for *Snow and Ice* by Kay Davies and Wendy Oldfield. Finally, read about weird and wacky weather and the causes behind strange weather phenomena in *Pink Snow and Other Weird Weather* by Jennifer Dussling.

After any weather reading, watch the weather on television and read about weather in the newspaper. Invite your young meteorologist to write and present a forecast for any kind of weather.

REQUIRED:
• Library/bookstore visit
• Paper and pencil

OPTIONAL:
• Newspaper

A+ ACTIVITIES FOR SECOND GRADE

SPINACH SHIRTS

SKILL: Experimentation

Dye is used for coloring materials. Natural dyes are made from many raw materials, including fruits, vegetables, leafy plants, and insects. Without rounding up the insects, you can make dye at home.

Provision yourselves with a fruit or vegetable that yields a colorful juice. Berries, spinach, red cabbage, and onion skins work well. Since the dye might stain surfaces, fill the bottom of an *old* pot with water. Add a selected fruit or vegetable to the pot, taking care when working at the stove. Bring the contents to a slow boil, cooking until the fruit or vegetable softens and the water colors. To remove residue, pour the dye through a strainer into an *old* container.

After the dye cools, add a spoonful of coarse salt to the container. Salt sets the dye and prevents running. Place a piece of white fabric into the die and let stand for three hours. Remove the fabric and dry on a protected work surface.

Repeat the process with other fruits and vegetables to make a range of colors. Use the natural dyes to add vibrant color to old and faded T-shirts, napkins, and dish towels.

REQUIRED:
- Fruits/vegetables
- Water
- Pot
- Container
- Strainer
- Spoon
- Salt
- Fabric

SPONGE TO SOIL

SKILLS: Prediction/Experimentation/Observation/Recording Data/Drawing/Making Comparisons

Every seed carries a supply of food. Initially, a seed needs water, sunlight, and appropriate climate to grow. Ultimately, a seedling must be planted in soil to ensure growth. Concretely demonstrate this concept with a Sponge to Soil experiment.

Provision yourselves with a sponge, dish, spray bottle, journal, pencil, plastic wrap, and mustard seeds (readily available at the supermarket).

Dampen the sponge and place it on the dish. Scatter the mustard seeds on the sponge. Place the dish on a sunny windowsill. Predict what might happen to the mustard seeds over time. Record both the date and your prediction in the journal.

Spray water on the sponge periodically each day to maintain dampness. To retain moisture, carefully cover the sponge with plastic wrap each night.

Encourage your second grader to observe, record, and draw any changes to the mustard seeds over a two-week period. Always include the date of observations made. Compare the appearance and growth of the mustard plants from day to day. Transplant the mustard plants to soil for continued growth.

REQUIRED:
- Sponge
- Dish
- Spray bottle
- Journal
- Pencil
- Plastic wrap
- Mustard seeds

ZIPLOC GREENHOUSE

SKILLS: Experimentation/Prediction/Observation/Recording Data/Drawing/Making Comparisons

Witness seed germination right on your own window by creating a Ziploc Greenhouse. Two inches from the bottom of a plastic Ziploc bag, staple from the left edge to the right. Dampen a paper towel. Slide the paper towel into the bag so that the bottom edge touches the staples. Drop several thumbelina, alyssum, lobelia, magic carpet, ageratum, or marigold seeds into the bag. Seal the bag and tape it to a sunny window. Predict what might happen to the seeds over time. Record both the date and your prediction in a journal.

Encourage your second grader to observe, record, and draw any changes to the seeds over a one-week period. Always include the date of observations made. Transplant the new plants to soil when they have two or three double leaves.

As a variation, tape several greenhouses to your window, each containing a different seed. Observe and compare the growth rate of each seed. Finally, share books such as *A Seed Is a Promise* by Claire Merrill or *The Tiny Seed* by Eric Carle to learn more about seeds and how they grow.

REQUIRED:
- Ziploc bag
- Stapler
- Paper towel
- Seeds
- Journal/notebook/pad
- Pencil

OPTIONAL:
- Library/bookstore visit

NO SEEDS NEEDED

SKILLS: Vocabulary Development/Prediction/Experimentation/Observation/Recording Data/Drawing

Did you ever find a potato or onion under your sink that has grown shoots? Don't throw it away! Amaze your child with the discovery that some plants grow without seeds.

Through a process called *vegetative propagation,* plants *regenerate* themselves. Concretely demonstrate vegetative propagation with a carrot, jar, flowerpot, knife, toothpicks, water, and potting soil.

Fill the jar with water. Slice the top quarter from a carrot. Insert four toothpicks around the carrot. Suspend the carrot in the jar so that the bottom rests in the water. Predict what might happen to the carrot over time. In a journal, record both the date and your prediction.

Record and draw any changes observed. When shoots grow to 1" from the base of the carrot, transfer the carrot to a pot of soil. Care for the carrot plant daily. Record and date all observations. Before long, enjoy the vegetables of your labor!

REQUIRED:
- Jar
- Carrot
- Toothpicks
- Water
- Journal
- Pencil
- Flowerpot
- Potting soil
- Knife

GREEN THUMB SHIRLEY

SKILLS: Vocabulary Development/Experimentation/Observation

Did you know you can grow a pineapple plant, an avocado tree, and an African violet plant at home? Green Thumb Shirley, the most amazing gardener we know, has proven that anything is possible with plants. Follow Shirley's easy steps and amaze your child as Shirley has amazed us!

Just below its base, carefully remove the *crown* of a pineapple, the group of small leaves at the top. Sit the crown, with ½″ of soil around its perimeter, in a planter of potting soil or an outside garden in warm climates. Water, but do not saturate, the soil, keeping it well drained. Soon, the beginnings of a pineapple plant will appear from the center of the crown.

Fill a container with water. Remove the pit from an avocado and insert toothpicks around the pit's base. Balance the pit atop the container so that its base rests in the water. When roots appear, transplant to a pot or outside garden in warm climates. Tend your avocado tree as it grows.

Remove a healthy leaf from an African violet. Insert the stem in *humus*, rich soil. Provide moderate sunlight and water. Watch as tiny leaves form around the stem.

Do as Shirley does to add lush greenery to your home.

REQUIRED:
- Planters
- Container
- Water
- Soil
- Toothpicks
- Pineapple
- Avocado
- African violet

NATURE LINKS

SKILLS: Vocabulary Development/Sequencing/Drawing/Cutting/Expressive Language

An *ecosystem* is a community and its surroundings: a meadow, a pond, a woodland. The science of *ecology* enhances our understanding that the plants and animals in an ecosystem depend upon each other for survival.

Create Nature Links to demonstrate concretely that living things in an ecosystem are connected. Cut a plant from construction paper. Label the plant "producer." Next, cut a picture of a rabbit. Label the picture "herbivore," plant-eater. Finally, cut a picture of a fox. Label the picture "carnivore," meat-eater.

Show the interdependence of these three components of a meadow ecosystem by punching a hole(s) on the right edge of the plant and the left and right edge of the rabbit. Attach the plant and the rabbit with yarn. Punch a hole(s) on the left edge of the fox. Attach the rabbit and the fox with yarn. In so doing, you've illustrated that the new growth that the plant produces feeds the rabbit, which, in turn, feeds the fox.

Invite your child to explain to all family members the interdependence of living things in an ecosystem.

REQUIRED:
- Construction paper
- Pencil
- Crayons/markers
- Safety scissors
- Hole punch
- Yarn/ribbon/string

SCIENCE ACTIVITIES

BACKYARD BEAUTIES

SKILLS: Vocabulary Development/Observation/Drawing/Recording Data/Making Comparisons

Butterflies are insects. They have three body parts—*head, thorax, abdomen*—and six legs. Their wings, attached to the thorax, are covered with tiny scales.

There are more than twenty thousand different species of butterflies in the world. They come in all colors and range in size from as tiny as a fingernail to as large as a man's hand. While butterflies and moths are alike, butterflies are identified by their slender, hairless bodies; bright colors; and long, slender antennae, each with a knob at the tip.

Work with your second grader to make a *lepidopterist*'s journal of the butterflies you see in your yard or neighborhood. Use a notebook, journal, or papers stapled together in book form. Draw and color each kind of butterfly you see. Observe its appearance and behavior. Record your observations.

Visit your local library to match and compare your findings to those in a book such as *Butterflies and Moths* by Bobbie Kalman and Tammy Everts.

REQUIRED:
- Notebook/journal
- Paper and pencil
- Crayons/markers

OPTIONAL:
- Stapler
- Library/bookstore visit

METAMORPHOSIS MOBILE

SKILLS: Vocabulary Development/Sequencing/Drawing/Cutting

Butterflies pass through the same four stages. A monarch butterfly, for example, presses a tiny *egg* onto a leaf of a milkweed plant. A few days later, a small *caterpillar* or *larva* hatches. For about two weeks, the caterpillar feasts on the milkweed leaf. As it grows, the caterpillar *molts,* breaking out of its old skin, several times.

Now the caterpillar hangs upside down from the stem of a leaf. Its skin splits again and falls off, leaving a wrapped, blanketlike form called the *chrysalis* or *pupa.* The chrysalis changes until it is transparent. Inside, the white dots and orange and black lines of the growing butterfly are visible. Soon the chrysalis wiggles and splits open. The monarch butterfly emerges!

Together, demonstrate the marvelous phenomenon of change by making a Metamorphosis Mobile. Draw, color, and cut out pictures of the egg, caterpillar, chrysalis, and monarch butterfly. Use a needle and thread to connect each stage to the base of a hanger, attaching from left to right.

Hang the mobile for all family members to admire as your young lepidopterist explains the four stages of *metamorphosis.* Read about metamorphosis in a book such as *Monarch Butterfly* by Gail Gibbons.

REQUIRED:
- Paper and pencil
- Crayons/markers
- Safety scissors
- Needle and thread
- Hanger

OPTIONAL:
- Library/bookstore visit

BUTTERFLY LINE

SKILLS: Vocabulary Development/Sequencing/Drawing/Cutting/Written Expression/Poetry

A teeny egg sticks to a leaf,
A caterpillar hatches.
It eats and eats, until it molts,
Onto a stem it latches!

A blanket forms, the chrysalis,
It wraps a wondrous surprise.
In just two weeks, wiggle and split,
Butterfly, before your eyes!

REQUIRED:
• Paper and pencil
• Crayons/markers
• Safety scissors
• Hole punch
• Yarn/ribbon/string

Concretely demonstrate the stages of metamorphosis by creating a Butterfly Line. Draw, color, and cut out pictures of the egg, caterpillar/larva, chrysalis/pupa, and butterfly. Enlarge the size of the tiny egg so that it can be seen and manipulated.

Punch a hole(s) on the right edge of the egg and the left and right edge of the caterpillar. Attach the two figures with yarn, ribbon, or string. Continue in this manner to attach the chrysalis and the butterfly.

Using the model above, work together to create a poem that describes the process of metamorphosis. Display the butterfly line for all to admire as your child poetically presents the marvel of metamorphosis.

MIGRATION MAP

SKILLS: Map Skills/Imaginative Thinking/Written Expression/Point of View

The migration of the monarch butterfly from northern areas of the United States to southern areas of the United States and Mexico is a fascinating phenomenon! Monarch butterflies that hatch in the middle of the summer live for eight to nine months. These butterflies migrate or travel to warmer climates as autumn approaches. As the monarch travels, sometimes nearly one hundred miles a day at nearly twelve miles per hour, others join it. At times, more than one thousand monarchs travel together, flying to the places their ancestors flew. The monarchs remain in their southern home until spring returns. Then they migrate north to the milkweed plants to begin the cycle again!

Invite your child to plan an itinerary for a monarch butterfly as it travels from north to south. Examine a map of North America together. Use common pins to plot the route that your butterfly follows from a northeast state to Florida, from a north central state to Mexico, or from a northwest state to southern California.

Finally, write a travel log, sequentially describing the migration from a butterfly's point of view.

REQUIRED:
• Map of North America
• Common pins
• Paper and pencil

SCIENCE ACTIVITIES

SEEING IS BELIEVING!

SKILLS: Vocabulary Development/Observation/Recording Data/Drawing

Seeing Is Believing! What better way to demonstrate the process of metamorphosis than to witness it firsthand! Give your second grader the wonderful opportunity to watch a caterpillar form a chrysalis and then emerge as a Painted Lady butterfly.

Order a Butterfly Garden, an award-winning product, from Insect Lore. The Butterfly Garden kit includes a butterfly house, butterfly feeding kit, and three to five caterpillars with food and instructions on their care.

The Butterfly Garden is available year-round in the continental United States. If you order the kit in winter, request that it come with a certificate for the caterpillars. When spring arrives and the temperature is sixty degrees or more in the daytime, mail the certificate to Insect Lore. The caterpillars will arrive in approximately ten days.

Encourage your child to record observations and draw pictures of the caterpillars as they change. When the Painted Lady butterflies emerge, observe them for up to a week before releasing them to the world!

Insect Lore
P.O. Box 1535
Shafter, California 93263
1-800-LIVEBUG

Web site: *www.insectlore.com*
E-mail: *insect@lightspeed.net*

REQUIRED:
- Butterfly Garden
- Paper and pencil
- Crayons/markers

SYMMETRICAL ETCH

SKILLS: Vocabulary Development/Drawing/Painting/Symmetry

A butterfly is a *symmetrical* creature. The left side of its body matches the right.

After reading a butterfly book or observing butterflies in your yard or neighborhood, design a butterfly of your own, keeping symmetry in mind. Whenever you purchase fruit, vegetables, or meat packaged on a styrofoam tray, wash and recycle the tray! Cut square or rectangular etching boards from the trays.

Work with your second grader to sketch a symmetrical butterfly on the tray. Use the pencil lightly as you form the head, antennae, thorax, abdomen, and wings. Be careful to match the left side to the right as you form the design on the wings.

Trace over the sketch several times to make a hollow outline of the butterfly. Be careful not to pierce the tray.

Paint over the drawing, using a brush or small roller. Notice that the hollowed outline stays free of paint. Carefully press the painted side to a blank sheet of white construction paper. The outline of the butterfly will appear before you!

Use the butterfly print to make placements, wrapping paper, or greeting cards.

REQUIRED:
- Styrofoam trays
- Pencil
- Paint
- Paintbrush/roller
- Construction paper

OPTIONAL:
- Library/bookstore visit

CAITLIN'S CRITTERS

SKILLS: Imaginative Thinking/Constructing

A student named Caitlin taught us how to make pipe cleaner critters. She learned to make them from a book such as *Pipe Cleaners Gone Crazy: A Complete Guide to Bending Fuzzy Sticks* by Laura Torres and Michael Sherman.

To make a caterpillar, set aside six 12″ pipe cleaners, the fuzzier the better. Fold one pipe cleaner in half. Wrap another pipe cleaner tightly around a pencil. Pull the coiled pipe cleaner off the pencil. Slide the coiled pipe cleaner down one side of the folded pipe cleaner to the fold to make the bottom segment of the caterpillar. Wrap a second pipe cleaner tightly around the pencil to make a coil. Remove from the pencil and slide down both sides of the folded pipe cleaner to meet the bottom segment. Coil and slide the remaining pipe cleaners to form the body of the caterpillar. Curl the ends of the original folded pipe cleaner as antennae.

Challenge your second grader to try other critters. A butterfly or moth is easy to make. Use three or four pipe cleaners, two loosely twisted together and coiled around a pencil for the body and one or two twisted through the body to form the wings and antennae.

REQUIRED:
• Pipe cleaners

OPTIONAL:
• Library/bookstore visit

BUTTERFLIT

SKILLS: Connecting Science & Literature/Imaginative Thinking/Written Expression/Drawing/Cutting

Through the fantasy of children's literature, we learn about butterfly behavior. At the same time, authors provide insight into our reactions to the beautiful butterfly and the special place it holds in our hearts. Visit your library or local bookstore to enjoy butterflies in literature.

In *I Wish I Were a Butterfly,* a tale of friendship and self-esteem by James Howe, a little cricket longs to be a pretty butterfly. A lamb learns to accept the differences of others and the importance of freedom and independence in *The Lamb and the Butterfly* by Arnold Sundgaard. Join Emilio and his *abuelo* (grandfather) as they watch butterflies each sunny morning in *Butterfly Boy* by Virginia Kroll. Discover *The Butterflies' Promise* in the book of the same name by Julie Ovenell-Carter. Delight in the joy a young girl feels as she and her grandfather rescue a caterpillar that soon becomes a Painted Lady butterfly in *Butterfly House* by Eve Bunting.

After sharing a butterfly book, coauthor and illustrate an original story about a butterfly. Combine fact and fantasy as you weave a tale of wonder. You may want to write your story on paper cut in the shape of a butterfly.

REQUIRED:
• Library/bookstore visit
• Paper and pencil
• Crayons/markers

OPTIONAL:
• Safety scissors

SCIENCE ACTIVITIES

DISCOVER A DINO

SKILLS: Vocabulary Development/Sculpting/Drawing/Imaginative Thinking/Measurement

Serious research on dinosaurs did not begin until the first half of the 1800s when, in England, a couple found the large teeth and bones of a giant reptile they named *Iguanodon*. The discovery of Iguanodon by Gideon and Ann Mantell accompanied the discovery of *Megalosaurus* and *Hylaeosaurus*. In 1841, a renowned scientist, Sir Richard Owen, gave these creatures the group name "dinosaurs," a word that means "terrible lizards."

Invite your second grader to Discover a Dino. Using Sculpey or clay, mold a single tooth or bone. From that single *fossil*, draw the skeleton of a new dinosaur. Be sure to include a skull, four leg bones, a backbone, and a tailbone.

From the skeleton, draw and color the dinosaur, covering the body with *scales*. Below the drawing, write the dinosaur's name, length, and weight. Finally, designate whether the dinosaur you've "discovered" is a meat-eater, carnivore, or a plant-eater, herbivore.

To enhance familiarity with dinosaurs, share a book such as *Eyewitness Books, Dinosaur* by David Norman and Angela Milner.

REQUIRED:
- Sculpey/clay
- Paper and pencil
- Crayons/markers

OPTIONAL:
- Library/bookstore visit

BACKDROP HABITAT

SKILLS: Imaginative Thinking/Drawing/Cutting/Sculpting

When dinosaurs roamed the Earth, there were no people, buildings, or highways anywhere. There were sweeping plains, wooded forests, expansive deserts, lakes, ponds, streams, swamps, trees, bushes, ferns, boulders, rocks, and pebbles.

Recreate the environment of the dinosaurs by making a Backdrop Habitat. Use any medium to transform the interior of a shoebox into a prehistoric scene.

Leaves, berries, ferns, and sticks can be made from paper or pipe cleaners. Boulders and rocks can be made from clay. Swamps and streams can be made from crinkled plastic wrap or tissue paper. Use nontoxic craft glue to attach all parts. To authenticate the scene, you may want to gather and attach pebbles, sand, leaves, grass, and sticks.

When the backdrop is complete, sculpt a dinosaur from Sculpey or clay. Stand your dinosaur before the backdrop to bring the world of the "terrible lizards" back to life.

REQUIRED:
- Shoebox
- Art supplies
- Safety scissors
- Nontoxic glue
- Sculpey/clay

OPTIONAL:
- Leaves/grass/sticks

A+ ACTIVITIES FOR SECOND GRADE

FOSSIL FEET

SKILLS: Vocabulary Development/Observation/Sculpting

Fossils are the remains of animals and plants from long ago. Bones, teeth, plants, insects, and even footprints have lain in the ground for millions of years and become fossils that are as hard as rock.

When scientists called *paleontologists* discover dinosaur fossils, they work very carefully to remove them from the ground. It is from the study of these fossils that we learn about prehistoric life on Earth.

Join your second grader to make fossil feet from Sculpey or clay. Roll out a portion of clay on the work surface. Then use a knuckle or blunt end of a pencil to make an imprint of a dinosaur foot. Make a large, rounded footprint of a plant-eater or a smaller, pointed, three-toed footprint of a meat-eater. If you use Sculpey, bake the footprint according to directions.

The next time you visit the beach or lakeside, make and examine footprints and handprints in the sand. Also observe footprints you see in both wet and dry sand. Determine from the size and shape of the print whether it was made by a human being—adult, child, or toddler; by a dog, large or small; or by a bird, web-footed or clawed.

REQUIRED:
- Sculpey/clay
- Pencil

OPTIONAL:
- Beach/lake visit

AN INCREDIBLE TAIL

SKILLS: Vocabulary Development/Imaginative Thinking/Drawing/Sculpting/
Making Comparisons/Expressive Language

The dinosaurs that used their tails to defend themselves were four-footed plant-eaters. Some of these plant-eaters, *Sauropods,* used their long, thin tails as whips. Others, *Ankylosaurs,* had armored tails equipped with bony clubs. Finally, *Stegosaurs,* or plated dinosaurs, had tails with sharp spikes.

To design An Incredible Tail for a dinosaur, refer to a book such as *Dinosaurs Everywhere!* by Carol Harrison. Work together or independently to draw or mold from clay or Sculpey a long, whiplike tail, a clubbed tail, or a spiked tail. Compare your designs and explain the way in which you believe the tail weapon worked.

REQUIRED:
- Sculpey/clay
- Paper and pencil
- Crayons/markers

OPTIONAL:
- Library/bookstore visit

FOSSIL FUN

SKILLS: Vocabulary Development/Following Directions/Recording Data

Fossils are the remains of animals and plants from long ago. A fossil could be an insect or a leaf or the imprint of an animal or plant. Over millions of years, fossils become hard as rock.

With art plaster, you can have Fossil Fun without waiting millions of years to see the results. Mold a lump of modeling clay into a cuplike structure. With care, press a stick, leaf, shell, acorn cap, or any natural item into the bottom of the clay cup. Gently remove the item, making sure the imprint is visible.

According to the directions, prepare the art plaster in a plastic or paper disposable cup. Mix with a plastic spoon. Carefully pour the mixture into the clay cup to cover the imprint. Set aside until hard.

With care, "unearth" your "fossil." Lift the plaster impression out or peel away the clay. Encourage your young paleontologist to create and store a collection of fossils, dating and recording information about each one.

REQUIRED:
- Art plaster
- Leaf/stick/acorn/shell
- Clay
- Paper cup
- Plastic spoon

OPTIONAL:
- Notebook
- Pencil
- Storage container

THE BIG DIG

SKILLS: Vocabulary Development/Drawing/Cutting

Paleontologists are scientists who dig up dinosaurs. They study fossils to learn about the appearance and habits of the reptiles that once inhabited Earth.

In a book such as *Digging Up Dinosaurs* by Aliki, we learn that the job of digging for fossils is not easy. It demands a team of experts, including a *paleontologist,* who studies plants and animals; a *geologist,* who studies rocks and fossils; a *draftsman,* who draws pictures; *workers,* who remove the fossil from rock; and a *photographer,* who takes pictures of the fossils found.

Give your child the chance to reconstruct a dinosaur from its bones. Draw, trace, print out, or photocopy a picture of a dinosaur skeleton. Cut the skeleton into parts. Scatter the parts about your home, placing each under a pillow, book, or magazine. Then begin The Big Dig. Give clues, as necessary, to help your young paleontologist find the bones to fit together.

As an added treat, if you happen to live near a museum with a dinosaur exhibit, pay a visit.

REQUIRED:
- Picture of a dinosaur skeleton
- Safety scissors

OPTIONAL:
- Library/bookstore visit
- Museum visit

REPTILIAN RESTAURANT

SKILLS: Vocabulary Development/Brainstorming/Imaginative Thinking/Making Comparisons/
Written Expression/Drawing

The dinosaurs with sharp, pointed teeth like those of *Tyrannosaurus*, or a sharp, hard beak like that of *Oviraptor,* were meat-eaters, carnivores. The dinosaurs with short, flat teeth like those of *Triceratops,* or long, blunt teeth like those of *Diplodocus*, were plant-eaters, herbivores. Most dinosaurs were herbivores.

Invite your second grader to create an imaginary menu for a carnivore and one for an herbivore, too. Work together to invent such delicious delicacies as fricasseed froggies, poached *Protoceratops*, and leg of lizard for the *carnivorous* dinosaurs, and fried fern salad, baked berry buns, and pine needle popovers for the *herbivorous* dinosaurs.

For each menu, fold a piece of construction paper in half like a greeting card. Put the name of your Carnivore Cafe or Herbivore Eatery on the front cover. Print the menu inside. Use teeth or claws as currency for carnivores and flower petals or acorn caps as currency for herbivores. Add drawings as desired.

When the menus are complete, compare the beverages, appetizers, salads, entrees, and desserts created. Note the differences in the dietary preferences of carnivores and herbivores.

REQUIRED:
- Paper and pencil
- Crayons/markers

GRAPH-A-SAUR

SKILLS: Vocabulary Development/Graphing/Recording Data/Application/
Making Comparisons/Addition/Subtraction

By studying fossils, paleontologists can determine the length of dinosaurs. They have learned that some, like *Compsognathus,* were small—28 inches long—while others, like Diplodocus, were enormous, nearly 90 feet long.

Read a dinosaur book such as *The Time Trekkers Visit the Dinosaurs* by Kate Needham. Make a graph to record the length of each dinosaur you view. Use a ruler to make an 11-column, 10-row graph. Make the first column wide enough to print dinosaur names. Along the base of the graph, from left to right, indicate the length in feet by marking column lines "10 feet," "20 feet," "30 feet," and so on to "100 feet."

Read about a dinosaur. Print its name in column one. When you discover the dinosaur's length, color the bar beside its name to the appropriate length.

When the graph is complete with 10 dinosaur names and lengths, challenge each other to use the data to answer questions such as: "Which dinosaur was the longest?" "Which dinosaur was the shortest?" "Which dinosaur was 10 feet shorter than Tyrannosaurus?" "Which dinosaur was 20 feet longer than Protoceratops?"

REQUIRED:
- Dinosaur books
- Paper and pencil
- Ruler

OPTIONAL:
- Library/bookstore visit

DINOSAUR BANK: Stegosaurus—25 feet   Protoceratops—5 feet   Tyrannosaurus—50 feet
Spinosaurus—40 feet   Troodon—6 feet

ALLOSAURUS TO ZEPHYROSAURUS

SKILLS: Vocabulary Development/Brainstorming/Recording Data

Believe it or not, there are dinosaurs and other prehistoric reptiles whose names begin with letters from *A* to *Z!* As you share dinosaur reading and research with your second-grade paleontologist, keep an *A* to *Z* register of reptile names.

Label the pages of a notebook, pad, or journal from *A* to *Z*, one letter per page. Begin the register by brainstorming and recording prehistoric reptile names. Beside each name, record facts that identify the dinosaur or reptile. Include information such as habitat, dietary preference, and size. Over time, as you share dinosaur books of fact and fiction, your second grader is sure to accumulate information about prehistoric reptiles from *A* to *Z*.

REQUIRED:
- Notebook/pad/journal
- Pencil
- Dinosaur books

OPTIONAL:
- Library/bookstore visit

Next time you visit the library, enjoy *The Dinosaur Alphabet Book* by Jerry Pallotta, a colorful and informative dinosaur ABC.

DINO DIALOGUE

SKILLS: Vocabulary Development/Brainstorming/Researching/Note Taking/Point of View/Oral Expression

Invite your second grader to work on your paleontology team. Read about a favorite dinosaur using a book such as *Prehistoric Animals* by Peter Zallinger.

Before reading, brainstorm three to five questions to research. Write each question on an index card. Focus questions on specific information your young paleontologist seeks, such as size, habitat, diet, and physical characteristics. Take notes on each index card to answer the question posed.

After learning all about the dinosaur, invite your child to play the part of the dinosaur while you play the part of the paleontologist. Hold a dialogue with the dinosaur, engaging your child in a lively discussion. A sample script follows.

Paleontologist: Hello there, Mr./Ms. Dinosaur, and welcome to the twenty-first century! What kind of dinosaur are you?

Dinosaur: I am a Stegosaurus and I'm mighty hungry at the moment.

Paleontologist: Can I get you something to eat?

Dinosaur: That would be terrific! I'd really enjoy the leaves of a palm tree right about now!

REQUIRED:
- Library/bookstore visit
- Index cards
- Paper and pencil

Encourage your young "dinosaur" to use the notes taken as an aid to answering your questions.

LITERASAURUS

SKILLS: Connecting Science & Literature/Vocabulary Development/Imaginative Thinking/Written Expression/Drawing

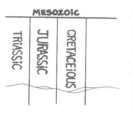

Dinosaurs lived during the *Mesozoic Era*, an era divided into three time periods, including *Triassic,* about 250 million years ago; *Jurassic,* about 200 million years ago; and *Cretaceous*, about 150 million years ago. Although dinosaurs had become extinct by the end of the Cretaceous Period, dinosaurs live on in the imaginations of children. Share dinosaur stories with your young paleontologist to learn facts about these fascinating reptiles through fantasy.

In Marcus Pfister's *Dazzle the Dinosaur,* cheer for Dazzle, an imaginary dinosaur who restores the true home of the *Maiasauruses,* the "Good Mother Lizards," by driving off an imaginary Dragonsaurus. Visit the neighborhood dinosaurs in *Patrick's Dinosaurs,* and learn of the life and times of dinosaurs in *What Happened to Patrick's Dinosaurs?* both by Carol Carrick. See what happens as a dinosaur hatches in *The Dinosaur Who Lived in My Backyard* by B. G. Hennessy and *The Enormous Egg* by Oliver Butterworth. Solve dinosaur mysteries in *Cam Jansen and the Mystery of the Dinosaur Bones* by David A. Adler and *Nate the Great and the Sticky Case* by Marjorie Weinman Sharmat.

REQUIRED:
- Library/bookstore visit
- Paper and pencil
- Crayons/markers

After sharing Literasaurus, encourage your child to write and illustrate an original dinosaur tale by weaving fact and fantasy.

HELLO, WHALE!

SKILLS: Vocabulary Development/Brainstorming/Written Expression/Drawing

Amazingly, prehistoric whales had four legs and lived on land. Fifty million years ago, as whales moved into water, their bodies gradually changed to adapt to the environment. Had they not changed, whales might be *extinct* today. Instead, approximately seventy-six kinds of whales, dolphins, and porpoises are members of an order of animals called *cetacea*. Unfortunately, some of the animals in this order and other wild animals are in trouble. They can't find safe places to live or enough food to eat. Human beings rather than natural phenomena are responsible for the *endangerment* of animals around the world.

REQUIRED:
- Library/bookstore visit
- Paper and pencil
- Crayons/markers
- Safety pins
- Safety scissors
- Envelope
- Stamp

Enhance your child's awareness of our responsibility to animals. Share books such as *Endangered Animals* by Gallimard Jeunesse and Sylvaine Perols or *Will We Miss Them?* by Alexandra Wright to learn about endangered animals such as the manatee, red wolf, koala, and mountain gorilla.

Discuss what you can do to help. Begin a Save the Animals Campaign, making buttons and posters to build awareness. Write to a newspaper or science magazine to express concern about an endangered animal in your area.

SCIENCE ACTIVITIES

THEN THERE WERE NONE

Dinosaurs lived on Earth for 140 million years until they disappeared 65 million years ago. While no one knows what happened to the dinosaurs, there are many possible ideas or theories to explain why these reptiles became extinct.

Since the imagination of second-grade thinkers is sparked when they are given the opportunity to consider possibilities and maybes, ask your second grader to come up with a theory to explain what might have eliminated the dinosaurs. Provide thought starters as needed to initiate the discussion. Ask your child to consider possible causes such as disease or changes in climate.

Welcome and encourage any ideas presented and share your ideas, too. Then, share a book such as *What Happened to the Dinosaurs?* by Franklyn Mansfield Branley to discover whether or not anyone else has considered one of the theories you proposed.

In your travels, visit actual dinosaur sites or museums for a prehistoric experience.

The Dinosaur Museum
754 South 200 West
Blanding, UT 84511
1-435-678-3454
Web site: *www.dinosaur-museum.org*
E-mail: *dinos@dinosaur-museum.org*

Dinosaur State Park
400 West Street
Rocky Hill, CT 06067
1-860-257-7601
Web site: *www.dinosaurstatepark.org*
E-mail: *fdpa@webmaster.snet.net*

REQUIRED:
• Your time
OPTIONAL:
• Library/bookstore visit

PRESERVE AND PROTECT

SKILLS: Written Expression/Business Letter

Discover how your family can help to Preserve and Protect animals, plants, and natural communities. Write a letter to one of several organizations dedicated to research, rescue, protection, and preservation of animals and their environment.

Review the six parts of a business letter: the heading, inside address, salutation/greeting, body, closing, and signature. Whether handwriting or typing, state your ideas clearly and make requests politely. Ask what you can do to help. Adopt a whale, bison, heron, or an acre of the rain forest. Rescue a reef or sponsor a manatee. Preserve the nesting ground of the sandhill crane. Take a stand and send a letter.

Center for Coastal Studies
59 Commercial Street
P.O. Box 1036
Provincetown, MA 02657
1-508-487-3622
Web site: *www.provincetown.com/coastalstudies*
E-mail: *ccc@coastalstudies.org*

International Wildlife Coalition
70 East Falmouth Highway
East Falmouth, MA 02536
1-508-548-8328
Web site: *www.iwc.org*
E-mail: *iwcadopt@capeonramp.com*

The Nature Conservancy
4245 North Fairfax Drive
Suite 100
Arlington, VA 22203
1-703-841-5300
Web site: *www.tnc.org*
E-mail: *comment@tnc.org*

National Audubon Society
700 Broadway
New York, NY 10003
1-212-979-3000
Web site: *www.audubon.org*
E-mail: *webmaster@list.audubon.org*

REQUIRED:
• Stationery
• Pen/pencil
• Envelope
• Stamp

THE GREAT OUTDOORS

SKILLS: Observation/Attributes/Recording Data/Drawing/Making Comparisons

Discover The Great Outdoors with your child. Go for a hike in your yard, city park, or town forest. Walk at the beach or beside a lake. Sharpen observation skills to enhance your second grader's awareness of the environment.

Review safety rules as you provision yourselves with a journal, pencil, magnifying glass, binoculars, insect net, pail, digging implement, drinking water, and any other useful gear. Remember that the property of city, state, and national parks belongs to everyone and must be respected. Follow all posted rules for hiking and collecting.

When on the trail, challenge your second grader to find things based on texture and color: a pinecone, rough and brown; a rock, smooth and gray. Find things based on shape: an oval leaf, a round dandelion. List items observed from *A* to *Z*. Look for birds, lizards, fish, frogs, squirrels, insects. Note the different kinds of trees, plants, and ground cover. Sketch and record observations of particular interest to you. Be sure to include the date so that the next time you hike in the same area, you are able to make comparisons of changes observed.

REQUIRED:
• Hiking gear
• Journal/notebook/pad
• Pen/pencil

STICKY SQUARES

SKILLS: Experimentation/Observation/Making Comparisons/Surveying

Pollutants dirty our environment and affect the health of human beings, animals, and plants. The air we breathe is polluted by unwanted by-products such as chemicals from factories; exhaust from cars, trucks, and buses; and fertilizers and pesticides sprayed by farmers. These chemicals build up and pollute the air. The amount of pollution found in the air depends on where you live. Take a pollution survey to determine how much air pollution exists in your neighborhood.

Cut two 6″ squares from cardboard. Cut a large hole in the center of each square. Cover each hole with clear tape. Poke a hole in the top of each square. Tie a length of string through each hole. Hang one square from a tree branch close to your home. Hang the second square in another location in your neighborhood.

Examine the squares on a daily basis. Observe and compare the pollutants that have attached themselves to the tape on each square. After one week, bring the squares home and observe the pollutants with a magnifying glass. Were the pollutants the same in each area surveyed?

REQUIRED:
• Cardboard
• Safety scissors
• Tape
• String

LEND A HAND

An empty juice bottle sits on the kitchen counter. Newspapers are piled in a wicker basket by the couch. Magazines collect on the coffee table. An empty tuna fish can sits atop the wastebasket beside a cardboard pizza box, crumpled foil, soda cans, and an outgrown pair of sneakers. Trash! We are running out of places to put all the things we throw away.

Lend a Hand in efforts to reduce the amount of solid waste generated every day in homes, schools, offices, and businesses across our country. Talk about what you can do as a family to contribute to reducing what we use, reusing what we can, and recycling items into new materials.

Include your child in the responsibility of sorting and rinsing, when appropriate, glass, plastic, cardboard, and metal containers for recycling. Invite your child to participate in the visit to the recycling center. Suggest that you donate clothes, shoes, and toys that you've outgrown to a local shelter or philanthropic agency and books you've read and outgrown to a needy school, hospital, or child care facility.

By heightening awareness of the need to reduce, reuse, and recycle, you play an essential role in preserving and conserving the resources of Earth.

REQUIRED:
• Recyclable materials

HERBERT'S CORK SHOP

SKILLS: Recycling/Brainstorming/Imaginative Thinking/Painting

One of the most conscientious recyclers and creative artisans we know is our friend Herbert. He recycles corks in useful and artistic ways! While Herbert uses corks to make trivets, coasters, and bulletin boards, your child can use corks to make sailboats, insects, animals, fishing bobbers, robots, castles, or bridges.

Save your corks! While examining them, mention that corks are made from the bark of the cork oak tree, which grows in Portugal, Spain, and Italy.

Provision yourselves with paint, paintbrushes, craft glue, beads, pipe cleaners, toothpicks, colored paper, and cloth swatches. For a sailboat, stick a toothpick in the top center of a cork. Attach a triangular sail cut from cloth and set sail. Make a caterpillar by gluing a line of corks together. Attach pipe cleaners as antennae and legs and beads as eyes. Paint the corks authentically or fancifully. Hatch a butterfly by gluing three corks together, top to bottom, for the head, thorax, and abdomen. Paint the corks and let dry. Shape pipe cleaners into wings and attach. Add eyes and antennae. For a fishing bobber, paint bright stripes around a cork and attach to a fishing line.

Do as Herbert does! Use your imagination to transform versatile corks.

REQUIRED:
• Corks
• Art supplies
• Nontoxic glue
• Safety scissors

LIGHTS OUT!

SKILLS: Vocabulary Development/Surveying/Recording Data/Conserving

Thunder booms, lightening flashes, wind screeches, snow rages, and the lights go out! We light candles, illuminate flashlights, create a cozy atmosphere, and make the best of a power outage . . . for a little while. The cozy effect wears thin when we want to listen to music, heat a pot of soup, cool or heat the room, or watch television. When energy is gone, specifically electrical energy, which we use most, we realize how much we depend upon energy to keep us comfortable and meet our needs. *Energy* is the ability to make things happen!

Provide your child with a pad and pencil to complete an electrical energy survey in your home. Work your way from room to room. Make a list of everything, from the toaster to the ceiling fan, that depends upon electricity to operate.

To conserve energy, ask your second grader to conduct a Lights Out! campaign in your home. When the compact disc player is blaring with no one listening, turn it off! When the television is on with no one watching, turn it off! When the bathroom light is on with no one in the room, turn it off! When the front porch light is left on in the daytime, turn it off!

REQUIRED:
• Pad and pencil

COOL, CLEAR WATER

SKILLS: Vocabulary Development/Experimentation/Observation

In *The Search for Delicious* by Natalie Babbitt, a poll is taken to determine the meaning of delicious. Subjects in the kingdom decide that Cool, Clear Water is the perfect definition.

In order to provide people, animals, and plants with the clean water they need to live, all of us must take responsibility for keeping our oceans, rivers, lakes, ponds, and streams clean. When water is *polluted* by harmful wastes, trash, soil, food, and sewage, that water must be treated so that it is once again clear and clean.

At a water-treatment plant, dirty or polluted water is filtered to make it clear. Water is *aerated* and treated with chemicals to kill germs. Before water leaves a treatment plant, it is tested to ensure that it is safe to drink.

Concretely demonstrate water *filtration*. Stir pepper, dry rice, sand, and pebbles into a glass of water. Use a rubber band to attach a coffee filter or paper towel over a second glass or container. Slowly pour the dirty water onto the filter. Observe and discuss what happens, noting that the water that passes through the filter becomes clear, leaving the residue on the filter.

REQUIRED:
• Two glasses
• Coffee filter/paper towel
• Rubber band
• Small grainy substances

OPTIONAL:
• Library/bookstore visit

A+ ACTIVITIES FOR SECOND GRADE

WISE WATER WATCHER

SKILLS: Brainstorming/Written Expression

Water, water everywhere . . . Did you know that water covers more than 70 percent of Earth's surface and is the most common substance on our planet? Because water "recycles" itself, evaporating into the air from oceans, lakes, and rivers and returning to Earth in some form of precipitation, Earth always has water. Yet, as our demand for water increases, we need to make better use of this essential resource.

Talk with your child about the importance of conserving water, emphasizing that all human beings, plants, and animals need water to survive. Brainstorm a list of all the ways in which we use and depend upon water. Working from your list, design Wise Water Watcher signs to post strategically about your home, on the front of a dishwasher, above a sink, beside the washing machine, or on a bathroom cabinet. On each sign, include a short reminder to help all family members use water wisely.

Please turn water off while you brush your teeth!

Shorten shower time, please!

Turn the faucet all the way off, please!

In your home, do your part to ensure that we always have clean water to meet our needs.

REQUIRED:
- Paper
- Permanent marker
- Tape

E-SHIRT

SKILLS: Brainstorming/Imaginative Thinking/Written Expression/Drawing/Application

While Earth Day, April 22, is a day set aside each year since 1970 to enhance public awareness of environmental issues, each of us can contribute to protecting our air, land, and water from January to December.

Talk with your child about the need to protect our resources. Brainstorm ideas of what you can do individually and collectively to keep Earth clean and healthy. Weave your ideas together to write an original Protect the Earth slogan. Design an illustration to accompany the slogan.

Invite each family member to choose a plain T-shirt from his or her wardrobe to transform into an E-Shirt. Insert cardboard to separate the front of the shirt from the back. Use waterproof markers to copy your slogan and design on your Earth shirt. Wear the shirt proudly, not only on Earth Day but on many days throughout the year. Be sure to practice what your E-Shirt preaches by doing your part to reduce, reuse, and recycle. Pick up litter you see in a park; turn off lights, appliances, and entertainment units when not in use; fix leaky faucets; write letters to voice your concerns about the safety of our planet.

Celebrate Earth Day 365 days a year!

REQUIRED:
- Paper and pencil
- T-shirts
- Waterproof markers
- Cardboard

PAPER MAKER

Paper is made when wood chips are boiled in water, drained, pressed, dried, and rolled. Give your second-grade Paper Maker the opportunity to manufacture homemade paper.

Provision yourselves with newspaper, tissue paper, two sheets of white construction paper, a large pot, a strainer, and a rolling pin. Spread newspaper on a work surface.

Shred the tissue paper. Make a pulplike substance by mixing the tissue paper with warm water. Pour the mixture through a strainer to drain the water. Lay one sheet of construction paper on the newspaper. Spread the mixture on the construction paper. Place the second sheet of construction paper over the mixture. Use the rolling pin to squeeze out excess water. Set aside to dry.

Finally, test your homemade paper. Can you write on it? Is it smooth or rough? Does it tear easily?

As an alternative, repeat the experiment with tissue paper of five or six colors. Use the colorful homemade paper for gift wrap or greeting cards. Additionally, while the paper is still wet, decorate with seeds or dried flowers or leaves for a woodsy effect.

REQUIRED:
- Newspaper
- Tissue paper
- Construction paper
- Pot
- Strainer
- Rolling pin
- Water

OPTIONAL:
- Seeds/flowers/leaves

ENVIRONREAD

Reinforce the need to be environmentally aware by sharing nonfiction books about environmental preservation. Read about the factors that contribute to the pollution of Earth and what you and your second grader can do to help.

Discover why and how to care for our planet by reading *Earth: Where Would We Be Without It?* by Kathy Kranking or *Take Care of Our Earth* by Gare Thompson. Find out how to help preserve nature in *Nature in Danger* by Sally Morgan and Rose Harlow. Understand the need for strong, healthy trees in *Be a Friend to Trees* by Patricia Lauber. Read about the lush rain forest and the need to care for it in *Why Save the Rain Forest?* by Donald Silver. Find out about landfills and recycling in *Where Does the Garbage Go?* by Paul Showers. Learn about the importance of maintaining a clean water supply in *Clean Water (Earth at Risk)* by Karen J. Barss. Finally, read about animals affected by changes in the environment in *Animals in Danger* by Gare Thompson or *Tammy Turtle, A Tale of Saving Sea Turtles* by Suzanne Tate.

Sharing books of this kind is sure to make your child environmentally aware.

REQUIRED:
- Library/bookstore visit

LOST IN SPACE

Children often learn about the solar system during second grade. Boost your young astronomer's familiarity with space terms by creating and completing a word search.

Do a fast-paced, back-and-forth brainstorm to gather words for the search. Make a list of words generated, printing neatly. You say, "Earth." Your child says, "Mars." You say, "moon." Your child says, "star." Continue until you have a list of 15 words. Give your child the list.

Draw a 6″ square on a sheet of graph paper. As your second grader reads one word to you, print that word—vertically, horizontally, or diagonally, one letter per square—within the bounded area. Repeat the process until all words have been printed.

Randomly print letters, one letter per square, until each square in the bounded area holds a letter. Now challenge your child to find and circle all the words that are Lost in Space.

WORD BANK: planet, Mercury, Venus, Earth, Mars, Jupiter, Saturn, Uranus, Neptune, Pluto, sun, moon, comet, asteroid, meteor, galaxy, orbit, rotate, crater, star, shuttle, rocket, astronaut, gravity, constellation, astronomer

REQUIRED:
• Paper and pencil
• Graph paper

STARGAZE

Starlight, starbright, first star I see tonight.
I wish I may, I wish I might,
Have the wish I wish tonight.

When did you last take time to gaze at the stars with your child? On a clear night, find a few minutes to Stargaze.

Pack up a blanket and a thermos of hot chocolate or lemonade. Just before it gets dark, at dusk, go outside to look for stars as they appear in the night sky. As each family member finds a first star, recite the poem and make a wish.

Remain outside as it gets dark to observe the moon and the stars. Comment on the phase of the moon. Look for the North Star in the north sky. Depending on the time of year and where you live, search for constellations, including the Big Dipper, the Little Dipper, and the hunter, Orion. You may even see a shooting star or meteor.

If you happen to live near a planetarium, follow up your stargazing with a visit.

REQUIRED:
• Blanket

OPTIONAL:
• Planetarium visit
• Refreshments

SKY BOX

SKILLS: Observation/Imaginative Thinking/Drawing

Twinkle, twinkle, little star,
How I wonder what you are . . .

JANE TAYLOR

The little star is actually a giant ball of hot, glowing gases.

People have always been fascinated by stars—discovering them, telling tales of their origins, wishing upon them, and finding their way by them. People have also named stars and constellations, groups of stars that form patterns in the sky.

Learn more about and view constellations in books such as *The Big Dipper* and *The Sky Is Full of Stars,* both by Franklyn Mansfield Branley. Use this background knowledge to make a Sky Box.

On a sheet of paper, draw a configuration of stars to form a new constellation. Name the constellation. Line the inside of a shoebox with black construction paper. Hold the shoebox horizontally with the opening facing you. Working together, use a nail to poke holes in the back wall of the shoebox to match the configuration of stars in your constellation.

Pull the shades and turn out the lights. Illuminate a flashlight from behind the Sky Box. Gaze into the Sky Box to view your constellation.

REQUIRED:
- Paper and pencil
- Shoebox
- Construction paper
- Safety scissors
- Nontoxic glue
- Nail

OPTIONAL:
- Library/bookstore visit

MOON WATCH

SKILLS: Vocabulary Development/Observation/Recording Data/Drawing

The moon takes 29½ days to orbit Earth. During the moon's orbit, the moon appears to change. The changes, or *phases,* are caused by the amount of sunlight reflected by the moon toward Earth. The moon has eight phases. Over the course of a month, Moon Watch to observe and record five phases: the *waxing* (increasing) *crescent moon, half moon, full moon, half moon,* and *waning* (decreasing) *crescent moon.*

Make a Moon Watch book from two sheets of folded white paper. Tape the right edge of the first folded sheet to the left edge of the second. Fold accordion style, front to back. Print the title, "Moon Watch," and the name of the moon watcher on the cover.

Check your newspaper for the date of the waxing crescent moon. On that day, moon watch from a window or your yard. Observe, discuss, and draw the waxing crescent moon on the first interior page. Label the page "Waxing Crescent Moon." Encourage your child to record observations.

Follow the same procedure as the moon moves through its phases. Enhance the month-long Moon Watch by reading *Papa, please get the moon for me* by Eric Carle.

REQUIRED:
- Paper and pencil
- Crayons
- Tape
- Newspaper

OPTIONAL:
- Library/bookstore visit

MAN IN THE MOON

SKILLS: Vocabulary Development/Imaginative Thinking/Sculpting/Drawing/Making Comparisons

Has your child ever wondered, "Who is the Man in the Moon?" Has your child ever asked, "Is the moon really made of cheese?"

The dusty and rocky surface of the moon is pocked with *craters* that were formed billions of years ago by falling chunks of metal and rock called *meteorites*. The craters give the moon's surface the look of a man's face or a slice of cheese.

Invite your child to join you as you imagine what the Man in the Moon would look like were he to exist. Provide clay, Play-Doh, or Sculpey, a modeling clay that can be baked in your oven for preservation. Work independently to sculpt your vision of the Man in the Moon. Begin with a smooth ball of clay. Use knuckles or the eraser end of a pencil to depress craters to form a face. Compare the results. As an option, draw the Man in the Moon.

Enjoy more imaginative space travel by sharing *Regards to the Man in the Moon* by Ezra Jack Keats.

REQUIRED:
- Clay/Play-Doh/Sculpey

OPTIONAL:
- Library/bookstore visit
- Paper and pencil
- Crayons/markers

LIGHTWEIGHT

SKILLS: Vocabulary Development/Measurement/Weight/
Recording Data/Calculator/Division/Making Comparisons

The moon's *gravity* is one-sixth of the earth's gravity. An object that weighs 30 pounds on Earth weighs 5 pounds on the moon. Challenge your child to determine the moon weight of each member of your family.

Weigh your child. Record your child's Earth weight on a sheet of paper. Work together, using a calculator to determine your child's weight on the moon. A child who weighs 72 pounds on Earth weighs 12 pounds on the moon, or 72 ÷ 6. A child who weighs 100 pounds on Earth weighs approximately 17 pounds on the moon, or 100 ÷ 6. Record your child's moon weight beside your child's Earth weight.

Repeat the process to give your second grade *astronomer* the opportunity to determine the moon weight of each family member. Discuss and compare all results.

REQUIRED:
- Scale
- Paper and pencil
- Calculator

SCIENCE ACTIVITIES

DAYLIGHT, DARK NIGHT

SKILLS: Vocabulary Development/Experimentation/Observation

Earth *rotates*, spins or turns, on its *axis*. It takes Earth 24 hours, one day, to make one complete *rotation*. A young student on *The Magic School Bus, Lost in the Solar System* by Joanna Cole tells us, "When one side of the Earth faces the sun, it is daytime on that side. When that side turns away from the sun, it is night."

Demonstrate the concept of day and night concretely. You need a flashlight and a sphere—an orange, tennis ball, basketball, or globe.

Stand facing your child. Tell your child to imagine that the sphere is Earth and the flashlight is the sun. As you hold "Earth," your child shines the "sun" directly at Earth. Explain that it is daytime on the side of Earth that faces the sun and night-time on the side of Earth that doesn't face the sun.

Slowly rotate the sphere to demonstrate how day becomes night. Emphasize that it takes 24 hours, one day, for Earth to make one complete rotation.

REQUIRED:
• Sphere
• Flashlight

OPTIONAL:
• Library/bookstore visit

SUNRISE, SUNSET

SKILLS: Observation/Drawing

There is nothing more special than a beautiful sunrise. The birds chirp to welcome a new day. There is nothing more special than a glorious sunset. The birds chirp to wish all a goodnight.

Have you ever stopped to consider that the sun doesn't really rise, move across the sky from east to west, or set! Rather, it is Earth's rotation on its axis that makes the sun appear to rise, move, and set.

Check your newspaper for the time of sunrise. Set the alarm, gather the family, pack the juice and muffins, and head outside to watch a new day begin. Listen to the welcoming birds and enjoy the splash of color across the horizon.

Notice that the sun does appear to rise.

Check your newspaper for the time of sunset. Gather the family once again to watch the day draw to a close. Again, you'll be entertained by the music of the birds as you watch the sun sink slowly in the west. Notice that the sun does appear to set, followed by a vibrant pink and purple sky.

Invite your second grader and all family members to color or "collage" Sunrise, Sunset scenes to capture the beauty of dawn and dusk.

REQUIRED:
• Newspaper

OPTIONAL:
• Crayons/markers
• Pastel tissue paper
• Nontoxic glue
• White construction paper
• Juice/muffins

SILLY SOLAR SYSTEM SENTENCE

SKILLS: Sequencing/Imaginative Thinking/Sentence Construction

Can you remember which planet is closest to the sun? Do you know which planet is farthest from the sun? Is Venus next to Earth or beside Mars?

Help your child remember the order of the nine planets of our solar system from closest to the sun to farthest away by making up a Silly Solar System Sentence.

Use the first letter of each planet, *M*ercury, *V*enus, *E*arth, *M*ars, *J*upiter, *S*aturn, *U*ranus, *N*eptune, and *P*luto to write a sentence whose words begin with *M, V, E, M, J, S, U, N, P,* in that order.

Refer to the sentence as a helpful and concrete mnemonic device to recall the names of the planets in order from Mercury to Pluto.

*M*r. *V*incent *e*ats *m*int *j*elly *s*itting *u*pon *N*ancy's *p*orch.

*M*any *v*ery *e*ager *m*ice *j*ump *s*hyly *u*nder *N*athan's *p*illow.

*M*ost *v*isitors *e*ach *m*orning *j*ust *s*it *u*pon *n*ine *p*lanets.

REQUIRED:
• Paper and pencil

SPACE SHOT

SKILLS: Vocabulary Development/Sequencing

Put on the sunscreen, pack a parka, and travel from the sun to each planet, beginning with Mercury, the planet closest to the sun, and ending with Pluto, farthest from the sun. As you travel the planetary path, familiarize your child with the names and order of planets while dodging asteroids, comets, and meteors!

Make the Space Shot gameboard from a file folder. Open the folder vertically. In the lower left-hand corner, draw a yellow circle labeled "Sun." In the upper right-hand corner, draw a smaller circle labeled "Pluto." Draw a winding path of 15 stars and 8 circles to connect the Sun to Pluto. Beginning in the lower left-hand corner, label the circles, in order: "Mercury," "Venus," "Earth," "Mars," "Jupiter," "Saturn," "Uranus," and "Neptune," one planet per circle. In the stars, write messages such as: "Pulled by gravity; go back 2." "Chase comet; thrust ahead 3." "Caught in asteroid belt; lose 1 turn." "Discover new star; go ahead 2." Use buttons or coins as game pieces.

Place game pieces on the Sun. Alternate turns. Toss a die, move that number of spaces, read the message, and act accordingly. Land on a planet and take another turn. The first player to reach Pluto is the winner.

REQUIRED:
• File folder
• Pencil/marker
• Die
• Game pieces

PLANETARY POSTCARDS

SKILLS: Facts & Details/Expressive Language/Written Expression/Drawing/Oral Reading Fluency

In July 1969, American astronaut Neil Armstrong visited the moon. At the start of the twenty-first century, invite your second-grade astronaut to visit one of the planets.

In preparation for the voyage, share a book such as *Postcards from Pluto, A Tour of the Solar System* by Loreen Leedy. Join six children as they travel about the solar system, writing postcards to friends and relatives at home. Learn basic facts about the sun and the planets. Discuss the information gathered in concrete terms that your second grader can understand.

Encourage your child to design, write, and "send" you a postcard from one of the planets as you do the same from another. Draw an illustration of the planet on one side of a 4″ × 6″ index card. Divide the other side in half, reserving the left portion for the message; the right, for the address. Include factual information about the planet in the message.

Place the Planetary Postcards in your mailbox and retrieve with the next delivery of your mail. Alternate turns reading each other's postcards aloud. Comment on the amazing planets visited and described.

REQUIRED:
- Paper and pencils
- Crayons/markers
- Index cards
- Library/bookstore visit

PLANET PRO

SKILLS: Vocabulary Development/Researching/Referential Writing/Drawing/Sculpting

An astronomer is a scientist who studies celestial bodies. Invite your second grader to work on your astronomy team to research a favorite planet. Visit your local library to find two or three books such as *The Planets in Our Solar System* by Franklyn Mansfield Branley to bring home.

Before reading the books, brainstorm three to five questions to research. Write each question on an index card. Focus questions on specific information your young astronomer seeks, such as size, location, duration of day and year, appearance and number of moons. Keep the topics manageable. Take notes on each index card to answer the question posed. Work together to organize the cards so that the information is logically sequenced.

Develop a topic sentence that states the main purpose of the research: "Jupiter is a fascinating planet." Then write the report, including the information gathered to support the main idea. Conclude with a sentence such as, "It is clear that the largest planet in our solar system is extraordinary." Bind the report in book form. Encourage your child to draw illustrations, add pictures, or make a clay model of the planet.

REQUIRED:
- Library visit
- Index cards
- Paper and pencil

OPTIONAL:
- Crayons/markers
- Safety scissors
- Clay
- Magazines
- Hole punch
- Yarn/ribbon/string for binding

AGING GRACEFULLY

SKILLS: Calculator/Multiplication/Division/Making Comparisons

 It takes Earth about 365 days to orbit the sun. An Earth year is thus 365 days. The closer a planet is to the sun, the shorter the duration of that planet's "year." The farther a planet is from the sun, the longer the duration of that planet's "year."

Use the chart below to determine your child's age on each planet.

Planets	Length of Year
Mercury	88 days
Venus	About 225 days
Earth	About 365 days
Mars	About 2 Earth years
Jupiter	12 Earth years
Saturn	About 30 Earth years
Uranus	84 Earth years
Neptune	165 Earth years
Pluto	248 Earth years

Record your child's Earth age. Label the age, "Earth Age." Work together using a calculator to determine your child's age on each planet. A child who is 7 years old on Earth is 210 years old on Saturn (7 × 30 years). A child who is 8 years old on Earth is about 2 years old on Mercury. (Multiply 8 × 88 days = 704 days. Divide 704 days by 365 days = 1.9 years or about 2 years old.) Record your child's age on each planet. Discuss and compare results.

For added challenge, calculate the age of another family member on each planet.

REQUIRED:
• Paper and pencil
• Calculator

HANDS-ON PLANET

SKILLS: Researching/Facts & Details/Constructing/Painting

Planet facts and details are astounding! Mercury is covered with craters. Venus is engulfed in poisonous yellow clouds. Nearly three-quarters of Earth's surface is water. Mars is the red planet. Jupiter has colorful stripes. Saturn is surrounded by rings. Uranus, a blue green gas planet, has at least 15 moons. Neptune is a giant gas planet. Pluto is the smallest planet.

Perhaps your second-grade astronomer is fascinated by one of the planets in particular. Construct the planet using factual information, imagination, a balloon, flour, water, newspaper, and paint. Inflate a round balloon and set aside. Tear strips of newspaper to dip into a liquid paste of flour and water. Pat the wet strips onto the entire surface of the balloon in layers. When dry, paint the planet using photos or illustrations as a guide.

Encourage your child to use recycled materials to enhance the authentic appearance of the planet. For example, after painting Venus, drape it in wispy cotton painted yellow to replicate the sulfuric acid contained in its clouds.

With imagination sparked, your second grader may want to construct every planet! Vary the size of balloons as appropriate.

REQUIRED:
- Balloon
- Newspaper
- Flour
- Water
- Paint and paintbrush
- Reference books

OPTIONAL:
- Recycled materials
- Safety scissors
- Library/bookstore visit

BLAST-OFF BOOKS

SKILL: Connecting Science & Literature

Enjoy any one of myriad books to learn more about the solar system.

Join Ms. Frizzle and her students as they step aboard *The Magic School Bus, Lost in the Solar System* by Joanna Cole, or travel with Amanda in *Amanda Visits the Planets* by Gina Ingoglia. Fly kites on windy Jupiter and play hide-and-seek among Saturn's moons as you explore space with a group of playful dogs in *Dogs in Space* by Nancy Coffelt. Finally, enjoy the chapter book *Planet Pee Wee* by Judy Delton to discover what a group of students do to win a trip to Camp Blast-Off.

Enhance your child's knowledge of the sun and other stars by reading books such as *Stars* by Seymour Simon and *I Can Read About the Sun and Other Stars* by Richard Harris. Discover amazing facts about comets, meteors, and asteroids in a book such as *Comets, Meteors, and Asteroids* by Seymour Simon.

Learn about the phases of the moon in *What the Moon Is Like* by Franklyn Mansfield Branley.

Whatever your selection, your second grader is sure to be starstruck by the wealth of information found in Blast-Off Books.

REQUIRED:
- Library/bookstore visit

CEREAL BOX ROBOT

SKILLS: Brainstorming/Drawing/Imaginative Thinking/Constructing/Written Expression

While most robots are computer-controlled machines that look nothing like human beings, anthropoid robots, like those featured in science fiction movies and television programs, resemble mechanical people.

Build an anthropoid Cereal Box Robot together. For the torso, cover an empty cereal box with foil or shiny wrapping paper. Cover a smaller box, such as an empty box of instant rice, with tissue paper to attach as the head. For arms and legs, use spaghetti boxes, shoeboxes, or paper towel or toilet paper tubes cov-
ered in shiny paper. Use paper fasteners to connect two boxes or tubes for jointed arms and legs. Attach paper-covered recycled yogurt containers as hands and feet, with pipe cleaners, lollipop sticks, or Popsicle sticks as fingers and toes. Recycled parts from broken devices, nuts, bolts, screws, and buttons function well as facial features, dials, switches, and levers. Encourage imaginative thinking as you gather and use an array of materials.

When your robot is complete, write a short paragraph that tells its name and function. As an option, construct a more conventional robot that does not resemble a human being.

REQUIRED:
- Paper and pencil
- Recycled materials
- Shiny paper
- Nontoxic glue
- Stapler/tape
- Safety scissors
- Paper fasteners

INNER WORKINGS

SKILL: Observation

Have you ever wondered what is inside a clock, watch, computer, or radio? Examine the Inner Workings of broken or unwanted mechanical and electrical devices in your home.
Together, find and disassemble an old, unwanted wristwatch. Inside a mechanical watch, find and examine the springs and wheels. Speculate how the springs and wheels work together to make the watch run efficiently. Inside a digital watch, find and examine the microchip and battery.

Unplug and disassemble a broken telephone. Locate the circuit board, the area in which the components of the telephone's electronic circuit are housed. Point out the metal tracks on the board that connect all of the components.

Examine the inside of an old computer mouse. Handle the ball that helps move the mouse. Unplug and examine the inside of the computer itself. Locate the microchips that store information in the form of electronic charges.

By disassembling and examining devices around you, your second grader will have enhanced understanding of how things work.

REQUIRED:
- Broken/unwanted devices

IN A HEARTBEAT

SKILLS: Vocabulary Development/Experimentation/Counting/Recording Data/Prediction/Making Comparisons

The heart pumps blood to each part of the body. When resting, an adult's heart beats approximately 60 to 70 times per minute. When exercising, an adult's heart beats more than 150 times per minute to ensure that each muscle receives enough oxygen and nourishment to work efficiently. Demonstrate the difference between *resting heart rate* and *active heart rate*.

Place two fingers on either side of the windpipe to feel the pulse of blood traveling to and from the heart. Set a timer to 60 seconds. Count the number of beats. Record this number as the resting heart rate. Compare your child's resting heart rate to yours. Predict and record whether the heart rate will increase, decrease, or stay the same after two minutes of exercise.

Next, set the timer to two minutes and run in place. Immediately following the exercise, reset the timer to 60 seconds and count the number of beats again. Record this number as the active heart rate. Compare active heart rate to resting heart rate for you and your child. Does the heart beat faster after exercise? Does an adult's heart beat faster than a child's? Discuss all findings.

REQUIRED:
- Paper and pencil
- Timer

PRACTICAL PYRAMID BUILD

SKILLS: Vocabulary Development/Drawing/Categorizing

Protein-rich, vitamin-enriched, fat-free, low-fat, polyunsaturated fat, saturated fat, cholesterol-free, low-sodium . . . what does it all mean? When you and your child discuss *nutrition*, the science that deals with food and how the body uses it, you need only focus on the importance of a balanced diet.

Since health is directly affected by what we eat, the United States Department of Agriculture developed the Food Guide Pyramid to demonstrate recommended amounts to eat from each of the major food groups. Build a food pyramid for your kitchen. Draw a large triangle on construction paper. Make three horizontal lines to split the pyramid into four sections. Label the largest section at the base, "Grains—bread, cereal, rice, pasta." Use a vertical line to split the next section in half. Label the left portion "Vegetables" and the right, "Fruits." Moving up, split the next section in half, labeling the left "Dairy—milk, butter, yogurt, cheese," and the right, "Meat—chicken, beef, pork, fish, eggs." Label the smallest section at the top, "Fats—oils, sweets."

Post the completed pyramid in the kitchen on the refrigerator door so that your young *nutritionist* can remind everyone of the foods necessary to ensure a balanced diet.

REQUIRED:
- Paper and pencil
- Ruler

PRACTICAL PYRAMID TALLY

SKILLS: Categorizing/Tallying

Once you have built and posted a Food Guide Pyramid as described in Practical Pyramid Build, invite your young nutritionist to put a tally mark in the appropriate area of the pyramid for each food served at breakfast, lunch, and dinner. At the end of the day, total the tally to determine whether your diet on that day was a balanced one including recommended portions of grains, fruits, vegetables, dairy products, meat products, and fats. The number of tally marks in each section of the pyramid should decrease as you move from bottom to top. If all areas are represented, with the greatest number of portions moving from bottom to top, your diet for that day was balanced.

To learn more about nutrition and recommended daily portions in each food group, visit the library or bookstore to share books such as *The Food Pyramid (True Books, Food & Nutrition)* by Joan Kalbacken or *The Edible Pyramid: Good Eating Every Day* by Loreen Leedy.

REQUIRED:
• Paper and pencil
• Three meals

OPTIONAL:
• Library/bookstore visit

PAPER PLATE NUTRITION

SKILLS: Brainstorming/Imaginative Thinking/Cutting/Sorting/Tallying

A balanced diet includes foods from each of the five major food groups. Work with your young nutritionist to make three paper plate collages, each showing a menu for a healthy meal at breakfast, lunch, and dinner.

Look for pictures of grains, including bread, cereal, rice, and pasta; fruits; vegetables; dairy products; and meat products in recyclable magazines and newspapers. Cut out a collection of pictures to spread before you. The labels from product bags, boxes, and cans also work well. Sort pictures and labels into the five food groups.

Brainstorm a breakfast menu. Look through your collection to select the meal. Arrange the pictures and labels on one paper plate. Attach with glue when satisfied with the design. Repeat the process for lunch and dinner, too!

When all three collages are created, do a tally of grains, fruits, vegetables, dairy products, and meat products included in your menus. Determine whether or not you have created a balanced diet for the day.

To follow up the artistry, actually prepare each paper plate meal for your family's good health and nutrition. Then enjoy a book such as *Gregory the Terrible Eater* by Mitchell Sharmat.

REQUIRED:
• Paper plates
• Magazines/newspapers
• Safety scissors
• Nontoxic glue

OPTIONAL:
• Library/bookstore visit
• Three meals

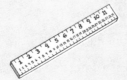

SOCIAL STUDIES

Stand before a pond or puddle. Toss a small stone into the water. Watch one circular ripple surround the stone. See the ripple journey outward to form a second, a third, and a fourth. The stone is your child; the first ripple, your family; the second, your neighborhood; the third, your country; the fourth, your world.

The activities that follow take you and your child on a journey from self-awareness to social action, from pride of self and family to celebration of our global community. Because celebration of and respect for others comes from self-pride and self-respect, we begin with a focus on your child and family. You'll have the opportunity to chronicle each year of your child's life with pictures, write self-pride poetry, design T-shirt dreams of freedom, establish a family creed, construct a Family Totem Pole, meet your ancestors, and make a peek-a-boo model of your home.

From self and family, the journey takes you to your neighborhood. Profile Positive Impact People who have, by their example, inspired you to acts of kindness that benefit others. Learn more about the events that shape your community. Get the scoop in newspapers and children's magazines, and speak up and be heard to clean up a park or enhance safety at a pedestrian crossing.

Next, journey to your country. Because second graders appreciate other times and places, create the rock art of the Ancient Ones, the first inhabitants of North America. Adopt a magical, musical name in the tradition of our Native American forebears, and catch a dream with the Chippewa. Keep a sailor's log of a voyage with Columbus; time travel to the settlement of Plymouth and observe Thanksgiving with a Cornucopia of Thanks. Create a collage of your state; get to know a president and run a political campaign as you learn about your country, then and now.

Finally, journey the world. Enhance map skills with compass rose creations and a world map gameboard. Capitalize on your second grader's eagerness to learn about people and customs of other cultures. Explore a country each month without leaving your home, and enjoy a fashion parade of traditional costumes from continent to continent. Feast on international foods and construct the igloo of the Eskimo, the tepee of the Plains tribes, the wigwam of the Algonquian, and the hogan of the Navajo. Build the pagoda of Asia and the round house of Africa. Finally, celebrate the children of our global community. Create a tree for children, each leaf and fruit the face of one of the inheritors of our world.

AUTOBIO-LINE

SKILLS: Sequencing/Brainstorming/Written Expression/Drawing/Cutting

Celebration of and respect for others comes from celebration of and respect for self. During second grade, children enjoy learning about the culture and tradition of people from around the world. They also enjoy sharing information about themselves.

In celebration of and respect for who you are, work together to create a chronological Autobio-Line of your second grader. Brainstorm ideas before deciding upon symbols to pictorially represent each year of your child's life. Using construction paper, draw, cut out, and decorate each picture. Punch holes on the right edge of the first-year picture and the left and right edges of the second-year picture. Attach the two pictures with yarn or ribbon. Continue in this manner until you have a line of seven or eight connected pictures, one for each year of your child's life.

Look at family photos. Talk about milestones for each year. Work together to write on separate sheets of paper a short paragraph to tell about each year. Attach each paragraph to its corresponding picture.

When the Autobio-Line is complete, display for the family to share. Add a picture and a paragraph at birthday time each year.

> **REQUIRED:**
> • Construction paper
> • Safety scissors
> • Hole punch
> • Yarn/ribbon
> • Paper and pencil
> • Crayons/markers
>
> **OPTIONAL:**
> • Family photos

SELF-PRIDE POETRY

SKILLS: Brainstorming/Written Expression

Each of us is unique and special. Each of us is celebrated yearly on the day of our birth. Extend that celebration to every day by writing and sharing Self-Pride Poetry.

Poems capture feelings, emotions, imaginations, and dreams. In a range of structures and shapes, poems often express thoughts that would otherwise remain unspoken. Encourage your child and each family member to celebrate the self by writing a poem.

Suggest that your second grader try an acrostic. Each line of the poem begins with the letters, in sequence, of your child's name. Before writing, talk about what makes your child unique. List activities enjoyed: sports, stamp collecting, reading, painting. List physical characteristics: golden skin, curly hair, green eyes, long legs. List personal qualities that demonstrate character: kind, sensitive, patient, responsible, funny. Weave your ideas together, playing with language, so that your child's name becomes the structure for the poem.

As she plays her guitar,
Notes dance. She sings of
New hope when
Evening sunsets paint the sky.

> **REQUIRED:**
> • Paper and pencil

As an option, write free verse, rhyme, or shape poems. The structure is secondary to the poetic celebration of self. When each member of the family has completed a poem, set aside time to share and celebrate who you are.

DREAM WORKS

SKILLS: Brainstorming/Imaginative Thinking/Written Expression/Drawing/Application

The Declaration of Independence reads, "We hold these truths to be self-evident; that all men are created equal." The great civil rights leader, Dr. Martin Luther King, Jr., believed in these words and worked unceasingly to validate them in practice. Dr. King's dream for equality should be celebrated 365 days a year.

Talk with your child about equal rights. Brainstorm ideas of what you can do to ensure that all people have the same opportunities and rights in regard to education, housing, healthcare, jobs, and recreation. Emphasize the importance of having freedom to pursue your dreams.

Transform a plain white T-shirt into a "D-shirt." First, draw your dream. Insert cardboard to separate the front of the shirt from the back. Use waterproof markers to copy your drawing on the front of the shirt. On the back, write a phrase to state your dream: "I dream of designing buildings." "I dream of exploring outer space." "I dream of composing a symphony." "I dream of curing diseases." "I dream of sailing ships." "I dream of saving endangered animals."

As an option, draw dreams on posters, placemats, hats, and homemade greeting cards.

REQUIRED:
- Paper and pencil
- T-shirts
- Waterproof markers
- Cardboard

OPTIONAL:
- Construction paper
- Hats
- Crayons/markers

ROUND ROBIN DREAMS

SKILLS: Brainstorming/Expressive Language

While the third Monday in January is set aside each year to honor slain civil rights advocate, Dr. Martin Luther King, Jr., one need not wait until that day to reflect and act upon his dream of equality for all people. When children recognize the value that adults place upon respect for human differences, children embrace this value as well. They carry respect for human differences forward into the twenty-first century as they become the caretakers of our planet.

Talk with your child about Dr. King and share . . . *If You Lived at the Time of Martin Luther King* by Ellen Levine. Discuss personal dreams; dreams for family and friends; dreams for your community, your country, and the world. Consider what you can do individually and collectively to celebrate our world of differences.

Share Round Robin Dreams in the car on the way to visit relatives, at a restaurant while waiting for your order, at an airport gate while waiting to board a plane. Go around the group as each family member shares a dream.

Finally, celebrate diversity as you read stories such as *The Araboolies of Liberty Street* by Sam Swope or *All the Colors of the Earth* by Sheila Hamanaka.

REQUIRED:
- Your time

OPTIONAL:
- Library/bookstore visit

SOCIAL STUDIES ACTIVITIES

FAMILY RIGHTS

SKILLS: Brainstorming/Written Expression

The Constitution of the United States begins with 10 amendments known as the Bill of Rights. These amendments protect the rights of all American citizens. Our rights include the right to talk about ways to improve government and the right to express personal opinions, beliefs, and ideas. Discuss the need for these rights and what might happen if these rights were revoked. Then, work with your child to create a Bill of Rights for your family.

Brainstorm rights that both you and your second grader feel are important for all family members. Begin each statement with: "Each family member has the right to . . ." Ideas might include: "express hopes and dreams," "express opinions," "suggest family activities," "offer ideas for family celebrations." Share the list with everyone in the family so that everyone takes part in developing the document.

Decorate a large sheet of construction paper headed, "Our Family's Bill of Rights." Neatly copy the list of rights generated. Post the document in a prominent place so that everyone can put good thinking to practice.

REQUIRED:
- Paper and pencil
- Construction paper
- Crayons/markers

FAMILY TOTEM POLE

SKILLS: Vocabulary Development/Brainstorming/Imaginative Thinking/Sculpting/Painting

Native American families and clans acknowledged, celebrated, and recorded family history on a *totem pole,* a large log of up to 60 feet, erected in front of the home. The carved figures, stacked one on top of the other, represented ancestral beings called *totems.* Work together to design and build a miniature totem pole for your family.

Provision yourselves with a supply of Sculpey, a modeling and baking clay that is available in craft shops. Prior to sculpting, encourage all participants to sketch one segment of the totem pole. Decide who is sculpting whom. Include one segment for each family member and pet.

Work individually and collaboratively to sculpt figures of approximately the same size. Use a range of colors, adding hair, eyes, nose, mouth, and limbs. Use toothpicks to add texture.

Stack the totems on a cookie sheet. Preheat the oven to 275° Fahrenheit and follow directions provided for baking.

Remove from the oven and cool. Place your totem pole in a position of honor in celebration of your family.

For a glimpse of an authentic totem pole of the Tsimshian tribe of the Pacific-Northwest, read *Totem Pole* by Diane Hoyt-Goldsmith.

REQUIRED:
- Paper and pencil
- Sculpey
- Cookie sheet
- Toothpicks

OPTIONAL:
- Library/bookstore visit

GENERATION TO GENERATION

SKILLS: Cultural & Family Awareness/Expressive Language/Written Expression

A photograph of a young couple standing by a fence hangs on the wall. You see it every day but rarely stop to look at the people who look out at you. The picture was taken nearly a century ago in a country different from your own. The people are your great-great-grand-parents on their wedding day. You never met them. You may not even know their first names. They are your ancestors, those who came before you.

Take time to introduce your child to the grandparents and parents of your parents through pictures, if available, and anecdotes. Talk about the origins of your family so that your child recognizes the connection from Generation to Generation. Keep the stories of your family's roots alive as you yourselves add new chapters.

Work with your second grader to update family photo albums by adding captions and dates to old entries and new. The people and places in the photos are a lasting record of your branch on the family tree.

Finally, share the stories of families who emigrate to America in *The Keeping Quilt* by Patricia Polacco and *Grandfather's Journey* by Allen Say.

REQUIRED:
- Photographs
- Picture albums
- Pen/pencil

OPTIONAL:
- Library/bookstore visit

HOME SWEET HOME

SKILLS: Drawing/Cutting

Click your heels together three times like Dorothy in *The Wizard of Oz* and say, "There's no place like home, there's no place like home . . ." To celebrate your home, create a lift-up peek-a-boo model of your home.

Use a large piece of construction paper, your choice of color, as the outside of the model. Hold the paper vertically. Fold in half from top to bottom. With the fold at the top, draw and cut out your home, leaving the fold intact so that you can lift up the paper.

Trace your home onto a piece of white construction paper. Cut out and paste inside the folded paper. On the white paper, draw and color the inside of your home. Add stairways, rooms, closets, furniture, and knickknacks, taking care to include details.

With the interior design complete, on the front of your home, cut out three sides of doors and windows that lift up or out to give a peek at the interior. Finally, glue the back of the colored model to a larger sheet of paper. Using art supplies, add outdoor trimmings to depict your yard or neighborhood. Invite all family members to "tour" your model of Home Sweet Home.

REQUIRED:
- Construction paper
- Safety scissors
- Nontoxic glue
- Pencil
- Crayons/markers
- Art supplies

DREAM HOUSE

SKILLS: Surveying/Recording Data/Imaginative Thinking/Drawing/Constructing

According to Mr. Plumbean of *The Big Orange Splot* by Daniel Manus Pinkwater, "My house is me and I am it. My house is where I like to be and it looks like all my dreams."

Do as Plumbean does. Design and draw a house that is a reflection of all your dreams. As the architect who designs the structure, your child surveys each member of the family to discover and record dreams and wishes. Perhaps Mom dreams of being a famous golf pro, Dad a renowned chef, Sister an accomplished artist, and Brother a talented musician. Remind your child to include personal wishes and dreams in the survey.

With wishes in hand, discuss possibilities: a golf-bag chimney, muffin-shaped windows, painted sidewalks, a violin-shaped front door, and, for your child, the future astronaut, the whole house shaped like a rocketship.

Use art supplies to draw or construct your family Dream House. Recycled boxes and juice and milk containers work well as basic structures. When the house is complete, let it serve as a model. On your next day at home, each family member can draw or construct an individual dream house to create a fantasy community.

REQUIRED:
- Paper and pencil
- Art supplies
- Recycled containers

OPTIONAL:
- Library/bookstore visit

POSITIVE IMPACT PEOPLE

SKILLS: Brainstorming/Written Expression/Drawing

A hero, as defined in the dictionary, is a person of distinguished courage or ability, admired for brave deeds and noble qualities. A hero as depicted on television and in movies is often one who leaps tall buildings or rids a community of some kind of menace. A hero, in actuality, is one whom we admire and acknowledge for examples set in dependability, sensitivity, perseverance, courage, intelligence, and kindness.

Tell your second grader about people who have had a positive impact on you. Mention a teacher who encouraged you; a coworker who praised you; a grandmother who took time to show interest in your accomplishments; a father who celebrated your piano playing even when you missed a note; a scientist, sports figure, musician, author, or actor who inspired you.

Ask your youngster to name a person of positive impact. As you draw a portrait of your hero, ask your child to do the same. When you write a paragraph that explains why this person is your hero, ask your child to write one, too. Attach your paragraphs to the corresponding portraits. If the designated hero is someone you know or someone you can contact, present your work in tribute and recognition.

REQUIRED:
- Paper and pencil
- Crayons/markers

ACTS OF KINDNESS

SKILLS: Brainstorming/Application

Your child may know that not all people in the world have homes, clothing, and food. Some people do not have the comforts that many take for granted.

Brainstorm ways to help people in need. Gather old clothes from family members and neighbors. Donate clothing, blankets, linens, and personal hygiene products to an agency such as the Salvation Army or Morgan Memorial Goodwill Industries, Inc. Collect canned goods for a local food drive. Gather unwanted toys, books, and games in good condition to donate to a local shelter or daycare center. On Halloween, collect money for UNICEF, the United Nations Children's Fund, or donate surplus candy to needy children in your community. After a family gathering, deliver surplus food to a local soup kitchen.

Encourage your second grader to be an active member of the community who, through acts of kindness and generosity, sets an example for others.

UNICEF Headquarters
UNICEF House
3 United Nations Plaza
New York, NY 10017
1-212-326-7000
Web site: *www.unicef.org*

Salvation Army National Headquarters
615 Slaters Lane
P.O. Box 269
Alexandria, VA 22313
1-800-SAL-ARMY
Web site: *www.salvationarmyusa.org*

Morgan Memorial Goodwill Industries, Inc.
1010 Harrison Avenue
Boston, MA 02119
1-800-664-6577
Web site: *www.goodwill.org*

REQUIRED:
• Your time

EVENTS OF THE DAY

SKILLS: Facts & Details/Current Events

Second graders are curious about events that shape the community, country, and world.

Peruse the front page of your local newspaper. Point out, read, and discuss headlines. Browse sections of the newspaper to find, read, and discuss stories that focus on community, national, and world news.

While the newspaper is a rich resource, developmentally appropriate publications specifically written for young readers are available at newsstands and by subscription.

Consider magazines such as *Time for Kids (News Scoop Edition)* and *Sports Illustrated for Kids*. These wonderful resources include stories on a range of topics from the environment to the Women's World Cup.

Whatever resources you use, your child will benefit from a daily dose of current events.

Time for Kids
1271 Avenue of the Americas
New York, NY 10020
1-800-777-8600
Web site: *www.timeforkids.com*
E-mail: *privacy@pathfinder.com*

Sports Illustrated for Kids
PO Box 6001
Tampa, FL 33660
1-800-423-7771
Web site: *www.sikids.com*
E-mail: *sikids_inbox@sikids.com*

REQUIRED:
• Newspaper or magazine

SPEAK UP AND BE HEARD!

SKILLS: Brainstorming/Written Expression

A community is a group of people living in the same locality and under the same government. In order for a community to thrive, its residents must embrace a common set of values.

Consider this. On the day after a local election, children arrive at school to find the front lawn littered with campaign posters of the previous day. The children express concern that the posters left in the yard are not only an eyesore but also a safety hazard to anyone who might trip on the debris. What can they do?

Supervised, the children work to remove the litter. Then they write a letter to the editor of the local newspaper. A few days later they are delighted to see their letter in print and satisfied to know their concerns are heard.

In any situation of concern that arises in your neighborhood or community, encourage your child to Speak Up and Be Heard. Work together to plan, draft, and send a letter to the proper authority so that the issue in question can be resolved in a timely and sensible manner. The broken swing in the park will be fixed, the sidewalk repaired, the stop sign posted.

REQUIRED:
• Paper and pencil
• Envelope
• Stamp

A+ ACTIVITIES FOR SECOND GRADE

ROCK ART

SKILLS: Vocabulary Development/Imaginative Thinking/Drawing/Painting

Throughout the southwestern portion of the United States, in New Mexico, Arizona, Colorado, and Utah, pictures of people, turtles, snakes, deer, birds, plants, handprints, and spirits have been found painted on or chipped into stone. The painted images are *pictographs*. The chipped images are *petroglyphs*. Both are the art of the first people to inhabit North America thousands of years ago. The images are magical, a recording of the spiritual and daily life of the Ancient Ones.

Share *Stories on Stone, Rock Art: Images from the Ancient Ones* by Jennifer Owings Dewey. Learn more about these ancient creations as you view illustrations of the primitive drawings of *paleo-Indians*. Then, try your hand at drawing or painting images on stone.

Collect small solid-color rocks or stones with smooth, flat surfaces. Sketch drafts of drawings to put on the stones. Use felt tip pens or acrylic paints to transfer your work to the rocks. Either replicate the images of the Ancient Ones or paint images that depict some aspect of family life today. Who knows? Perhaps one day thousands of years from now, your Rock Art will be discovered by those who follow.

REQUIRED:
- Paper and pencil
- Paint/paintbrush
- Felt tip pens
- Rocks/stones

OPTIONAL:
- Library/bookstore visit

MAGICAL, MUSICAL NAMES

SKILLS: Brainstorming/Imaginative Thinking

Enjoy the magic and music of Native American legends, stories handed down from generation to generation.

In the Blackfeet Indian tale *The Legend of Scarface,* adapted by Robert San Souci, Scarface, a boy with a scarred cheek, selflessly saves Morning Star. Father Sun touches Scarface on his cheek and bids him return to his village. ". . . [H]e was called 'Scarface' no longer, but 'Smoothface.'"

In the Algonquian Legend *Little Firefly,* written and adapted by Terri Cohlene, a maiden, "Little Burnt One," endures the mistreatment of her sisters with patience and grace. She is rewarded the gift of love and acceptance and finally known by her true name, "Little Firefly."

In Tomie dePaola's retelling of the Comanche tale *The Legend of the Bluebonnet,* an orphaned girl, "She-Who-Is-Alone," sacrifices her most special possession in order to save her people. The little girl is then known as "One-Who-Dearly-Loved-Her-People."

In honor of special qualities and deeds, confer a new name on your child as your child confers a new name on you. As you share the new names chosen, be sure to explain the reason for their selection.

REQUIRED:
- Library/bookstore visit

CATCH A DREAM

SKILLS: Imaginative Thinking/Constructing

In the tradition of the Chippewa Indians of the Lake Superior region, keep the legend of the Dreamcatcher alive. Believing that both good and bad dreams fly through the air until they find their destination, the Chippewa people slept beneath a Dreamcatcher. The nightmares got caught in the web while the good dreams found their way to the person below.

Make a simple Dreamcatcher from a 5 inch to 8 inch ring, embroidery hoop, or pliable twig tied into a ring. Wrap and glue yarn all around the ring. Cut a supply of yarn strips. Tie the ends of one strip to either side of the ring. Repeat the process several times, weaving the strings into a weblike configuration. Keep an open area in the center. Dangle beads and feathers as desired, hang over the bed, and sleep tight.

See a Dreamcatcher at work and follow illustrated directions to make one in *Grandmother's Dreamcatcher* by Becky Ray McCain. Contact *Bob's Dreamcatchers* to make or purchase an authentic Dreamcatcher.

Bob's Dreamcatchers
c/o Bob Allison
P.O. Box 4252
Hopkins, MN, 55343

Web site: *www.members.tripod.com*
E-mail: *bobsdreamcatchers@rocketmail.com*

REQUIRED:
- Ring
- Yarn/ribbon/string
- Safety scissors
- Nontoxic glue

OPTIONAL:
- Library/bookstore visit
- Beads
- Feathers

SAILOR'S LOG

SKILLS: Imaginative Thinking/Written Expression/Point of View

Your child probably knows basic facts about the first voyage of Christopher Columbus from Spain to the New World. Add to your child's knowledge about Columbus by sharing books such as *Christopher Columbus* by Stephen Krensky or *Christopher Columbus: A Great Explorer* by Carol Green.

Having learned about the challenges of those aboard the Nina, the Pinta, and the Santa Maria, work together to write three entries in a Sailor's Log from the point of view of a crew member. Authenticate the aged look of the log by folding heavy watercolor paper into eighths. Unfold and brush lightly with cold tea. Blot damp spots with a paper towel and dry thoroughly.

Make the first entry, dated August 3, 1492, one of optimism and excitement as the voyage begins. Write the second entry, dated sometime in September 1492, as one of uncertainty and concern. Record the final entry, dated October 12, 1492, as one of thanks and relief as the sailor on watch calls out, "Land Ho!" and the ships reach what is now known as the West Indies.

For an example of a logbook written by a child at sea, share *Bluewater Journal, the Voyage of the Sea Tiger* by Loretta Krupinski.

REQUIRED:
- Library/bookstore visit
- Watercolor paper
- Tea
- Pencil

TIME TRAVELER

SKILLS: Facts & Details/Making Comparisons/Brainstorming/Point of View/Written Expression

In September 1620, the Mayflower set sail from England bound for North America. The Pilgrims sought freedom to worship as they chose, something they had been unable to do in England. Coming ashore in what is now Massachusetts, the Pilgrims established the settlement of Plymouth.

It was only by working together that these people were able to survive. Everyone contributed to the development of the new community. Adults and children worked diligently from dawn till dusk to provide food, shelter, and clothing for all.

For a factual view of a typical day in the life of a Pilgrim child, read *Samuel Eaton's Day: A Day in the Life of a Pilgrim Boy* and *Sarah Morton's Day: A Day in the Life of a Pilgrim Girl*, both by Kate Waters. Compare the typical day of a Pilgrim child to that of your child. Focus on chores, recreational activities, friendships, and family life.

Invite your child to join you as you time travel to the settlement of Plymouth. Work together to brainstorm and write, from the point of view of a Pilgrim child and adult, journal entries at the end of a long day of farming, milking, wood chopping, or butter churning.

REQUIRED:
- Library/bookstore visit
- Paper and pencil

CORNUCOPIA OF THANKS

SKILLS: Interviewing/Written Expression/Drawing/Cutting/Vocabulary Development

In the United States and Canada, a day is set aside to give thanks for blessings received during the year. Americans celebrate Thanksgiving on the fourth Thursday of November. Canadians celebrate Thanksgiving on the second Monday of October.

Two weeks prior to the holiday, encourage your child to interview family members and friends who will attend your Thanksgiving celebration. From construction paper, work together to cut the shapes of fruits and vegetables, including apples, pumpkins, corn cobs, and squash. On each shape, print "I am thankful for." Next guide your child in drawing and cutting a large, open horn, a traditional symbol of nature's bounty called the *cornucopia* or *horn of plenty*.

Encourage your second grader, with paper fruits, veggies, and pencil in hand, to chat in person, on the phone, or on-line with each expected guest. Simply ask, "Please complete the sentence, 'I am thankful for . . .'" As the guest responds, your second grader completes the sentence on a chosen shape, including the guest's name.

On Thanksgiving, paste all the fruits and veggies onto the cornucopia so that the writing is visible. When everyone is seated, begin your celebration with a reading of the Cornucopia of Thanks.

REQUIRED:
- Construction paper
- Pencil/pen
- Nontoxic glue/tape

QUEST 1600

SKILLS: Brainstorming/Imaginative Thinking/Drawing/Written Expression

The White House at 1600 Pennsylvania Avenue, Washington, D.C., is home to the president of the United States. This residence can be home to any United States citizen who runs for and is elected to the presidency.

Brainstorm issues to include in your child's campaign for the office of president. Select and record ideas that involve environmental awareness, education, food, housing, health care, jobs, and respect for human differences.

Design a poster that focuses on one aspect of your campaign. Draw and write about the need to conserve our water supply and protect our lakes, rivers, and oceans or about the need for safe, clean, and inclusive schools. Create a poster that focuses on plans to ensure that all citizens have food, housing, and work or that celebrates respect for the world community.

To learn more about the presidency, read a book such as *The Presidency* (*True Books: Government*) by Patricia Ryon Quiri or write a letter to the president at 1600 Pennsylvania Avenue, Washington, DC 20500. Visit the White House Web site at www.whitehouse.gov/WH/kids.

REQUIRED:
• Paper and pencil
• Construction paper
• Crayons/markers

OPTIONAL:
• Library/bookstore visit

PICK A "PRES"

SKILLS: Brainstorming/Researching/Written Expression/Drawing/Cutting

We see images of former presidents engraved, printed, or sculpted on coins, dollar bills, and mountains. We hear names of former presidents in the names of libraries, bridges, streets, and airports. Who were these leaders and what did each accomplish as president of the United States? To find out, visit your library and Pick a "Pres" to research.

Before researching, brainstorm three to five questions. Write each question on an index card. Focus questions on specific information your young historian seeks, such as the selected president's birthday, home state, dates of presidency, party affiliation, beliefs, objectives, and achievements. Keep the topics limited and manageable. Take notes on each index card to answer the question posed. Together, organize the cards so that the information is logically sequenced.

Develop a topic sentence that states the main purpose of the research: "Abraham Lincoln was an extraordinary president." Write the report, including the information gathered to support the main idea. Conclude with a sentence such as, "It is clear that Abraham Lincoln was a great contributor to his country." Bind the report in book form. Encourage your child to draw or to cut out pictures of the president studied.

REQUIRED:
• Library/bookstore visit
• Index cards
• Paper and pencil

OPTIONAL:
• Crayons/markers
• Safety scissors
• Magazines
• Hole punch
• Yarn/ribbon/ string for binding

OKLAHOMA ◆ ◆ ◆ OK!

SKILLS: Visual Memory/Map Skills

Play Oklahoma . . . OK to learn the names of the 50 states and their abbreviations.

Cut 50 index cards in half. Write the states and abbreviations below, one per card.

Alabama = AL	Alaska = AK	Arizona = AZ
Arkansas = AR	California = CA	Colorado = CO
Connecticut = CT	Delaware = DE	Florida = FL
Georgia = GA	Hawaii = HI	Idaho = ID
Illinois = IL	Indiana = IN	Iowa = IA
Kansas = KS	Kentucky = KY	Louisiana = LA
Maine = ME	Maryland = MD	Massachusetts = MA
Michigan = MI	Minnesota = MN	Mississippi = MS
Missouri = MO	Montana = MT	Nebraska = NE
Nevada = NV	New Hampshire = NH	New Jersey = NJ
New Mexico = NM	New York = NY	North Carolina = NC
North Dakota = ND	Ohio = OH	Oklahoma = OK
Oregon = OR	Pennsylvania = PA	Rhode Island = RI
South Carolina = SC	South Dakota = SD	Tennessee = TN
Texas = TX	Utah = UT	Vermont = VT
Virginia = VA	Washington = WA	West Virginia = WV
Wisconsin = WI	Wyoming = WY	

Spread 15 state cards facedown on the right side of the table and the corresponding abbreviation cards facedown on the left. Turn over one card from each section. If it's a match, keep the cards and go again. Otherwise, return cards to their original position. Alternate turns. The winner is the player with more pairs at the end.

Each time you play, add more cards.

REQUIRED:
- Index cards
- Safety scissors
- Pencils

ART OF THE STATE

SKILLS: Researching/Cutting/Drawing/Written Expression

1000 Main Street
Young America, MN

Your second grader probably knows that the United States of America is comprised of 50 unique states and that you live in one of them. Invite your child to create a collage about your state.

Write a letter to your state's Bureau of Tourism. Request brochures about historical, natural, cultural, and recreational features. Visit a travel agency for brochures about your state's landmarks and cities. Check your state's Web site and visit your library to borrow a book such as the *Children's Atlas of the United States*. Find facts of interest from all sources. Write the facts on colorful swatches of cloth or paper. Cut pictures from the brochures you accumulate that show places of interest. From your reading, draw pictures of your state's flag, flower, bird, and tree. Keep all state memorabilia in a folder until you have completed a sizable collection.

Decoratively print the name of your state across the top of a large sheet of construction paper. Arrange and glue all accumulated material onto the paper. Display the collage so that any family member can add to it at any time.

REQUIRED:
- Library visit
- Construction paper/cloth
- Pencil
- Crayons/markers
- Safety scissors
- Brochures
- Nontoxic glue

COMPASS ROSE REMINDER

SKILLS: Map Skills/Vocabulary Development/Imaginative Thinking/Drawing

As second graders begin to use maps more regularly, they need to recognize and remember the clockwise order of the *compass rose*. While we often say and hear *North, South, East,* and *West,* the compass rose in clockwise order is *North, East, South,* and *West.*

View a map with your child. On a separate sheet of paper, draw and decorate a circle to represent a compass rose. As you write *N* at 12:00 on the circle, show your young *cartographer* north on the map. Write *E* at 3:00 on the circle; show east on the map. Next print *S* at 6:00; show south on the map. Finally, write *W* at 9:00; point out west on the map.

To enhance recall of the clockwise order of directions on a compass rose, use the first letter of each direction—*North, East, South, West*—to write a sentence whose words begin with *N, E, S, W,* in that order. Your child may already know, "*Never Eat Shredded Wheat.*" Now create an original sentence as a helpful and concrete mnemonic tool. When "*Noisy Egrets Scream Wildly,*" your child is sure to remember which direction is which!

REQUIRED:
- Map
- Paper and pencil
- Crayons/markers

WAY TO GO!

SKILLS: Map Skills/Following Directions

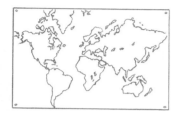

Way to Go! is a hands-on game that exposes your child to a world map and reinforces awareness of compass points.

Put a large world map on the wall at eye level or open to a world map in an atlas. Ask your young geographer, with eyes closed, to touch the map at any point. Then, with eyes open, see where you are.

Ask, "What country are you in?" Your child responds, "I'm in Switzerland." Ask your child to name the country that is just south of Switzerland. Your child slides a finger south on the map and notes that Italy is just south of Switzerland.

Alternate turns. If you point to Brazil, your second-grade geographer asks, "What country are you in?" You answer, "I'm in Brazil." Your child asks, "What is just east of Brazil?" You slide a finger east and note that the Atlantic Ocean is just east of Brazil.

Continue play to build map skills and directional awareness. As an option, post a map of the United States or Canada. Ask questions specific to the states or provinces: "What state is due north of Oregon?" "What province is due west of Ontario?"

REQUIRED:
• World map

OPTIONAL:
• Map of the United States
• Map of Canada

COUNTRY OF THE MONTH

SKILLS: Map Skills/Recording Data/Vocabulary Development/Drawing

Travel around the world without boarding an airplane or cruise ship. Make one country the center of exploration for a month.

Select a country from a map or atlas. Print the name of the country on a file folder. In your exploration of France, for example, serve French foods, including croissants, French bread, brie cheese, and crepes. Find and draw pictures of the French flag and traditional costumes. In a book such as *500 Really Useful French Words and Phrases* by Carol Watson and Philippa Moyle, learn words and phrases to record in your file.

Visit or write to a travel agency for brochures on France to read and store in your file. Borrow a book from the library such as *France* by Donna Bailey and Anna Sproule and learn from a young girl all about life in this beautiful European country. Read about a famous French artist in *Pierre Auguste Renoir (Getting to Know the World's Greatest Artists)* by Mike Venezia. Enjoy literature set in France, such as *Eloise in Paris* by Kay Thompson.

At the completion of your *Tour de France,* review the contents of your folder before setting out on another journey.

REQUIRED:
• Atlas/map
• File folder
• Paper and pencil
• Crayons/markers

OPTIONAL:
• Library/bookstore visit
• Brochures
• Food

FASHION PARADE

SKILLS: Observation/Collecting/Drawing/Cutting

While their wearing may be reserved to celebrations and festivals, the traditional costumes of the cultures of the world, as diverse as the people, climates, and customs of the world, deserve a place in an international fashion parade of design.

Collect, sketch, and display the clothing of people from around the world to include in a fashion portfolio. Make your portfolio from a notebook or from sheets of construction paper folded in half and stapled as a booklet. Label the cover with a title that celebrates the costumes of the world.

Cut out pictures of costumes and accessories from magazines and travel brochures to add to your portfolio. Beneath each, write the country of origin.

As you share books set in countries around the world, draw and color the outfits worn by characters. Include the costumes of bullfighters seen in *Ferdinand* by Munro Leaf, the winter wear of a Norwegian girl in *Trouble with Trolls* by Jan Brett, or the daily attire of African villagers in *A Story, A Story* by Gail E. Haley.

Bring cultures and customs into your home with clothing from around the world.

> **REQUIRED:**
> - Magazines/travel brochures
> - Construction paper/ notebook
> - Safety scissors
> - Nontoxic glue
> - Crayons/markers
> - Pencil
> - Stapler
>
> **OPTIONAL:**
> - Library/book- store visit

INTERNATIONAL EATS

SKILLS: Vocabulary Development/Observation/Following Directions

The foods of the world are as diverse as the people of the world—a celebration of textures, colors, and flavors! Cast routine to the wind as you use literature and the spirit of adventure to sample the international buffet.

Join Maria as she helps her mother knead the dough, *masa,* for *tamales,* a traditional Mexican food in *Too Many Tamales* by Gary Soto. Help Tony make pizza in his father's Italian restaurant, *Little Nino's Pizzeria,* in the book of the same name by Karen Barbour. Enjoy *latkes,* traditional potato pancakes, with Bubba Brayna and Old Bear in *The Chanukkah Guest* by Eric A. Kimmel. Learn about *anzac biscuits, mornay, minties, vegemite, pavlova,* and *lamington* as you travel about Australia with Grandma Poss and Hush in *Possum Magic* by Mem Fox.

When you next dine out, select a restaurant that specializes in foods from a country and culture different from your own. Focus on the cultural decor of the restaurant and peruse the language of the menu.

At home, follow recipes for ethnic dishes. At the grocery store, take time to look at ethnic foods. Add zip to your diet and cultural awareness to your family with food.

> **REQUIRED:**
> - Library/bookstore visit
> - Dinner out
> - Cookbooks/ingredients
> - Grocery store visit

CONDOS, CABINS, AND COOPS

SKILLS: Brainstorming/Categorizing/Making Comparisons

Houses protect people and animals from natural elements. They provide shelter from rain, snow, heat, cold, wind, and possible danger. Enhance your child's awareness that houses serve the same purpose despite their varied structures.

Draw a person on a sheet of paper headed "Houses for People" and an animal on another headed "Houses for Animals." Brainstorm types of houses inhabited by people and record beneath the drawing of the person. Suggest that your child picture houses from your neighborhood, places you've visited, background knowledge, and books you've read so that the list is as varied as the structures people inhabit from many cultures.

Brainstorm types of houses inhabited by animals. Suggest that your child consider different habitats and climates, generating ideas from background knowledge, animals common to your area, and books you've read.

When lists are complete, talk about similarities and differences of the houses on your lists. Read *A House Is a House for Me* by Mary Ann Hoberman to confirm and extend your ideas.

PEOPLE HOUSE BANK: one-family, two-family, apartment, mobile home, houseboat, pueblo, wigwam, tepee, hogan, ranch, farm house, igloo, chalet, castle, pagoda

ANIMAL HOUSE BANK: burrow, barn, cave, hive, sty, kennel, hutch, pen, hole, nest, water

REQUIRED:
• Paper and pencil

OPTIONAL:
• Library/bookstore visit

DWELLING DISPLAY

SKILLS: Cutting/Drawing/Making Comparisons

Log cabins, pagodas, igloos, chalets, tepees, and apartments are all houses with unique styles and structures. Take notice of the similarities and differences of houses by creating a collage.

Provision yourselves with recyclable magazines, postcards, travel brochures, newspapers, scissors, glue, crayons, and markers. Have fun as you cut, draw, arrange, and glue different styles of houses onto a piece of construction paper.

Upon completion, make comparisons of the houses included. Facilitate the discussion by asking questions: "Are all houses the same size?" "Do all houses protect inhabitants from the weather and other possible dangers?" "Are all houses built from the same materials?" "Are all houses decorated in the same fashion?"

Display the completed collage in a special place in your home so that other family members can admire your work and add to it at any time.

REQUIRED:
• Construction paper
• Recyclable print materials
• Safety scissors
• Nontoxic glue
• Crayons/markers

 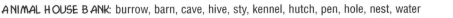

HUFF AND PUFF HOUSES

SKILLS: Connecting Social Studies & Literature/Recording Data/Making Comparisons

The wolf huffed and puffed and blew down houses of straw and sticks. Only the house of brick remained in *The Three Little Pigs* by Paul Galdone. The rich treasury of children's literature offers your child the opportunity to view houses made from a range of materials dependent on culture, climate, inhabitant, available materials, and imagination.

As you read together, keep a running record of dwellings visited. Record the title, author, and main character of each book and the type of house, shelter, or dwelling pictured or described. Make comparisons of structures to determine common and unique characteristics.

Marvel at a home fashioned from earth in *This House Is Made of Mud, Esta casa está hecha de lodo* by Ken Buchanan. Delight in rock and box houses constructed by children in *Roxaboxen* by Alice McLerran. Build castles like those in *Jethro and Joel Were a Troll* by Bill Peet. Visit woods where a house once stood in *Home Place* by Crescent Dragonwagon. Share the happiness and sorrow of *The Little House* by Virginia Lee Burton. See a garden cottage restored to its original beauty in *Mandy* by Julie Edwards.

The houses and dwellings of literature build a diverse and marvelous community!

REQUIRED:
- Library/Bookstore visit
- Paper and pencil

ARCHITECTURE EXPLORATION

SKILLS: Vocabulary Development/Constructing

People of different cultures build homes of different styles. Availability of materials, climate, and possible dangers are factors considered when building a house.

Provide your child with the opportunity to construct houses of different cultures.

"*Igloo*" is the *Inuit,* or *Eskimo,* name for shelter. Igloos are made from packed snow cut into blocks. Make an igloo by gluing sugar cubes together in a spiral. Make the spiral smaller at the top to form a dome. Construct a tunneled entrance.

A *tepee* is a house commonly inhabited by the Plains tribes of North American Indians. Tepees are made from buffalo skins stretched over poles. Make a tepee by securing small sticks to a base in the shape of a cone. Tie the sticks at the top and cover with fabric or paper and other decorative materials. For the entrance, cut a slit near the base of the tepee.

A *wigwam* is a house inhabited by the *Algonquians.* Wigwams are oval domes made from poles tied with bark. Make a wigwam from an inverted recyclable plastic container covered with layers of bark and grass. Cut an entrance slit at the base of the wigwam.

REQUIRED:
- Sugar cubes
- Nontoxic glue
- Sticks/bark/grass
- Fabric/paper
- Plastic container
- Safety scissors
- Art supplies

MORE ARCHITECTURE EXPLORATION

The *pagoda* of China, Japan, southeastern Asia, and parts of India is a tower whose three to fifteen stories decrease in size from bottom to top. Each story of a pagoda has an overhanging roof with edges curved upward. Decorate a box as a pagoda. Layer pipe cleaners to create a tiered roof.

A *hogan* is a traditional *Navajo* dwelling. Made from logs and dirt, a hogan is six sided, eight sided, or round. Construct walls from twigs, stacked and secured with glue or string. Leave space for an entrance. For the roof, lay sticks across the top of the walls and cover with soil.

The *Kikuyu* people of *Kenya* live in round houses that have straw and mud brick walls and thatched roofs. Use clay to shape the round house. Roll a piece of construction paper into a cone to fit on top as the roof. Cover the cone with grass.

Replicate a log cabin with pretzel sticks glued to a recycled half-pint milk carton. Transform an empty box into a chalet, castle, apartment building, or house with imagination and art supplies.

Set up all completed homes to create the architecture of our world community.

REQUIRED:
- Recyclable materials
- Sticks/soil/grass
- Clay
- Art supplies

PIÑATA PLAY

Bring the zest and vitality of a Mexican tradition to your next family celebration by making a *piñata*, a brightly decorated figure containing candy and small gifts.

In preparation for making a piñata, share *The Piñata Maker/El Piñatero* by George Ancona. Read about the culture of the people and the making of a piñata as you visit Tio Rico, the craftsman in a small Mexican village.

Construct your piñata from a cardboard box. Fill the box with wrapped candies and party favors before sealing with tape. Turn the box over. Use tape to attach sturdy twine to the center of the bottom of the box.

Invite family members to join the fun as you decorate the piñata. Use crepe paper or tissue paper to cover the surface. Bunch the paper and attach with glue. For animal figures, cut eyes, ears, snout, mouth, beak, tail, legs, wings, whiskers, and horns from construction paper or cloth. Attach with glue.

Hang the piñata from the ceiling. Take turns trying to open the piñata by hitting it with a stick while blindfolded. Candies and party favors shower all guests when the piñata is finally broken.

REQUIRED:
- Library/bookstore visit
- Box
- Packing tape
- Candy/party favors
- Nontoxic glue
- Twine
- Safety scissors
- Art supplies
- Stick

OLD-TIME FLYERS

SKILLS: Imaginative Thinking/Constructing/Drawing/Painting

Three thousand years ago, the Chinese flew silk kites to frighten enemies. Today, people the world over fly kites for pleasure. Experience the joy of kite flying in books such as *The Emperor and the Kite* by Jane Yolen or *Huan Ching and the Golden Fish* by Michael Reeser. Then, work together to design and construct a kite.

A *flat kite* is basic. Tie four thin wooden stakes in the shape of a diamond. Secure a fifth stake across the diamond. Attach tissue paper, nylon, or silk to the frame with strong tape. Decorate with waterproof markers or paint. Dry thoroughly before attaching a tail made from tied strips of cloth.

A *delta kite* is easy to construct. Tie three stakes in a triangle. Secure a fourth stake from the center of the base to the top. Attach light fabric to the body of the kite with tape. Decorate, dry, and add a tail.

A *box kite,* elaborate and stable, has a square, rectangular, or triangular frame. Tie stakes into the preferred three-dimensional shape. Secure light fabric around the frame. Decorate, dry thoroughly, attach a tail, and fly!

REQUIRED:
- Paper and pencil
- Thin wooden stakes
- Tape
- Safety scissors
- Fabric/tissue paper
- Markers/paint

OPTIONAL:
- Library/bookstore visit

A TREE FOR CHILDREN

SKILLS: Respecting Human Differences/Collecting/Drawing/Cutting/Written Expression

Children, children everywhere,
children dark and children fair,
children of all shapes and sizes,
children springing odd surprises,
children chasing, running races,
children laughing, making faces . . .

JACK PRELUTSKY

Work together to make a mural in celebration and recognition of the children of the world. Along the bottom margin of a large sheet of white poster paper, draw and color the upper portion of the world. Use crayons or construction paper to make a large tree whose roots embrace the world. Cut leaves and fruits of all colors and shapes to glue on the branches of the tree.

Draw and color or, from recyclable magazines, cut out faces of children of all ages and races. Glue the face of a child to each leaf or fruit of the tree. Then, as a special tribute, plant a tree in your child's name, in honor of the children of the world, through Trees for Life, an organization that plants fruits trees to give people in developing countries a source of food.

Trees for Life
3006 W. St. Louis
Wichita, KS 67203
316-945-6929
Web site: *www.treesforlife.org*
E-mail: *info@treesforlife.org*

REQUIRED:
- Poster/construction paper
- Crayons/markers
- Magazines
- Safety scissors
- Nontoxic glue
- Paper and pencil

BIBLIOGRAPHY

Adler, David A. *Cam Jansen and the Mystery of the Carnival Prize*. New York: Dell Publishing, 1984.

Adler, David A. *Cam Jansen and the Mystery of the Dinosaur Bones*. New York: Puffin Books, 1987.

Adler, David A. *Cam Jansen and the Mystery of Flight 54*. New York: Puffin Books, 1992.

Adler, David A. *Cam Jansen and the Mystery of the Monster Movie*. New York: Dell Publishing, 1984.

Adler, David A. *A Picture Book of Jackie Robinson*. New York: Holiday House, 1997.

Adler, David A. *A Picture Book of Thomas Alva Edison*. New York: Holiday House, 1996.

Aliki. *Digging Up Dinosaurs*. New York: Ty Crowell Co., 1988.

Ancona, George. *The Piñata Maker/El Pinatero*. New York: Harcourt Brace, 1995.

Babbitt, Natalie. *The Search for Delicious*. New York: Farrar, Straus & Giroux, 1991.

Bailey, Donna, and Anna Sproule. *France*. Austin, TX: Raintree/Steck-Vaughn, 1990.

Baker, Leslie. *The Third-Story Cat*. Boston: Little, Brown and Company, 1987.

Bang, Molly. *The Paper Crane*. New York: Mulberry Books, 1985.

Barbour, Karen. *Little Nino's Pizzeria*. New York: Harcourt Brace, 1990.

Barss, Karen J. *Clean Water (Earth at Risk)*. Broomall, PA: Chelsea House Publications, 1992.

Baum, L. Frank. *The Wizard of Oz*. New York: Henry Holt & Company, Inc., 1988.

Bemelmans, Ludwig. *Madeline's Rescue*. New York: Viking Press, 1953.

Bolognese, Don. *Little Hawk's New Name*. New York: Scholastic Inc., 1995.

Bourgeois, Paula, and Brenda Clark. *Franklin's New Friend*. New York: Scholastic Inc., 1997.

Branley, Franklyn Mansfield. *The Big Dipper*. New York: Harper Collins Juvenile Books, 1991.

Branley, Franklyn Mansfield. *Down Comes the Rain*. New York: Harper Collins Juvenile Books, 1997.

Branley, Franklyn Mansfield. *Flash, Crash, Rumble and Roll*. New York: Harper Collins Juvenile Books, 1999.

Branley, Franklyn Mansfield. *The Planets in Our Solar System*. New York: HarperTrophy, 1998.

Branley, Franklyn Mansfield. *The Sky Is Full of Stars*. New York: HarperTrophy, 1983.

Branley, Franklyn Mansfield. *What Happened to the Dinosaurs?* New York: Harper Collins Juvenile Books, 1991.

Branley, Franklyn Mansfield. *What the Moon Is Like*. New York: HarperTrophy, 1986.

Brett, Jan. *Town Mouse Country Mouse*. New York: Putnam Publishing Group, 1994.

Brett, Jan. *Trouble with Trolls*. New York: Scholastic Inc., 1992.

Briggs, Raymond. *Jim and the Beanstalk*. New York: Coward-McCann, Inc., 1970.

Brown, Jeff. *Flat Stanley*. New York: Scholastic Inc., 1974.

Brown, Marcia. *Once a Mouse*. New York: Atheneum, 1972.

Buchanan, Ken. *This House Is Made of Mud, Esta casa está hecha de lodo*. Flagstaff, AZ: Rising Moon Publications, 1991.

Bunting, Eve. *Butterfly House*. New York: Scholastic Trade, 1999.

Burns, Marilyn. *The Greedy Triangle*. New York: Scholastic Inc., 1995.

Burns, Marilyn. *Spaghetti and Meatballs for All! A Mathematical Story*. New York: Scholastic Inc., 1997.

Burton, Virginia Lee. *The Little House*. Boston: Houghton Mifflin, 1942.

Butterworth, Oliver. *The Enormous Egg*. Boston: Little Brown & Co., 1993.

Calhoun, Mary. *Cross Country Cat*. New York: Mulberry Books, 1979.

Calhoun, Mary. *Henry the Sailor Cat*. New York: Mulberry Books, 1998.

Carle, Eric. *Papa, please get the moon for me*. New York: Scholastic Inc., 1986.

Carle, Eric. *The Tiny Seed*. New York: Scholastic Inc., 1987.

Carle, Eric. *Walter the Baker*. New York: Scholastic Inc., 1972.

Carlstrom, Nancy White. *Goodbye Geese*. New York: Scholastic Inc., 1991.

Carrick, Carol. *Patrick's Dinosaurs*. Boston: Houghton Mifflin Co., 1983.

Carrick, Carol. *What Happened to Patrick's Dinosaurs?* Boston: Houghton Mifflin Co., 1986.

Cassie, Brian, and Jerry Pallotta. *The Butterfly Alphabet Book*. Watertown, MA: Charlesbridge Publishing, 1995.

Children's Atlas of the United States. New York: Rand McNally and Company, 1989.

Chinn, Karen. *Sam and the Lucky Money*. New York: Lee & Low Books, Inc., 1997.

Christopher, Matt. *All-Star Fever*. Boston: Little Brown & Co., 1997.

Christopher, Matt. *The Dog That Stole Home*. Boston: Little Brown & Co., 1996.

Cicero, Marcus Tullius. *Pro Archia Poeta I, 2,* (In Defense of Archias the Poet). Loeb Classical Library. Cambridge: Harvard University Press, 1957.

Clymer, Susan. *Scrawny the Classroom Duck*. New York: Scholastic Inc., 1991.

Clymer, Susan. *There's a Hamster in My Lunchbox*. New York: Scholastic Inc., 1994.

Coerr, Eleanor. *The Big Balloon Race*. New York: Harper Collins Juvenile Books, 1992.

Coffelt, Nancy. *Dogs in Space*. New York: Voyager Picture Book, 1996.

Cohen, Miriam. *Don't Eat Too Much Turkey*. New York: Dell Publishing, 1987.

Cohen, Miriam. *Second-Grade Friends*. New York: Scholastic Inc., 1993.

Cohlene, Terri. *Little Firefly, An Algonquian Legend*. Mahwah, NJ: Watermill Press, 1990.

Cole, Joanna. *The Magic School Bus, Lost in the Solar System*. New York: Scholastic Inc., 1990.

Cole, Joanna, and Stephanie Calmenson. *Bug in a Rug*. New York: Mulberry Books, 1996.

Cole, Joanna, and Stephanie Calmenson. *Miss Mary Mack and Other Children's Street Rhymes*. New York: Beech Tree Books, 1991.

Cooney, Barbara. *Island Boy*. New York: Puffin Books, 1991.

D'Aulaire, Ingri, and Edgar D'Aulaire. *Abraham Lincoln*. New York: Picture Yearling, 1987.

Dadey, Debbie, and Marcia Thornton Jones. *Triplet Trouble and the Bicycle Race*. New York: Scholastic Inc., 1997.

Dadey, Debbie, and Marcia Thornton Jones. *Triplet Trouble and the Class Trip*. New York: Scholastic Inc., 1997.

Dadey, Debbie, and Marcia Thornton Jones. *Trolls Don't Ride Roller Coasters (Adventures of the Bailey School Kids, Vol. 35)*. New York: Scholastic Inc., 1999.

Davies, Kay, and Wendy Oldfield. *Snow and Ice*. Austin, TX: Raintree/Steck-Vaughn, 1995.

Delton, Judy. *Blue Skies, French Fries*. New York: Dell Publishing, 1988.

Delton, Judy. *Bookworm Buddies*. New York: Bantam Doubleday Dell Books for Young Readers, 1996.

Delton, Judy. *Camp Ghost-Away*. New York: Dell Publishing, 1988.

Delton, Judy. *The Pee Wee Jubilee*. New York: Dell Publishing, 1989.

Delton, Judy. *Planet Pee Wee*. New York: Yearling Books, 1998.

Demarest, Chris L. *No Peas for Nellie*. New York: Macmillan Publishing Company, 1988.

DePaola, Tomie. *The Legend of the Bluebonnet*. New York: G. P. Putnam's Sons, 1983.

Dewey, Jennifer Owings. *Stories on Stone, Rock Art: Images from the Ancient Ones*. Boston: Little, Brown and Company, 1996.

Dorros, Arthur. *Abuela*. New York: E.P. Dutton, 1991.

Dragonwagon, Crescent. *Home Place*. New York: Aladdin Books, 1993.

Duke, Kate. *Aunt Isabel Tells a Good One*. New York: E.P. Dutton, 1992.

Dussling, Jennifer. *Pink Snow and Other Weird Weather*. New York: Grosset & Dunlap, 1998.

Edwards, Julie. *Mandy*. New York: HarperTrophy, 1971.

Fowler, Allan. *Can You See the Wind?* New York: Children's Press, 1999.

Fox, Mem. *Night Noises*. New York: Harcourt Brace, 1992.

Fox, Mem. *Possum Magic*. New York: Harcourt Brace, 1990.

Fox, Mem. *Wilfred Gordon McDonald Partridge*. New York: Kane Miller, 1985.

Freeman, Don. *Corduroy*. New York: Viking Press, 1976.

Friedman, Aileen. *A Cloak for the Dreamer*. New York: Scholastic Inc., 1995.

Friedman, Aileen. *The King's Commissioners*. New York: Scholastic Inc., 1995.

Galdone, Paul. *Henny Penny*. Boston: Houghton Mifflin, 1984.

Galdone, Paul. *The Monkey and the Crocodile: A Jataka Tale from India*. Boston: Houghton Mifflin, 1987.

Galdone, Paul. *The Three Billy Goats Gruff*. New York: Clarion Books, 1973.

Galdone, Paul. *The Three Little Pigs*. Boston: Houghton Mifflin, 1984.

Gelmen, Rita Golden. *More Spaghetti I Say*. New York: Scholastic Inc., 1992.

Gelmen, Rita Golden. *Why Can't I Fly?* New York: Scholastic Inc., 1986.

George, Christine O'Connell. *The Great Frog Race*. New York: Clarion Books, 1997.

Gibbons, Gail. *Monarch Butterfly*. New York: Holiday House: 1989.

Giff, Patricia Reilly. *The Beast in Ms. Rooney's Room (The Kids of the Polk Street School, 1)*. New York: Yearling Books, 1984.

Giff, Patricia Reilly. *Monster Rabbit Runs Amuck (The Kids of the Polk Street School, 15)*. New York: Yearling Books, 1991.

Giff, Patricia Reilly. *The Mystery of the Blue Ring*. New York: Young Yearling, 1987.

Giff, Patricia Reilly. *The Riddle of the Red Purse (Polka Dot Private Eye, No. 2)*. New York: Young Yearling, 1987.

Giff, Patricia Reilly. *Say "Cheese" (The Kids of the Polk Street School, 10)*. New York: Yearling Books, 1985.

Giff, Patricia Reilly. *Snaggle Doodles (The Kids of the Polk Street School, 8)*. New York: Yearling Books, 1985.

Giff, Patricia Reilly. *Spectacular Stone Soup (New Kids at the Polk Street School, 5)*. New York: Young Yearling, 1989.

Gobel, Paul. *The Girl Who Loved Wild Horses*. New York: Simon & Schuster, 1983.

Goldish, Meish. *101 Science Poems & Songs for Young Learners: With Hands-On Activities*. New York: Scholastic Inc., 1997.

Greene, Carol. *Christopher Columbus: A Great Explorer (Rookie Biographies)*. New York: Children's Press, 1989.

Gross, Ruth Belov (adapted from Hans Christian Anderson). *The Emperor's New Clothes*. New York: Scholastic Inc., 1994.

Gwynn, Fred. *The King Who Rained*. New York: Aladdin Paperbacks, 1988.

Haley, Gail E. *A Story, A Story*. New York: Atheneum, 1988.

Hall, Donald. *Ox-Cart Man*. New York: Viking Press, 1979.

Hamanaka, Sheila. *All the Color of the Earth*. New York: Morrow Junior Books, 1994.

Harper, Dan. *Telling Time with Big Mama Cat*. New York: Harcourt Brace & Company, 1998.

Harris, Richard. *I Can Read About the Sun and Other Stars*. New York: Troll Associates, 1996.

Harrison, Carol. *Dinosaurs Everywhere!* New York: Scholastic Inc., 1998.

Harshman, Terry Webb. *Porcupine's Pajama Party*. New York: Harper & Row, 1988.

Helldorfer, Mary-Claire. *The Mapmaker's Daughter*. New York: Atheneum, 1991.

Heller, Ruth. *Kites Sail High: A Book About Verbs*. New York: Grosset & Dunlap, 1988.

Heller, Ruth. *Many Luscious Lollipops: A Book About Adjectives*. New York: Grosset & Dunlap, 1989.

Heller, Ruth. *Merry-Go-Round: A Book About Nouns*. New York: Grosset & Dunlap, 1990.

Heller, Ruth. *Mine All Mine: A Book About Pronouns*. New York: Grosset & Dunlap, 1997.

Heller, Ruth. *Up, Up and Away: A Book About Adverbs*. New York: Grosset & Dunlap, 1991.

Henkes, Kevin. *Sheila Rae, The Brave*. New York: Scholastic Inc., 1987.

Henkes, Kevin. *Weekend With Wendell*. New York: William Morrow & Company, 1986.

Hennessy, B. G. *The Dinosaur Who Lived in My Backyard*. New York: Puffin Books, 1990.

Hoberman, Mary Ann. *A House Is a House for Me*. New York: Puffin Books, 1982.

Hodges, Margaret. *Saint George and the Dragon*. Boston: Little Brown and Company, 1984.

Hogrogian, Nonny. *One Fine Day*. New York: Simon & Schuster, 1971.

Holub, Joan. *Ivy Green, Cootie Queen*. Mahwah, NJ: Troll Communications L.L.C., 1998.

Hopkins, Lee Bennett. *Marvelous Math, A Book of Poems*. New York: Simon & Schuster, 1997.

Hopping, Lorraine Jean. *Hurricanes!* New York: Scholastic Inc., 1995.

Hopping, Lorraine Jean. *Tornadoes!* New York: Scholastic Inc., 1994.

Houston, Gloria. *My Great-Aunt Arizona*. New York: Scholastic Inc., 1992.

Howe, James. *I Wish I Were a Butterfly*. New York: Harcourt Brace & Company, 1987.

Howe, James. *Pinky and Rex and the Mean Old Witch*. New York: Avon Books, 1991.

Hoyt-Goldsmith, Diane. *Totem Pole*. New York: Holiday House, 1994.

Hutchins, Pat. *The Wind Blew*. New York: Aladdin, 1993.

Ingoglia, Gina. *Amanda Visits the Planets*. New York: Inchworm Press, 1998.

Jeunesse, Gallimard, and Sylvaine Perols. *Endangered Animals, A First Discovery Book*. New York: Scholastic Inc., 1995.

Johnston, Tony. *The First Day of School*. New York: Scholastic Inc., 1997.

Jones, Carol. *The Lion and the Mouse*. Boston: Houghton Mifflin, 1997.

Jorgensen, Gail. *Crocodile Beat*. New York: Scholastic Inc., 1988.

Joyce, William. *A Day with Wilbur Robinson*. New York: Scholastic Inc., 1990.

Kalbacken, Joan. *The Food Pyramid (True Books, Food & Nutrition)*. New York: Children's Press, 1998.

Kalman, Bobbie, and Tammy Everts. *Butterflies and Moths*. New York: Crabtree Publishing Company, 1994.

Keats, Ezra Jack. *Regards to the Man in the Moon*. New York: MacMillan Publishing Company, 1981.

Keats, Ezra Jack. *The Snowy Day*. New York: Viking Press, 1962.

Keenan, Sheila. *The Biggest Fish*. New York: Scholastic Inc., 1996.

Kellogg, Steven. *The Island of the Skog*. New York: Dial Books for Young Readers, 1993.

Kellogg, Steven. *Jack and the Beanstalk*. New York: Mulberry Books, 1997.

Kemp, Moira. *Humpty Dumpty*. New York: Dutton Lodestar Books, 1996.

Kennedy, X. J., and Jane Dyer. *Talking Like the Rain*. Boston: Little Brown and Company, 1992.

Kim, Grace. *The Amazing Panda Adventure*. New York: Scholastic Inc., 1995.

Kimmel, Eric A. *The Chanukkah Guest*. New York: Holiday House, 1988.

Kipling, Rudyard. *How the Leopard Got His Spots and Other Just So Stories*. Mineola, NY: Dover Publications, 1992.

Kline, Suzy. *Horrible Harry and the Dungeon*. New York: Scholastic Inc., 1996.

Kline, Suzy. *Horrible Harry and the Kickball Wedding*. New York: Scholastic Inc., 1992.

Kranking, Kathy. *Earth: Where Would We Be Without It?* New York: Golden Books Publishing Co., Inc., 1999.

Krensky, Stephen. *Christopher Columbus*. New York: Random House, 1991.

Kroll, Virginia. *Butterfly Boy*. Honesdale, PA: Boyds Mills Press, 1997.

Krupinski, Loretta. *Bluewater Journal, The Voyage of the Sea Tiger*. New York: HarperCollins, 1995.

Kunhardt, Edith. *Pompeii . . . Buried Alive!* New York: Random House, 1987.

Lauber, Patricia. *Be a Friend to Trees*. New York: Harpercollins Juvenile Books, 1994.

Leaf, Munro. *The Story of Ferdinand*. New York: Puffin Books, 1987.

Leedy, Loreen. *The Edible Pyramid: Good Eating Every Day*. New York: Holiday House, 1996.

Leedy, Loreen. *The Monster Money Book*. New York: Holiday House, 1992.

Leedy, Loreen. *Postcards from Pluto, A Tour of the Solar System*. New York: Holiday House, 1993.

Levine, Ellen. . . . *If You Lived at the Time of Martin Luther King*. New York: Scholastic Inc., 1990.

Little, William T., and John Peterson. *The Littles and Their Friends*. New York: Scholastic Inc., 1981.

Lobel, Arnold. *Ming Lo Moves a Mountain*. New York: Mulberry Books, 1993.

Lobel, Arnold. *Mouse Tales*. New York: Harper Trophy, 1978.

Lobel, Arnold. *Owl at Home*. New York: Harper Trophy, 1982.

Low, Joseph. *Mice Twice*. New York: Aladdin Books, 1986.

Lundell, Margo. *A Girl Named Helen Keller*. New York: Scholastic Inc., 1995.

Maccarone, Grace. *The Sword in the Stone*. New York: Scholastic Inc., 1992.

Maccarone, Grace, and Marilyn Burns. *Three Pigs, One Wolf and Seven Magic Shapes*. New York: Scholastic Inc., 1998.

Mahy, Margaret. *The Seven Chinese Brothers*. New York: Scholastic Inc., 1992.

Martin, Jaqueline Briggs. *Snowflake Bentley*. Boston: Houghton Mifflin, 1998.

McCain, Becky Ray. *Grandmother's Dreamcatcher*. Morton Grove, IL: Albert Whitman & Co., 1998.

McClosky, Robert. *Make Way for Ducklings*. New York: Viking Press, 1941.

McCully, Emily Arnold. *Mirette on the High Wire*. New York: Putnam Publishing Group, 1992.

McDermott, Gerald. *Arrow to the Sun: A Pueblo Indian Tale*. New York: Viking Press, 1977.

McGee, Marni. *Jack Takes the Cake*. Mahwah, NJ: Troll Communications L.L.C., 1998.

McKissack, Patricia C. *Flossie & the Fox*. New York: Scholastic Inc., 1986.

McLerran, Alice. *The Mountain That Loved a Bird*. New York: Simon & Schuster, 1985.

McLerran, Alice. *Roxaboxen*. New York: Scholastic Inc., 1991.

McNulty, Faith. *Dancing with Manatees*. New York: Scholastic Inc., 1994.

Medearis, Angela Shelf. *Picking Peas for a Penny*. New York: Scholastic Inc., 1990.

Merrill, Claire. *A Seed Is a Promise*. New York: Scholastic Inc., 1973.

Modesitt, Jeanne. *The Story of Z*. Saxonville, MA: Picture Book Studio, 1990.

Moore, Eva. *Buddy The First Seeing Eye Dog*. New York: Scholastic Inc., 1996.

Mora, Pat. *A Birthday Basket for Tia*. New York: Simon & Schuster, 1992.

Morgan, Sally, and Rosie Harlow. *Nature in Danger*. New York: Kingfisher, 1995.

Most, Bernard. *The Cow That Went Oink*. New York: Harcourt Brace, 1990.

Most, Bernard. *Where to Look for a Dinosaur*. New York: Harcourt Brace & Company, 1993.

Murphy, Stuart J. *Give Me Half!* New York: HarperCollins, 1996.

Needham, Kate. *The Time Trekkers Visit the Dinosaurs*. Brookfield, CT: Copper Beech, 1995.

Ness, Evaline. *Sam, Bangs and Moonshine*. New York: Henry Holt & Company, Inc., 1971.

Neuschwander, Cindy, and Marilyn Burns., *Amanda Bean's Amazing Dream*. New York: Scholastic Inc., 1998.

Nirgiotis, Nicholas. *Volcanoes, Mountains That Blow Their Tops*. New York: Grosset & Dunlap, 1996.

Norman, David, and Angela Milner. *Eyewitness Books: Dinosaur*. New York: Alfred A. Knopf, 1989.

Osborne, Mary Pope. *Afternoon on the Amazon (Magic Tree House, No. 6)*. New York: Random House, 1995.

Osborne, Mary Pope. *Buffalo Before Breakfast (Magic Tree House, No. 18)*. New York: Random House, 1999.

Osborne, Mary Pope. *Day of the Dragon King (Magic Tree House, No. 14)*. New York: Random House, 1998.

Osborne, Mary Pope. *Lions at Lunchtime (Magic Tree House, No. 11)*. New York: Random House, 1998.

Ovenell-Carter, Julie. *The Butterflies' Promise*. New York: Annick Press, 1999.

Pallotta, Jerry. *The Dinosaur Alphabet Book*. Watertown, MA: Charlesbridge Publishing, 1991.

Parish, Peggy. *Amelia Bedelia*. New York: Harper & Row, 1963.

Parish, Peggy. *Amelia Bedelia and the Surprise Shower*. New York: Harper Trophy, 1966.

Parish, Peggy. *Be Ready at Eight*. New York: Simon & Schuster, 1996.

Parlin, John. *Amelia Earhart: Pioneer of the Sky*. New York: Young Yearling, 1991.

Patterson, Dr. Francine. *Koko's Kitten*. New York: Scholastic Inc., 1985.

Peet, Bill. *Cowardly Clyde*. Boston: Houghton Mifflin, 1979.

Peet, Bill. *Cyrus the Unsinkable Sea Serpent*. Boston: Houghton Mifflin, 1982.

Peet, Bill. *Jethro and Joel Were a Troll*. Boston: Houghton Mifflin, 1990.

Peet, Bill. *The Whingdingdilly*. Boston: Houghton Mifflin, 1970.

Peterson, John. *The Littles and the Trash Tinies*. New York: Scholastic Inc., 1977.

Peterson, John. *The Littles Go Exploring*. New York: Scholastic Inc., 1978.

Pfister, Marcus. *Dazzle the Dinosaur*. New York: North South Books, 1994.

Pfister, Marcus. *Sun and Moon*. New York: Scholastic Inc., 1990.

Pinkwater, Daniel Manus. *The Big Orange Splot*. New York: Scholastic Inc., 1977.

Polacco, Patricia. *Appelemando's Dreams*. New York: Philomel, 1991.

Polacco, Patricia. *Babushka Baba Yaga*. New York: Philomel, 1993.

Polacco, Patricia. *Chicken Sunday*. New York: Philomel, 1992.

Polacco, Patricia. *Just Plain Fancy*. New York: Bantam Doubleday Dell Publishing Group, 1990.

Polacco, Patricia. *The Keeping Quilt*. New York: Simon & Schuster, 1988.

Polacco, Patricia. *Meteor*. New York: Philomel, 1999.

Polacco, Patricia. *Mrs. Katz and Tush*. New York: Bantam Books, 1992.

Quiri, Patricia Ryon. *The Presidency (True Books: Government)*. New York: Children's Press, 1999.

Rachin, Ann. *Beethoven (Famous Children Series)*. New York: Barrons Juveniles, 1994.

Raffi, and Nadine Bernard Westcott. *Down by the Bay*. New York: Crown Publishers, 1990.

The Random House Book of Poetry, selected by Jack Prelutsky. New York: Random House, 1983.

Rathmann, Peggy. *Officer Buckle and Gloria*. New York: Putnam Publishing Group, 1995.

Reeser, Michael. *Huan Ching and the Golden Fish*. Austin, TX: Raintree/Steck-Vaughn, 1988.

Rocklin, Joanne. *The Case of the Shrunken Allowance*. New York: Scholastic Inc., 1998.

Rocklin, Joanne. *Three Smart Pals*. New York: Scholastic Inc., 1994.

Rosenbloom, Joseph. *Deputy Dan Gets His Man*. New York: Random House, 1985.

Rylant, Cynthia. *Birthday Presents*. New York: Orchard Books, 1987.

Rylant, Cynthia. *Poppleton Forever*. New York: Scholastic Inc., 1998.

San Souci, Robert D. *The Legend of Scarface: A Blackfeet Indian Tale*. New York: Doubleday, 1996.

Say, Allen. *Grandfather's Journey*. Boston: Houghton Mifflin, 1993.

Scieszka, Jon. *Math Curse*. New York: Viking Children's Books, 1995.

Scieszka, Jon. *The True Story of the 3 Little Pigs by A. Wolf*. New York: Puffin, 1996.

Sharmat, Marjorie Weinman. *Nate the Great and the Sticky Case*. New York: Young Yearling, 1981.

Sharmat, Marjorie Weinman. *Nate the Great and the Stolen Base*. New York: Bantam Doubleday Dell Books for Young Readers, 1992.

Sharmat, Marjorie Weinman. *Nate the Great Saves the King of Sweden*. New York: Bantam Doubleday, 1997.

Sharmat, Mitchell. *Gregory, The Terrible Eater*. New York: Scholastic Trade, 1989.

Showers, Paul. *Where Does the Garbage Go?* New York: Harpercollins Juvenile Books, 1994.

Silver, Donald. *Why Save the Rain Forest?* New York: Julian Messner, 1993.

Silverstein, Shel. *A Giraffe and a Half.* New York: HarperCollins, 1981.

Simon, Seymour. *Comets, Meteors, and Asteroids.* New York: William Morrow & Company, 1994.

Simon, Seymour. *Stars.* New York: Mulberry Books, 1989.

Singer, Marilyn, and Jerry Pinkney. *Turtle in July.* New York: Atheneum, 1989.

Sobol, Donald J. *Encyclopedia Brown: Boy Detective.* New York: Bantam Skylark, 1985.

Soto, Gary. *Too Many Tamales.* New York: Putnam Publishing Group Juvenile, 1993.

Steig, William. *The Amazing Bone.* New York: Farrar Straus & Giroux, 1984.

Steig, William. *Dr. DeSoto.* New York: Scholastic Inc., 1982.

Steig, William. *Sylvester and the Magic Pebble.* New York: Simon & Schuster, 1989.

Steptoe, John. *Mufaro's Beautiful Daughters.* New York: Mulberry Books, 1993.

Stevens, Janet (adapted from Hans Christian Anderson). *The Princess and the Pea.* New York: Holiday House, 1988.

Stevens, Janet. *The Tortoise and the Hare.* New York: Holiday House, 1985.

Sundgaard, Arnold. *The Lamb and the Butterfly.* New York: Scholastic Inc., 1995.

Swope, Sam. *The Araboolies of Liberty Street.* New York: Random House, 1995.

Symes, R. F. *Rocks and Minerals.* New York: Alfred A. Knopf, 1988.

Tate, Suzanne. *Tammy Turtle, A Tale of Saving Sea Turtles.* Nags Head, NC: Nags Head Art, Inc., 1991.

Thompson, Gare. *Animals in Danger.* Austin, TX: Raintree/Steck-Vaughn, 1998.

Thompson, Gare. *Take Care of Our Earth.* Austin, TX: Raintree/Steck-Vaughn, 1998.

Thompson, Kay. *Eloise in Paris.* New York: Simon & Schuster, 1999.

Torres, Laura, and Michael Sherman. *Pipecleaners Gone Crazy: A Complete Guide to Bending Fuzzy Sticks.* Palo Alto, CA: Klutz Press, 1997.

Turkle, Brinton. *Do Not Open.* New York: E.P. Dutton, 1981.

Turner, Ann. *Dakota Dugout.* New York: Scholastic Inc., 1987.

Turner, Priscilla. *The War Between the Vowels and the Consonants.* New York: Farrar Straus Giroux, 1996.

Van Allsburg, Chris. *Jumanji.* Boston: Houghton Mifflin, 1981.

Venezia, Mike. *Pierre Auguste Renoir (Getting to Know the World's Greatest Artists).* New York: Children's Press, 1996.

Viorst, Judith. *Alexander and the Terrible, Horrible, No Good, Very Bad Day.* New York: Scholastic Inc., 1972.

Waddell, Martin. *Can't You Sleep, Little Bear?* Cambridge, MA: Candlewick Press, 1994.

Wallace, Barbara Brooks. *Argyle.* Honesdale, PA: Bell Books, 1987.

Ward, Lynd. *The Biggest Bear.* Boston: Houghton Mifflin, 1952.

Waters, Kate. *Samuel Eaton's Day: A Day in the Life of a Pilgrim Boy*. New York: Scholastic Trade, 1993.

Waters, Kate. *Sarah Morton's Day: A Day in the Life of a Pilgrim Girl*. New York: Scholastic Trade, 1993.

Watson, Carol, and Philippa Moyle. *500 Really Useful French Words and Phrases*. New York: Hippocrene Books, 1994.

Williams, Brenda. *Hills and Mountains*. Austin, TX: Steck-Vaughn Company, 1998.

Winter, Mio. *The Aesop for Children*. New York: Scholastic Inc., 1994.

Wood, Audrey. *Quick as a Cricket*. Auburn, ME: Child's Play International Ltd., 1990.

Wood, Jenny. *Volcanoes*. New York: Scholastic Inc., 1990.

Wright, Alexandra. *Will We Miss Them?* Watertown, MA: Charlesbridge Publishing, 1993.

Yolen, Jane. *Commander Toad and the Planet of the Grapes*. New York: The Putnam & Grosset Group, 1982.

Yolen, Jane. *The Emperor and the Kite*. New York: Putnam Publishing Group Juvenile, 1988.

Young, Ed. *Lon Po Po: A Red-Riding Hood Story from China*. New York: Scholastic Inc., 1990.

Zallinger, Peter. *Prehistoric Animals*. New York: Random House, 1981.

Zelinsky, Paul O. *Rapunzel*. New York: Scholastic Inc., 1997.

Ziefert, Harriet. *A New Coat for Anna*. New York: Alfred A. Knopf, Inc., 1986.

 # RESOURCES

Contact any of the resources provided below to enhance and extend exploration, discovery, and environmental awareness.

Center for Coastal Studies
59 Commercial Street
P.O. Box 1036
Provincetown, MA 02657
1-508-487-3622
Web site: www.provincetown.com/coastalstudies
E-mail: ccc@coastalstudies.org

The Dinosaur Museum
754 South 200 West
Blanding, UT 84511
1-435-678-3454
Web site: www.dinosaur-museum.org
E-mail: dinos@dinosaur-museum.org

Dinosaur State Park
400 West Street
Rocky Hill, CT 06067
1-860-257-7601
Web site: www.dinosaurstatepark.org
E-mail: fdpa.webmaster@snet.net

Insect Lore
P.O. Box 1535
Shafter, CA 93263
1-800-LIVEBUG
Web site: www.insectlore.com
E-mail: insect@lightspeed.net
International Wildlife Coalition

70 East Falmouth Highway
East Falmouth, MA 02536
1-508-548-8328
Web site: www.iwc.org
E-mail: iwcadopt@capeonramp.com

National Audubon Society
700 Broadway
New York, NY 10003
1-212-979-3000
Web site: www.audubon.org
E-mail: webmaster@list.audubon.org

The Nature Conservancy
4245 North Fairfax Drive
Suite 100
Arlington, VA 22203
1-703-841-5300
Web site: www.tnc.org
E-mail: comment@tnc.org

The Rock Garden
17 South Main Street
Branford, CT 06405
1-203-488-6699
Web site: www.rockgarden.com
E-mail: info@rockgarden.com

Contact any of the resources below to enhance awareness of the world community.

Bob's Dreamcatchers
c/o Bob Allison
P.O. Box 4252
Hopkins, MN 55343
Web site: www.members.tripod.com
E-mail: bobsdreamcatchers@rocketmail.com

Morgan Memorial Goodwill Industries, Inc.
1010 Harrison Avenue
Boston, MA 02129
1-800-664-6577
Web site: www.goodwill.org
E-mail: arubin@goodwill.org

Salvation Army National Headquarters
615 Slaters Lane
P.O. Box 269
Alexandria, VA 22313
1-800-SAL-ARMY
Web site: www.salvationarmyusa.org

Sports Illustrated for Kids
P.O. Box 6001
Tampa, FL 33660
1-800-423-7771
Web site: www.sikids.com
E-mail: sikids_inbox@sikids.com

Time for Kids
1271 Avenue of the Americas
New York, NY 10020
1-800-777-8600
Web site: www.timeforkids.com
E-mail: privacy@pathfinder.com

Trees for Life
3006 West St. Louis
Wichita, KS 67203
1-316-945-6929
Web site: www.treesforlife.org
E-mail: info@treesforlife.org

UNICEF Headquarters
UNICEF House
3 United Nations Plaza
New York, NY 10017
1-212-326-7000
Web site: www.unicef.org
E-mail: netmaster@unicef.org

The White House
1600 Pennsylvania Avenue
Washington, DC 20500
Web site: www.whitehouse.gov/WH/kids

ABOUT THE AUTHORS

Naomi E. Singer has been a teacher in Newton, Massachusetts, for more than twenty years. In her role as a language arts and reading specialist, she teaches in kindergarten through grade five at the John Ward School and the Cabot School. Naomi also works with faculty and staff to coordinate and integrate the language arts program into all other areas of the curriculum. Additionally, she facilitates parent meetings that focus on early literacy acquisition. Naomi is the coauthor of *A+ Activities for First Grade,* the author of several literature units for grades two through five, and the coauthor of a number of literature enrichment programs for kindergarten through grade three. Naomi holds a bachelor of arts degree with a major in English from the University of Connecticut and a master's degree in education from Lesley College in Cambridge, Massachusetts.

Matthew J. Miller has been a primary grade teacher in Newton, Massachusetts, since 1993. Matt was nominated for the 1998 Massachusetts Teacher of the Year Award. Currently, he is a member of the Cabot School Council, working with teachers, parents, and community members on this advisory committee to the principal. Matt is one of the authors of the Cabot School Web site and is a developer of curriculum at the first-grade level. Matt is the coauthor of *A+ Activities for First Grade.* He holds a bachelor of science degree with a major in education from Springfield College in Springfield, Massachusetts.

365 After-School Activities

Cynthia MacGregor

Trade paperback, $10.95
ISBN: 1-58062-212-7

What's the first thing your child does when he or she comes home from school? If your answer is "homework," you've got a very conscientious child. However, if the answer is "watch TV," *365 After-School Activities* has got some fun and creative suggestions for play activities, indoor and outdoor, artsy and athletic, and otherwise, solo and with friends, with or without parental involvement—in short, something for every child, every mood, every situation, every day!

Inside you'll find hundreds of activities, including:

- Alphabet Stories
- Balloon Volleyball
- Bottle-Cap Basketball
- Design a Flag
- Map Games

- Word Lightening
- Zoo's Who?
- Household Scavenger Hunt
- Top Ten Lists
- And much, much more!

365 Fun-Filled Learning Activities

Mary Weaver

Trade paperback, $10.95
ISBN: 1-58062-127-9

Children are curious and resourceful explorers who love to learn new things. *365 Fun-Filled Learning Activities* helps them enjoy investigating their world while acquiring the skills they need to prepare for and keep up with their school curriculum. Covering a broad base of language, math, science, and physical developmental skills, these fun activities will stretch their imaginations while building their knowledge of the world around them. Over time, practicing these skills will give them the tools they need both to succeed in school and enrich their play.

Inside you'll find hundreds of activities, including:

- Shopping for Words
- Alphabet Phonics Hunt
- Egg Carton Math
- Which Is Which?

- Miniature Gardens
- Vegetable Gardens
- Pressing Flowers
- And much, much more!

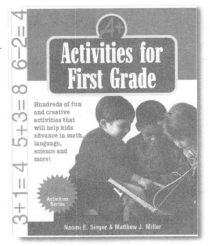